Prescriptiv~ ~~~y~~~~ ~~ ~~~~~~~
Joy, Peace and Purpose in Life

THR)VING
THROUGH
ADVERSITY

JUDITH PINKERTON

Companion to the Key2MEE Music App
for Mood Mastery

Music 4 Life, Inc.

Copyright © 2024 Judith Pinkerton. All rights reserved.

Published by Music 4 Life, Inc.

Distributed by Music 4 Life Technology, Inc.

8465 West Sahara Avenue, Suite 111-244, Las Vegas, Nevada 89117

info@themusic4life.com   1-855-MUSIC-RX

https://themusic4life.com

Music4Life® upholds copyright, which fuels creativity, encourages diverse voices, promotes free speech, and cultivates a vibrant culture. Thank you for purchasing an authorized edition of this book and respecting copyright laws by not reproducing, distributing, or transmitting it in any form or by any means, including photocopying, recording, or other electronic or mechanical methods, without prior written permission from the publisher, except for brief quotations in critical reviews and certain other noncommercial uses permitted by copyright law. For permission requests, please contact the publisher at the address provided above.

ISBN: 978-0-9745147-9-6

DISCLAIMER

This publication is designed to provide accurate and authoritative information on the subject matter covered. It is sold with the understanding that the author and publisher are not providing legal, financial, medical, or nutritional counseling services. The author and publisher are not liable or responsible for any loss or damage purportedly arising from any information or suggestions in this book. The information in this book should not be used as a substitute for professional advice from a licensed practitioner in your state.

When I present a disguised vignette of someone struggling with anxiety, anger, depression, or sadness, or when I illustrate how a particular technique works, I usually choose a positive and encouraging example that demonstrates recovery. Often, I highlight stories of individuals who improved significantly and relatively quickly. These examples offer the greatest potential for learning and can foster hope, which is essential for healing.

However, this should not be taken as a guarantee that the same techniques will be effective for you or someone you know. We are all unique and respond differently to various approaches. Additionally, while the techniques described in this book are powerful, not everyone who reads it or seeks professional treatment will experience rapid and dramatic changes.

Some more severe issues might require a longer course of treatment. This approach has proven to be incredibly rewarding, as a way forward always seems to emerge if you stay committed.

These trademarks are owned by Music 4 Life Inc.:

Music4Life

Music Medicine Pill

Mood Exercise Regimen

Chronic Comfort Zone

Mood Sequence Formula

USE MEE-Music Exercising Emotions

This trademark is owned by Music 4 Life Technology Inc.

Key2MEE

First edition 2024

DEDICATION

I n the journey of writing this book, I am profoundly aware of the multitude of influences and support systems that have shaped my path. This book reflects the collective love, encouragement, and wisdom I have received from those closest to me. It is with immense gratitude that I dedicate this work to the remarkable individuals who have been my pillars of strength and inspiration.

To my parents, Frank and Carol Pinkerton, who brought me into a world brimming with love and adventure and supported me unconditionally in all my endeavors. Their unwavering belief in me has been a driving force in my quest for excellence.

To my husband, Dr. Dennis D. Burkhardt, for his continual support of my heart, mind, body, and soul, along with our sons Thomas, Tim, and Michael, and our (grand)daughter Kaylan, for navigating the challenges of our blended family with resilience and grace. Their love and persever- ance have been a source of immense pride and joy. Special mention to my daughter Meghan, whose resolute battle with addiction has deeply influenced my professional journey. Her experiences have ignited within me a compassionate desire to understand and support those struggling with similar challenges, reinforcing my optimism for a brighter future for them and her.

To my younger siblings, Gary, Nancy, Jim, and Dan, who have consistently inspired me to explore new horizons and lead our family with courage and vision into the future.

And to God, whose Divine Presence has guided me through the tumultuous waters of life with serenity and purpose. This Divine Spirit empowers me to continue my journey with joy, mindful of a destination that craves clarity, and to embrace love in all its forms, especially in the face of adversity. God is my beacon of holiness, strengthening me to spread Divine love with unconditional presence throughout every aspect of my life.

This book embodies the profound impact each of you has had on my life and my work. Thank you for your unwavering support and for inspiring me to pursue my passions with a full heart.

ACKNOWLEDGMENTS

My heartfelt appreciation goes out to the thousands of clients who have provided invaluable feedback over the years. Your shared experiences and stories have been the lifeblood of this work, illuminating how the Music Medicine Protocol resonates in real lives. Through your candid insights and heartfelt testimonials, I have been able to refine and enhance the protocol shared within these pages. Each of your journeys has not only validated the power of music in healing but has also inspired me to continually evolve and innovate. This book is as much yours as it is mine, a testament to the transformative power of music and the shared commitment to well-being that binds us all. Thank you for your trust, your stories, and your unwavering support.

A tribute to Alyssa Janney, Music4Life's product development consultant, is in order. Alyssa's persistent encouragement and visionary approach pushed me to create the curriculum "6 Habits of Music Medicine for Highly Empowered People." This curriculum, beautifully brought to life in a card set she designed, teaches the key concepts of the Music Medicine Protocol and has been instrumental in spreading its benefits.

I also extend my deep appreciation to clinical psychologist Colonel Kevin McCal for his unwavering support of Music4Life® predating recognition of "invisible wounds," along with a dedicated team of military and civilian mental health providers. Their advice on both the book and the app has been invaluable, ensuring that the protocol meets the highest standards and can be effectively integrated into various settings.

Special thanks go to the dynamic branding duo Erin Saxton and Chad Lefevre. Your capability of redefining, redesigning, and recreating Music4Life not only identified the perfect book title and cover design but also captured the essence of this work to invite readers into a new system for a new world.

Kudos to Rick Duggan, co-author of the Key2MEE® Music App patent. Your willingness to delve deeply into my experiences and translate them into the app's patent application has been extraordinary. The support from your team at ConciergeSoftwareDesign.com has allowed the Music Medicine Protocol to evolve within the Key2MEE Music App, making this companion book a reality.

I am deeply indebted to the healthcare professionals, including treatment team colleagues, music therapists, interns, and students across the country. Your experiences implementing Music4Life's Music Medicine Protocol, shared during my presentations and trainings at conferences, universities, and online since the 1990s, have continually informed and enriched my work.

Finally, I would also like to thank Bobby Goodwin's team at Cosmic Creators. Jennifer and Gaby, your guidance with topics, organization, writing, editing, rewrites, flow, and design has been indispensable. Your creative solutions and unwavering support have kept me on course throughout this journey.

CONTENTS

FOREWARD

I t is with great honor and enthusiasm that I pen these words as the foreword to "Thriving through Adversity: Prescriptive Playlists to Reclaim Joy, Peace and Purpose in Life." When Judith approached me with the opportunity to contribute to this groundbreaking work, I was immediately drawn to the life-changing potential that lies within its pages.

The fusion of therapeutic tools and knowledge encapsulated in this book, coupled with the innovative Key2MEE® Music App, Heralds a new era in mental health care. The prospect of equipping compassionate and driven mental health providers with the means to integrate music into the healing process for their patients is truly exhilarating.

With over 30 years of experience as a psychologist in the military, I have witnessed suffering not only in emotionally distressed patients we treated but also in the dedicated medical professionals who treated them. Over the course of my career, as the military placed me in leadership positions at medical clinics, I shouldered the responsibility of care for active-duty members and their families. In those moments of challenge and adversity, I have seen firsthand the resilience and struggles of those who serve, striving to maintain stability amidst the turbulence of daily life. "Thriving through Adversity: Prescriptive Playlists to Reclaim Joy, Peace and Purpose in Life" emerges as a beacon of light, offering a roadmap to navigate the emotional, spiritual, and physical minefields that often accompany such endeavors.

My friendship with Judith began nearly two decades ago when she first introduced me to the concept of music therapy and its potential impact within the military. At that time, Music4Life® was just a concept. Little did I know then that I stood on the cusp of an innovative clinical movement that would touch the lives of thousands of individuals in the years to come.

Judith's unwavering dedication to sharing the power of music therapy through her Music Medicine Protocol is both inspiring and profound. It has impacted many diverse clinical populations for nearly 3 decades. Recently, I had the privilege of experiencing firsthand the therapeutic effects of her approach as I embarked on the Music Medicine Clinical Specialist Course. As part of that course, there is a requirement to either listen to a pre-formulated music playlist or one created for you with assistance from a certified music therapist once per day for 14 days. The impact of immersing myself in curated music playlists under Judith's guidance was nothing short of remarkable! It alleviated my physical pain and emotional distress, as well as fostered a newfound sense of well-being. The experience has left an indelible mark on my journey of self-discovery and healing through music and mood mastery.

Judith is rooted in music. She is a concert violinist and has played with top internationally known musicians. In 1986, she asked a loved one to listen to a recording of her violin music post-surgery. As a result, he did not need to take the expected medication to control negative symptoms like high blood pressure. From this discovery, her passion and far-reaching vision fueled the development of a revolutionary music-based, life enriching program in mobile format available to anyone. She expanded her knowledge base and clinical reach by becoming the first to receive a state-issued music therapy license in the US. Over the next two decades, Judith has treated more than 11,000 patients in many clinically diverse settings.

Through her innovative Music4Life® program and the forthcoming Key2MEE® mobile application, Judith is revolutionizing the landscape of music therapy, offering a holistic approach to emotion regulation and self-care. Her pioneering music therapy-informed strategies, honed over three decades of practice, provide a valuable alternative or complementary regimen to traditional medication, addressing a spectrum of emotional challenges, including anger, anxiety, depression, and grief.

"Thriving through Adversity: Prescriptive Playlists to Reclaim Joy, Peace and Purpose in Life," stands as a testament to Judith's evolution from musician to music therapist to entrepreneurial trailblazer. It weaves personal anecdotes, professional insights, and music therapy principles into a tapestry of empowerment and healing. Whether you are new to the concept of music therapy or a seasoned practitioner, this book promises to unlock the transformative potential of music as medicine, offering a treasure trove of tools, perspectives, and inspiration to enhance your practice and enrich the lives of those you serve. I wholeheartedly encourage you to delve into the pages of "Thriving through Adversity: Prescriptive Playlists to Reclaim Joy, Peace and Purpose in Life," embracing the wisdom and guidance it offers with an open mind and a receptive heart. May this book be a source of inspiration, enlightenment, and empowerment on your journey toward holistic well-being and healing.

Col Kevin McCal, Ph.D., MMCS

"Music should be an essential part of every analysis."

- Carl Jung, Psychiatrist (1875-1961)

"Music can lift us out of depression or move us to tears – it is a remedy, a tonic, orange juice for the ear. But for many of my neurological patients, music is even more – it can provide access, even when no medication can, to movement, to speech, to life. For them, music is not a luxury, but a necessity."

- Oliver Sacks, Neurologist (1933-2015)

INTRODUCTION

H ave you ever noticed how your favorite songs make you feel? Can a melody alone lift your spirits or soothe a troubled mind? Inspired by my transformative experiences with music, I wrote this book to explore music's significant impact on our resilience and mental health. Join me as we discover how the tunes you love can become a lifeline through life's challenges, demonstrating that sometimes, the right song is all it takes to turn the tide. In this journey, we unveil "the innovative Music Medicine Protocol," a system designed to address the emotional needs of our evolving world, made easily accessible through the Key2MEE® Music App.

"Thriving Through Adversity" is a groundbreaking exploration of music's significant impact on emotional healing and personal growth. Drawing from my extensive experience as a music therapist, I blend personal anecdotes with professional insights to create a compelling narrative highlighting music's transformative power. This book investigates how music can regulate emotions, support mental health, and aid in recovery from various life challenges. Readers will find practical techniques and real-life case stories demonstrating the use of music therapy in diverse contexts—from managing anxiety and depression to overcoming personal adversities like illness, addiction, and grief.

Recognizing the daily pressures we all face, from family obligations to professional demands, it becomes clear why maintaining emotional balance is more challenging than ever. Here, music steps in as an invaluable ally. In the upcoming chapters, you'll discover strategies to integrate music into your daily life as a therapeutic tool. Through these real-life applications, you'll see how music elevates your mindset and supports your emotional journey. As I've observed in my work with thousands of clients, individuals who integrate music into their daily lives enhance their well-being and transform the broader culture of music consumption.

This personal and communal transformation points to an important insight: actual change in the music industry begins at the grassroots level. By changing how individuals relate to and use music, we can shift the overall culture of music consumption. In my work with thousands of clients, I've seen happier people choose music supporting their emotional well-being, influencing industry trends from the ground up.

This commitment to grassroots change became even more personal after a revealing encounter that left me very frustrated with the music industry's focus on profit over well-being. I'll always remember a late-night conversation while on tour with an insider who managed significant artists. This person made a disturbing proclamation: "I have to do whatever it takes to keep them performing (sex, drugs, etc.)." This alarming attitude reminded me of Elvis' manager, Colonel Tom Parker, who insisted that Elvis continue performing despite his struggles, as depicted in the 2022 biographical drama. This conversation motivated me to continue focusing on working at the grassroots level of our country. However, the problem with moods being so out of control is that it's overwhelming. When one advisor mirrored my frustration, saying I was trying to boil the ocean, I realized I needed powerful voices. So, I'm enlisting all mental health providers to become knowledgeable about the deep effects of music listening habits.

My personal and professional experiences deeply influence the principles I advocate in my work. From navigating the complexities of raising a blended family and adopting my (grand)daughter to breaking new ground in music therapy, every challenge has enriched my understanding and approach to healing through music. This deep connection between my life's challenges and professional practice shapes the Music Medicine Protocol, making it a comprehensive tool for emotional healing. This same personal dedication to music's healing power underpins this book, designed to support mental health providers, their clients, and anyone struggling with emotional challenges such as anxiety, anger, depression, or sadness. Offering both inspiration and practical strategies, the book encourages integrating music into daily life to enhance emotional balance and resilience. It is structured flexibly, allowing readers to explore topics that resonate most with their needs. It is supported by the Key2MEE.com Music App, which guides users through the Music Medicine Protocol to build emotional resilience and master their moods.

As you read, consider how your life might change if you could decode the emotional messages within your favorite songs. When you download the Key2MEE® Music App from Apple or Google Play, the Emotional Profile Quiz is designed to help you decode your music listening habits with guidance about potential entrapment in Chronic Comfort Zones™. This exploration invites you to discover the healing power of music in your own life.

"When everything seems to be going against you, remember that the air-plane takes off against the wind, not with it." This quote from Henry Ford has always resonated deeply with me. Since I was ten, flying in bush planes taught me to navigate adverse conditions. My daily life was often fraught with challenges, but playing the violin provided a constant source of comfort and stability. Over the years, my musical journey expanded beyond classical music, leading me to explore various genres. This exploration sparked a compelling question: Is it the adverse conditions that create unsettledness and inspire music creation, or does music intensify this unsettledness, breeding more adversity? This cycle seems to escalate, fueling riots, shootings, violence, and even suicide.

The journey through this book begins with understanding the fundamental differences between music therapy and music medicine, setting the stage for a deeper exploration of their distinct roles in emotion regulation. From there, I share compelling stories illustrating how music therapy strategies can alleviate physical pain, soothe emotional distress, and enhance mental clarity. These stories demonstrate how prescriptive music adapts to individual healing journeys, providing lasting transformation. As we progress further into the book, I introduce the Music4Life® tools, harnessing the transformative power of music beyond traditional therapy. These tools offer strategies to enhance emotion regulation, resilience, and personal development, proving invaluable for mental health providers and anyone struggling with unsettledness. The concept of a healthy music diet then guides readers in personalizing their music choices to enrich daily living and navigate life's complex emotional landscape with greater harmony.

This focus on tailoring musical experiences to improve emotional well-being sets the stage for a personal revelation. The following sections of the book stress the importance of emotional fluidity and environment consciousness, emphasizing the need to carefully select music that mirrors emotions to facilitate effective emotional processing and healing. Here, I also share my journey of navigating multiple divorces and managing children with addictions, which led to my adoption of my (grand)child. These personal experiences powerfully illustrate how resilience and prescriptive music can transform adversity into opportunities for growth.

Further chapters explore how I developed the SMILE process, which deepened my passion and clarified my purpose. From traumatic experiences flying in Alaska to performing violin in Las Vegas shows and advocating for music therapy, this journey shows how to achieve goals against all odds. Inspired by my mother's motto, "Turn lemons into lemonade," the book demonstrates how to transform Adversity—whether it's emotional abuse, relocation, or professional challenges—into opportunities for growth.

Personal examples of harassment and discrimination are shared to illustrate how thriving through adversity with assertiveness, self-awareness, and strategic networking can lead to effective advocacy and empowerment. The balance between passion-driven purpose and family commitments is also discussed, with music weaving throughout my life's journey. From finishing school later in life to building a house and handling blended family struggles, these experiences provide insights into maintaining this balance.

The power of resilience and innovation is evident in transforming a "no" into a "yes" by aligning with core values, actionable behaviors, and mindfulness of boundaries. Lastly, the book reveals the importance of a synergistic network regimen inspired by my father's entrepreneurial spirit and offers strategies for pivoting and modeling a pioneering spirit in networking.

By the end of this book, you will learn to navigate life's challenges, discover your passion and purpose, and live it fully. Through personal stories and professional insights, I share how to turn adversity into growth opportunities, achieve goals against all odds, and create a balance between personal passions and family commitments. Take the next step, trust your inner guidance, and immerse yourself in the transformative power of music. This book encourages you to consider how we can reshape the culture of music creation and consumption to support a healthier and more balanced life. Together, we can make a difference, one note at a time, with the "Music Medicine Protocol" embedded in the Key2MEE® Music App, guiding us toward a new world.

1

THE POWER OF MUSIC ON HUMAN EMOTION AND PHYSIOLOGY

T hrough the tender strings of my violin, I've found a profound way to reach my father, whose journey through dementia has distanced him from the world he once knew. When cruising with my parents, I take my violin to support my dad's emotions and behavior positively. As my violin teacher, orchestra conductor, and flying/hunting buddy, we share many life experiences, and playing the violin is the easiest way to influence him. This instrument becomes a voice and a comfort, speaking to him in a language that dementia cannot silence. In these moments, with a bow in hand, I see the undeniable power of music to touch the heart and soul, to bring a smile to his face and a spark of recognition in his eyes. Music is more than melody; it's a lifeline, a reminder of joy and love that still flickers brightly amidst the shadows of his memory.

On one of our Caribbean cruise trips, we encountered another culture. Very little spoken language was exchanged with the string quartet from

Poland. They noticed my violin immediately upon boarding and invited me to play lead with them, after which they exclaimed that I was a wonderful mentor. It took me back to my Switzerland Music Conservatory days when music performance transcended language barriers.

Research has extensively explored the profound connection between music, emotions, and physical sensations, highlighting music's innate ability to transcend cultural barriers and evoke universally shared experiences. This intrinsic quality of music, deeply embedded in the fabric of human existence, speaks to its universal appeal and impact across diverse cultures (Reuell, 2018). A key focus of such studies is the phenomenon of Bodily Sensation Mapping (BSM), which illustrates the consistency of physical responses to music-induced emotions across different cultural contexts (Putkinen, 2024).

BSM involves documenting the physical sensations individuals experience in response to music, such as warmth, tingling, or pressure in various body parts. This method has revealed that music's acoustic and structural characteristics—its rhythm, melody, harmony, and dynamics—are intricately linked to emotion ratings and the physical sensations these emotions provoke, regardless of the listener's cultural background. These emotional ratings quantitatively measure the listener's emotional response to music, bridging the gap between subjective experience and objective analysis (Putkinen, 2024).

The consistent relationship between music's acoustic properties, the emotions it elicits, and its corresponding physical sensations across cultures reinforces that music's capacity to influence our emotional and physical states is a fundamental, universal aspect of human nature (Koivula, 2024).

This shows that the power of music is a universal language capable of eliciting deeply felt emotional and bodily responses that transcend cultural distinctions.

Historical Perspective on Music as a Healing Tool

Music's healing power has always been vital to human history and is deeply entrenched in our cultural and healing practices. Erin Seibert, M.A., MT-BC, a professionally trained and certified music therapist from the University of Evansville and Berklee College of Music, poignantly summarizes this enduring relationship between music and healing: "Music is one of the longest-standing self-prescribed therapies in history." Ancient Greek physicians, cognizant of music's profound effects on the human psyche and body, incorporated the lyre and flute into their treatments. These pioneering healers harnessed music's dynamic ability to influence physical and emotional well-being, applying its vibrational properties to various ailments, from digestive issues to mental health disorders and sleep problems. Aristotle, the eminent philosopher (384-322 BCE), recognized music's capacity to elicit potent emotions and advocated for its use in cleansing the soul. This perspective was echoed in ancient Egyptian traditions as well, where musical chants served as a healing modality for the ill (Meymandi, 2009).

The concept that our bodies are inherently rhythmic entities—characterized by heart and breathing rhythms, brain waves, and hormonal and circadian rhythms—highlights a natural synergy between music and human health. We walk in rhythm and talk in rhythm. So, it should be no surprise that our bodies and minds respond to music.

From the lyres of Ancient Greece to the sophisticated music therapy sessions of today, music has consistently served as a potent instrument of healing. Its ability to bridge temporal and cultural gaps while deeply affecting the mind and body points to music's timeless therapeutic potential. This historical perspective honors our ancestors' wisdom and paves the way for the continued integration of music into holistic health and wellness paradigms.

In contemporary times, the medical and neuroscience fields have revisited music's therapeutic promise with vigor. Investigations have broadened to encompass the cognitive health connections between music and various domains, including language development, memory enhancement, motor skills improvement, and emotion regulation. The American Music Therapy Association (AMTA) chronicles the evolution of music therapy from its roots in ancient healing rituals to its current recognition as an organized and structured form of therapy ("What is AMTA," n.d.)

The Neurochemistry of Music and Its Effects on the Brain

Investigating how music impacts our emotions and physical state prompts an intriguing question: How does music activate the central nervous system to alter our mood, cognition, and overall health? Through understanding music's effect on the brain, we uncover the intricate link between its elements and our biological and emotional well-being (Bowling, 2023).

Music stimulates the release of various neurochemicals responsible for pleasure, stress relief, immunity enhancement, and social bonding. There are four primary neurochemical systems affected by music (Chanda et al., 2013; Thaut et al., 2018).

Dopamine and opioids, which are linked with rewards, motivation, and pleasure, are released during enjoyable music-listening experiences, activating the brain's pleasure centers. This release highlights music's capacity to elicit feelings of enjoyment and satisfaction.

Music also influences stress and arousal-related hormones such as cortisol, CRH (corticotropin-releasing hormone), and ACTH (adrenocorticotropic hormone). It can decrease the release of these stress hormones, aiding individuals in coping with stressors more effectively.

Furthermore, serotonin and derivatives of POMC (pro-opiomelanocortin), which are associated with the body's immune response, are promoted by listening to music. This activity boosts the body's immunity, revealing the therapeutic potential of music to enhance immune function and promote overall health.

Additionally, exposure to music increases the release of oxytocin, known for its role in social affiliation, thereby fostering social connections and bonding among individuals. This effect of music on oxytocin release illustrates its importance in enhancing social bonds and emotional connections, further emphasizing the multifaceted benefits of music on human health and well-being.

Music has the incredible capacity to enhance neurochemical release, activate the brain's pleasure centers, reduce stress hormones, and improve immunity. Engaging with music involves a blend of empathic/emotional listening, aesthetic appreciation, and high-level cognitive processing, stimulating both the cortical and subcortical brain regions. This suggests that continuous and meaningful engagement with music can lead to neuro-plastic changes, potentially resulting in brain structural and functional modifications.

The Role of Brain Function in Music Processing

Debasish Mridha, M.D., once said, "Music can heal the wounds which medicine cannot touch." This perspective is supported by scientific research revealing how music interacts with brain areas like the basal ganglia, influencing emotional and physical health. Music can alleviate stress, enhance mood, and even improve cognitive and motor functions through its capacity to engage these neural pathways. By understanding music's role in both the scientific and healing realms, we appreciate its ability to enhance emotional well-being and physical recovery.

The basal ganglia are fundamental brain structures involved in various functions critical to movement, thought, and emotion. Primarily, they regulate motor control, smoothing and coordinating voluntary movements and managing the initiation and termination of actions. Beyond motor functions, the basal ganglia also play an essential role in cognitive processes such as decision-making, planning, and problem-solving, as well as in emotional processes, including reward processing, reinforcement learning, and habit formation. By influencing both motor and non-motor circuits within the brain, the basal ganglia contribute significantly to our ability to move, think, and feel (Chanda & Levitin, 2013).

The research shows that moving in rhythm with music can strengthen emotions, help people feel more connected to others, and improve movement in people with movement disorders. It points out that the basal ganglia, a part of the brain, plays a significant role in how music affects us emotionally and physically. This has opened up new ways to use music as therapy. It suggests that music with a specific rhythm could help with emotional and physical recovery. For example, particular beats can help people with Parkinson's disease move better or help anyone feel more relaxed and less stressed by affecting their emotions (Thaut et al., 2018).

In addition to these specific therapeutic uses, the broader implications of music on brain health are equally compelling. Brain health relies on the plasticity of our brains, which remain adaptable throughout life, adjusting to our bodies and environments. This adaptability allows us to thrive through healthy changes but can also lead to issues like addiction, mood disorders, and cognitive deficits when maladaptive changes occur. Fortunately, the brain's adaptability means suffering can often be temporary with the right therapeutic methods. Music therapy interventions promote positive neuroplasticity, coordinating both the recovery of diseased states and the improvement of healthy states (Tomaka, 2024).

This intricate relationship between music and the brain extends beyond therapy. When we listen to music, it's not just about enjoying the melody or the lyrics. Our brain engages in a complex process that involves deeply understanding and feeling the music and appreciating its beauty on a higher level. This process involves different parts of the brain working together, including the areas that process sound, help us make judgments about right and wrong, and control our emotions. Scientists believe regularly immersing ourselves in music, especially when we approach it with an appreciation for its beauty, can lead to lasting changes in our brains. This could mean changes in how our brain functions and even its structure, showing how powerful music can influence our brain health and emotional wellness.

In recognizing how music can shape our brains, we also see its potential in diverse contexts. For instance, the term "neurodivergent" describes individuals whose brain functions differently, leading to unique strengths and challenges. These differences can include medical disorders and learning disabilities, while strengths might include enhanced memory and visualization skills. "Neurodivergent" is not a medical term but a way to describe people without labeling them as "normal" or "abnormal." People without these brain function differences are called "neurotypical," meaning their strengths and challenges are not influenced by such differences (Cleveland Clinic, 2022).

One neurodiverse condition is dysgraphia, which is characterized by difficulty writing clearly and correctly, often involving syntax errors, illegible handwriting, odd spelling, and inaccurate word production. This condition requires complex cognitive functions, expressive language, and fine motor skills. Dysgraphia is linked to damage in brain areas involved in writing and language, such as the anterior cingulate, supramarginal gyrus, frontal gyrus, motor cortex, somatosensory cortex, and parts of the cerebellum, thalamus, and putamen (Cabrero et al., 2022).

Understanding these brain differences and how they interact with music can help create effective therapeutic approaches for individual needs. For instance, music therapy can be particularly beneficial for neurodivergent individuals, using their unique strengths to address their challenges. This shows how powerful and transformative music can be in enhancing brain health and emotional wellness.

To illustrate this point, consider the story of one executive who leads a venture development company at age 59 and describes himself as neuro-divergent with dysgraphia. "Before ADD/ADHD were recognized, I had difficulty taking notes, which resulted in poor retention and learning. My focus on writing removed my ability to remember what the teacher said."

What's even more interesting is his intense experiences with music, whether live or recorded, when masterfully and intensely executed. "The music powerfully resonates inside me, overwhelming me with emotion, making me cry, and I'm unable to speak." He cites Bach Gounod's "Ave Maria," played during his wedding on the pipe organ in New York City's Cathedral of St. John the Divine, as one such experience. Other standout moments occur when optimal acoustics are present, such as performances by The Grateful Dead, Paul Winters, Gyuto Monks, John Popper, Sugar Blue, and Stanley Clark. "When I play the didjeridu, I can create a transcendental experience, with my mind quieting, disconnecting, and changing the normal concept of myself."

For others, his story might support a greater understanding of personal experiences that are not well understood, illustrating how music can affect us so dramatically. By sharing his journey, we can explore how to deal with these profound emotional responses and harness music's effects for well-being. This narrative highlights the transformative power of music and its potential to enhance personal and emotional health, especially for those with neurodivergent traits.

Impact of Music on Emotion Regulation

The relevance of understanding music's role in emotion regulation has become a significant topic in psychology and therapy, particularly for young individuals with depressive tendencies. Individuals often use music for emotion regulation, employing strategies such as selecting music that contrasts with or mirrors their current emotional state to manage feelings (Stewart et al., 2019). Such insights illuminate the complex relationship between music and emotional states and underscore the importance of selecting appropriate music for effective mood management. Knowing which aspects of music can lead to positive changes and which might exacerbate negative emotions is crucial, particularly in music therapy, where therapists must customize interventions to maximize benefits.

The Music4Life® Music Medicine Protocol leverages the intrinsic healing properties of music, allowing individuals to independently manage their emotions through personalized music selections. This approach utilizing music therapy-informed techniques taps directly into the impact music listening has on the brain's emotion regulation areas (Moore, 2013). The success of this protocol relies heavily on individuals choosing music that aligns with their personal preferences and emotional needs.

Music therapy and music medicine might often be confused as the same practice, but there is a distinct difference between the two. While both involve the use of music for healing, their approaches and applications vary significantly. Music therapy requires a qualified therapist to use music within a clinical framework to achieve specific therapeutic goals, while the Music4Life Music Medicine Protocol involves the active or passive participation of a trained professional to tailor and implement music-based interventions, thereby empowering individuals to use prescriptive music on their own as a therapeutic tool. This sense of autonomy makes Music Medicine a valuable and accessible option for enhancing mental health and well-being in various settings, enabling more people to experience the benefits of music in a way that is uniquely suited to their individual needs. Simply put, in music therapy, the healing is facilitated by a qualified music therapist, while in Music Medicine, the music itself acts as the healing agent.

This personalized music therapy-informed protocol effectively addresses emotional challenges by tapping into music's unique ability to connect deeply with our emotions, promoting healing and balance. This method leverages individuals' specific emotional and psychological needs, demonstrating tailored musical experiences' profound impact on our well-being. During the early stages of the COVID-19 pandemic, music was able to help people manage their stress. A study spanning four countries reports that turning to music for emotional support helped 589 individuals cope with the stress and uncertainty of the pandemic. This effect was powerful among participants from India. Even though people with varying levels of depression and anxiety used music differently, everyone still experienced a positive shift in their mood. These insights reveal the universal appeal of music as a comforting and stabilizing force during the challenging times brought about by the pandemic (Hennessy et al., 2021).

Music significantly influences how we manage and understand our emotions. Research reveals that listening to music we enjoy or find familiar, sing, or improvise positively affects our brain in ways that help us regulate our emotions better. These activities have been shown to activate specific areas of the brain that are crucial for managing our feelings, suggesting that music can be a direct pathway to improving our emotional state. On the contrary, the research also points out that not all music experiences have the same effect. Complex, dissonant, or unexpected musical pieces might not always contribute to emotion regulation in the way we might hope. This is why it's important to select music that aligns with the listener's preferences and emotional needs, as the impact of music on emotional states can be highly individualized (Moore, 2013).

Music Genres and Emotion Regulation

The exploration into how different music genres contribute to emotion regulation reveals the intricate and personalized nature of music's impact on emotional states. One study (Cook et al., 2017) surveyed 794 university students, 74% females and 42% Caucasians, to explore their preferences across 14 music genres. These genres were grouped into four categories for analysis: reflective and complex (including jazz, classical, blues, and folk), intense and rebellious (such as alternative, rock, and heavy metal), upbeat and conventional (country, pop, religious, soundtracks), and energetic and rhythmic (rap/hip-hop, soul/funk, electronica/dance).

This study's results highlight specific music genres individuals prefer for emotion regulation. Pop, rap/hip-hop, soul/funk, and electronica/dance were commonly selected to enhance emotional arousal. Soul/funk music was especially effective at boosting positive emotions and reducing negative ones.

Further data analysis revealed demographic differences in musical tastes and how these preferences relate to emotion regulation strategies. Women showed a strong preference for upbeat and conventional music genres, using these selections for anxiety relief, mood improvement, and energy enhancement. Men, on the other hand, leaned towards genres that were reflective, complex, intense, and rebellious.

Racial and age-related variations in music preferences were also notable. The study found that different racial groups and ages gravitate towards different genres for emotion regulation, suggesting a complex interplay between cultural background, life experiences, and musical taste. For instance, younger participants and those from non-Caucasian backgrounds were more inclined towards energetic and rhythmic music like rap/hip-hop and soul/funk, which they used to elevate their mood and arousal levels. Conversely, as age increased, there was a tendency to prefer more reflective and complex music, indicating that older listeners might seek music that resonates with a broader range of emotional and cognitive experiences. Considering individual tastes and demographic characteristics is essential when leveraging music to regulate emotions. The diversity in music genre preferences and their application in managing emotions—ranging from using blues, jazz, and funk for positive and negative regulation to the varied strategies employed by different demographic groups—highlights music's broad applicability and complexity as a tool for emotional well-being.

The Music Medicine Protocol

The Music4Life® Music Medicine Protocol represents a sophisticated evolution in applying music therapy-informed techniques. This protocol encompasses a range of techniques and principles designed to optimize the therapeutic application of music across various contexts. One of the distinctive aspects of the Music4Life Music Medicine Protocol is its holistic approach to emotion regulation. It incorporates an understanding of music's physiological, psychological, and socio-cultural impacts, offering a comprehensive framework for therapeutic practice. It inspires innovation in therapeutic music applications by encouraging the exploration of music's full potential, considering all genres in promoting mental health and wellness.

During my early years of learning about music therapy, I set out to systematically explore and harness the therapeutic powers of music. This unrelenting passion led to the development of the Music4Life Music Medicine Protocol, a structured approach designed to optimize music for emotion regulation and healing. My path was fueled by a commitment to blend my firsthand experiences with solid scientific understanding, aiming to unlock music's full therapeutic potential through unique listening regimens.

Music Medicine Pills® and Their Application

A unique aspect of the Music4Life Music Medicine Protocol is the development of Music Medicine Pills, prescriptive music interventions designed to address specific emotional states. These "pills" are created through a rigorous assessment of music that aligns with the individual's therapeutic goals, providing a targeted approach to emotion regulation.

Music Medicine Pills® exemplify the practical application of music therapy principles, offering a personalized and accessible form of emotional support. Their use in therapy sessions and as part of self-care routines highlights the protocol's flexibility and potential as a healing empowerment tool. The impact of these music interventions on individual emotion regulation is profound, informing evidence of music therapy's effectiveness through a tangible, accessible format.

The field of music therapy employs a variety of techniques to address mental health issues, harnessing music's inherent therapeutic potential to facilitate emotion regulation and healing. More often now, music therapists are utilizing prescriptive playlists as a core technique to aid in emotion regulation. The selection process is grounded in understanding music psychology and its impact on the brain's emotional and cognitive processes. Music therapists can evoke specific emotional responses and facilitate a journey toward emotional balance and well-being by aligning music elements (such as tempo, rhythm, harmony, melody, plus lyrics) with the client's therapeutic needs.

The efficacy of prescriptive playlists lies in their ability to bridge the gap between music's therapeutic potential and its practical application in mental health care. This approach enables clients to engage with music actively or passively, promoting self-awareness, emotional processing, and coping strategies that extend beyond the therapy session.

Integrating Music into Everyday Life

With its universal nature, music weaves its melodies and harmonies into the fabric of our daily lives, offering solace, excitement, and a spectrum of emotions. In an era where access to music is virtually limitless, thanks to platforms like Spotify and YouTube, the challenge isn't finding music but how to integrate it meaningfully into our routines. As we navigate the rhythms of our everyday existence, from the rush of the morning to the quiet of the night, music has the potential to be more than just a backdrop. It can be a deliberate choice, a mindful practice that enriches every moment. By mindfully selecting and engaging with music, we can transform our daily experiences, making every note and lyric a step towards a more harmonious, emotionally balanced life.

In weaving music into the fabric of our daily lives, following a balanced music diet emerges as a guide. Practicing a balanced music diet involves choosing music that addresses our broad emotional continuum and being aware of how certain songs or genres may impact all our emotions and mental states. It encourages individuals to be intentional with their music listening habits, ensuring that music provides comfort and empowerment. This approach advocates for a mindful and diversified engagement with music, akin to a balanced diet for our emotional and psychological health. Just as we nourish our bodies with various foods to ensure physical well-being, our auditory experiences also benefit from a rich palette of music genres. Including an array of styles and sounds in our daily playlists serves a dual purpose: it prevents the auditory monotony from over-reliance on a single genre and opens our minds to the broad spectrum of emotions and experiences that music can evoke.

Diversity in music genres within daily playlists plays a crucial role in emotion regulation and personal well-being. Each genre carries its unique emotional signature and can evoke various responses. Incorporating a variety of music genres into our daily listening habits allows us to tap into different emotional states, providing a rich palette of emotional experiences. This variety isn't just about entertainment; it's about using music as a versatile tool to enhance the quality of our lives. A carefully curated playlist can be a morning energizer, an afternoon motivator, or an evening relaxant. We learn to select music that resonates with our current emotional state or aspirations through music hygiene, a concept explored in Chapter 4, enriching our daily routines. It encourages us to explore and integrate different music genres into our lives, underscoring the idea that music, in its diversity, can elevate the human experience, making each day more vibrant and emotionally fulfilling.

Addressing Chronic Comfort Zones

In using music as a daily companion for emotional wellness, it's crucial to recognize and navigate the concept of Chronic Comfort Zones[TM]. These danger zones represent habitual listening patterns that, while comfortable, may limit emotional growth or reinforce negative emotional states. This section explores strategies for identifying and overcoming listening habits that may have become toxic and customizing music selections for a positive emotional impact.

Toxic listening habits are patterns of music consumption that, over time, can contribute to emotional stagnation or exacerbate negative emotions. Examples include repeatedly listening to songs that reinforce feelings of

sadness, anger, or anxiety without fostering emotional processing or res-
olution. The first step in addressing these habits is identification—being
mindful of how certain music affects your mood and emotional state.

Overcoming toxic listening habits requires consciously diversifying one's
musical intake and choosing music that supports desired emotional outcomes. It involves stepping out of one's musical comfort zone to explore
genres or artists that might offer new emotional experiences and perspectives. Music therapists often guide individuals in this process, helping
them curate playlists incorporating lyric and mood analysis or re-creating
music, songwriting, and improvisation to process emotions with reflective,
positive reinforcement.

Customizing music selections involves more than just avoiding negative
triggers; it's about actively seeking out music that uplifts, soothes, or energizes, depending on one's current needs. This customization is based on
the understanding that music has the power to significantly influence our
broad emotional landscape.

The approach to customization is adapting the Music Medicine Protocol's Mood Sequence Formula™ to meet therapeutic goals. This formula
helps listeners curate playlists that transition from acknowledging current
emotional states to gradually introducing music elements that foster a shift
toward desired emotions. For instance, start with slow mournful blues to
resonate with sadness and then progressively move towards upbeat jazz or
pop (lyrics must match positive thoughts) to lift the mood.

The Mood Sequence Formula™

The Music Medicine Protocol's Mood Sequence Formula is a sophisticated approach to emotional processing through music. This approach guides listeners in navigating their emotional landscape, facilitating a journey from acknowledging current feelings to gradually shifting towards a more balanced, soothed, or positive state.

The Mood Sequence Formula is predicated on the belief that music can mirror our emotions, offering validation and understanding and then, crucially, lead us through those emotions toward healing or meeting peak performance goals. This process involves three primary steps:

1. Acknowledgment: The first step involves selecting music that resonates with the listener's current emotional state, offering recognition and validation. This acknowledgment is crucial for emotional authenticity and processing undesirable emotions, which could be found at any point along the broad emotional continuum.

2. Transition: After acknowledging current emotions, the listener transitions to music that may embody a more neutral emotional state. This music is introduced as a bridge to reduce the intensity of emotions and prepare the mind and body for a positive shift.

3. Upliftment: The final stage involves incorporating music with positive, uplifting qualities or matching the desired emotion. This music is chosen to enhance the desired emotion, which could instill hope and encourage a more optimistic outlook.

Exploring diverse genres invites us into a world where music resonates deeply with our emotions, reflecting the insight of Maria von Trapp, whose family's story inspired "The Sound of Music," famously stating, "Music acts like a magic key, to which the most tightly closed heart opens." This journey through different musical landscapes, from serene classical pieces to electrifying rock, allows us to see firsthand how varied sounds influence our feelings. It highlights music's unparalleled ability to connect with our innermost selves. Through this exploration, we honor the breadth of human expression and the transformative potential of music, as recognized by Maria von Trapp—the movie figure whose life exemplifies the profound impact music can have on our lives.

Music Medicine Pills®, crafted through the Mood Sequence Formula, offers a personalized approach to using music for emotional healing. Guided by a music therapist, individuals select songs that resonate with their emotional state and therapeutic goals, creating a tailored playlist for support and encouragement. Suzanne Hanser, EdD, MT-BC, an expert in music therapy, discusses the transformative power of music, noting it has the power to shift our moods, calm or energize, and validate experiences with self-empowerment. This approach showcases the effectiveness of music as a therapeutic tool, providing a structured way to enhance emotional health and resilience, essential in the journey toward mental well-being.

Dr. Hanser uses the Iso-Principle to match music to moods and gradually transitions the music to alter mood (Heiderscheit et al., 2015; Altshuler, 1948). She has collaborated with Pandora to help listeners create their own Mood Manager Playlist for loneliness, called "Lonely to Connected," on the Pandora music platform. This innovative use of a music therapy technique demonstrates the potential of curated playlists to significantly affect emotional states and promote healing (Hanser, 2021).

Theoretical Frameworks Supporting Music Therapy

Music therapy is grounded in psychological theories that explain its effectiveness in improving mental health and regulating emotions. This discipline utilizes the transformative power of music to achieve significant therapeutic outcomes, drawing upon a foundation of well-established psychological principles.

Behavioral theory, which suggests that behaviors are learned and can be modified, is vital to music therapy's approach to helping clients replace negative behaviors with positive ones through music-based interventions. Cognitive theory provides insight into how music therapy can alter negative thought patterns, offering clients new, healthier ways of thinking and relating to the world. Individuals are guided to challenge and change their cognitive processes through musical engagement (Madsen, 1968).

Humanistic theory emphasizes the importance of personal growth and self-actualization, aligning with music therapy's goal of fostering individual potential. It offers clients a space for creative expression, enabling them to explore their emotions and strengthen their sense of self through music (Hodges, 2020).

Neuroscientific approaches highlight how music affects brain function and structure, illustrating the biological basis of music therapy's impact. Research shows that music activates diverse brain areas involved in emotion, cognition, and sensory processing, demonstrating its decisive role in therapeutic settings (Thaut et al., 2014; Chen et al., 2022).

These psychological theories provide a solid framework for understanding how music therapy works. By leveraging the science of psychology with the art of music, music therapy effectively enhances emotion regulation and mental health recovery, proving a powerful tool in the therapeutic arsenal.

The Music Medicine Protocol is built on three theoretical principles that are critical to using music as a healing agent. The Iso Principle matches music to the listener's broad emotional continuum for immediate emotional resonance (Heiderscheit et al., 2015; Altshuler, 1948). Vectoring guides the transition from the current emotional state through the desired state, directing the therapeutic process (Shatin, 1970). The Entrainment mechanism ensures continuous engagement, facilitating an engaging emotional journey from start to finish (Rider, 1985).

Together, these principles guide the application of the Music Medicine Protocol to effectively manage stress and anxiety, reduce symptoms of anxiety, anger, depression and grief, and enhance mood stability. By substituting negative coping mechanisms with positive, music-based alternatives, it fosters improved emotional awareness and regulation. This approach, rooted in humanistic theory, empowers clients to explore and articulate their emotions, thus enhancing emotional intelligence and interpersonal relationships.

Additionally, the sessions stimulate cognitive processes, bolstering memory, attention, and problem-solving skills, with neuroscientific approaches highlighting the brain's response to musical stimuli. The theoretical framework behind music therapy validates its effectiveness. It empowers therapists to create music interventions tailored to their client's unique needs and psychological makeup, ensuring a personalized approach to mental health and emotional well-being.

Bridging the Gap Between Theory and Practice

As I've ventured deeper into the realm of music therapy, my work in real-world settings, particularly within residential addiction treatment centers, has underscored the intricate balance between theoretical knowledge and its practical application. My approach through the Music4Life® Music Medicine Protocol has been to stretch the boundaries traditionally set by music therapy's application in individual or small group contexts. By stepping into large group settings, accommodating 20-40 participants, I've challenged conventional norms, relying on a profound understanding of music therapy's core principles and a flexible, creative approach to meet the diverse needs of participants.

The Music4Life Music Medicine Protocol encapsulates various music therapy elements, from lyric analysis and music listening to facilitate emotional exploration to guided meditation with music as a backdrop for relaxation and deeper emotional insight. It also includes songwriting and music-making to encourage creative expression, psycho-education, and self-assessment exercises to bolster emotion regulation skills. This multi-faceted approach has enabled participants to engage with music therapy on several levels, creating a supportive group environment conducive to exploring and addressing emotional and psychological challenges.

Navigating the challenges of adapting music therapy for large groups, such as maintaining a therapeutic atmosphere and ensuring individual engagement, has been a journey of discovery and innovation. My work has demonstrated the potential of music therapy to transcend traditional settings and touch a broader audience, illustrating the practical application of music therapy theories and opening new avenues for its integration into therapeutic, educational, and community contexts. A key distinction between general mood management playlists, such as on Pandora (Hanser, 2021), and Music4Life's Music Medicine Protocol is the application of Mood Sequence Formulas™ with results potentially influencing physician-directed changes in medication usage, including reduction, cessation, or prescription (Wellman et al., 2015). This is facilitated by engaging the entrainment mechanism (Rider, 1985), which modulates music to effectively sequence emotions, vectoring from undesirable to desired emotions specifically identified in three different mood categories.

Reflecting on this journey, I'm reminded of Natalie Cole sharing these words with me: "People take music for granted, but it's instrumental in getting us through the day. It's not something you can capture in a bottle and use as medicine, but in a way you can." This sentiment resonates deeply with my experiences, highlighting music therapy's ubiquitous yet profound impact. Through my efforts and broader applications of music therapy, the tangible benefits of this therapeutic modality are increasingly evident, reinforcing its value in mental health care and beyond (Pinkerton, 1996, 2003).

As the landscape of music therapy and music medicine continues to evolve, driven by technological advancements and a deepening understanding of music's therapeutic potential, innovations like MedRhythms' digital therapeutics and LUCID's curated music selections are at the forefront of expanding access and personalization within the music therapy industry. These developments, coupled with the urgent need for evidence-based research highlighted by initiatives from institutions like the NIH, underscore the ongoing journey to harness music's full therapeutic potential. My work, rooted in the belief in music's healing power, aims to contribute to this evolving narrative, offering new possibilities for healing and growth through the universal nature of music.

Case Stories

Engaging with the Music4Life® Music Medicine Protocol has been an eye-opening experience, revealing the significant impact of music on healing and recovery. In the realm of oncology, the Music Medicine Pill® and Mood Exercise Regimen®, cornerstones of our protocol, have been revolutionary. This approach, which involves selecting music that harmonizes with the patient's healing journey, has significantly alleviated anxiety and enhanced overall wellness for cancer patients. It's a testament to music's intrinsic healing power, addressing not just the physical symptoms but also the emotional and psychological challenges that accompany a cancer diagnosis.

The positive feedback from oncology departments where the Music Medicine Pill has been introduced is incredibly affirming. Patients have reported a notable decrease in trait anxiety levels and a boost in their resilience, underscoring the protocol's success in navigating the complex emotional landscape of cancer treatment. These outcomes provide comfort and reinforce the potential of music therapy as an essential component of comprehensive healthcare. Some of my experiences are reported in "Brace for Impact: A Case for Emotional Fluidity," and have solidified my belief in music's ability to transcend traditional healing (Pinkerton, 2019).

Transforming Grief into Growth

Connie's journey through grief and physical pain illustrates the profound impact of personalized music therapy on healing and personal transformation. Amidst battling bone cancer, knee surgery recovery, and mourning the loss of her mother, Connie found herself in a cycle of constant pain and emotional detachment. Her condition had left her reliant on a wheelchair and walker, progressing to the use of a cane for mobility when she encountered a cancer support group where a guest music therapist introduced her to a personalized Music Medicine Pill® (MMP).

After committing to daily listening sessions with the MMP, Connie experienced remarkable improvements. Within two weeks, she walked into the music therapist's office unaided by a cane, signaling a significant turnaround in her physical health. More importantly, Connie's engagement with life was rekindled; her grief had subsided, and the once omnipresent physical pain had been dramatically reduced. Emboldened by her newfound strength, Connie embarked on previously unimaginable adventures—traveling and enrolling in classes, thus embracing life's opportunities with open arms.

Connie shared her story, shedding light on her struggle with multiple myeloma, a cancer affecting the bone marrow and causing severe bone pain exacerbated by arthritis. Despite her professional background in counseling and therapy, which taught her to maintain emotional equilibrium, the cancer seeped into her personal life, limiting her ability to experience joy or sorrow. The realization of her declining activity levels and the dominion pain had over her life prompted Connie to seek change.

A pivotal moment in Connie's music journey into recovery was the day she inadvertently left her cane behind while descending the stairs from her second-floor apartment. This moment of forgetfulness turned into a revelation—she didn't need the cane anymore. It marked the beginning of Connie's journey towards letting go of physical and emotional crutches, allowing herself to feel more deeply without the overshadowing presence of pain.

Connie's transformation underscores the power of music as a therapeutic tool, not just for managing physical discomfort but also for navigating the complex terrain of emotional healing. The personalized Music Medicine Pill® provided by Music4Life® emerged as a beacon of hope for Connie, significantly reducing her mood challenges and fostering relaxation and happiness. Her story is a testament to the potential of this Music Medicine Protocol to transcend traditional therapy forms, offering a holistic path to wellness and a renewed zest for life.

Comfort in the Skies and Beyond

During boarding a routine commercial flight, I sat between two individuals, each facing unique challenges. To my left, in an aisle seat, a woman was visibly shaken by anxiety, her unease manifesting in constant requests to the flight attendant for a blanket to provide warm comfort. In an effort to offer relief, I introduced her to a Music Medicine Pill®, an auditory therapeutic aid designed to reduce anxiety, elicit relaxation, and improve positive energy by processing through a Mood Sequence Formula™. Remarkably, in less than 30 minutes, the effects were evident. The woman, previously consumed by her anxiety, found warmth without needing a blanket, no longer requiring the flight attendant's attention. This transformation was so profound that it piqued the curiosity of the nurse seated to my right. Intrigued by the sudden change, she began to sketch out what she imagined were the physiological processes influenced by music therapy, astonished by the efficacy of such a non-traditional approach to calming anxiety. Recent research validates how this occurred with the entrainment mechanism influencing the psychophysiological relaxation response, wherein a stronger increase in peripheral blood flow contributes to feeling warmer (Kim et al., 2018).

In a contrasting yet similarly distressing scenario, our group was in a peculiar situation during a private jet flight on tour with Wayne Newton. We were the only aircraft granted permission to depart in the midst of severe weather. Amidst this backdrop of tension and unease, our drummer began to exhibit signs of a panic attack, a condition palpable through his pasty complexion, stiff posture, and difficulty engaging in conversation. In an attempt to alleviate his distress, I offered him the same Music Medicine Pill, which he accepted and experienced through headphones. The therapeutic impact of the music was swift and noticeable; within 30 minutes, he reported a significant improvement in his condition. His complexion regained its natural hue, his body relaxed, and he could converse freely and comfortably, sharing his experience of overcoming the panic that had momentarily overtaken him. These incidents, each occurring in the skies but under vastly different circumstances, underscore the transformative power of music applied as medicine, offering a glimpse into the potential of therapeutic music to provide solace and recovery in acute distress.

Harnessing the Power of Music for Emotion Regulation in Schools

Judy Poteete, a retired elementary school counselor, reflects on a pivotal moment in her career that reshaped her approach to supporting students with high anxiety and anger levels. About 15 years ago, Judy attended a workshop I led on the Music Medicine Protocol, a revelation that would significantly influence her work with children. The workshop introduced her to the transformative potential of music to affect emotional states, a theory she eagerly applied in her practice.

In her role, Judy frequently encountered students who entered her office or classroom exhibiting signs of excitement, anticipation, or restlessness. Drawing from the insights gained at the workshop, she began to experiment with a Music Medicine Pill® during her anger management, stress, and self-control groups. This innovative approach involved playing music that initially matched the students' high energy levels before gradually transitioning to more melodic, calming tones. The result was astonishing: the children's behavior mirrored the music's tempo, moving from agitation to calm.

The impact of the Music Medicine Pill was so profound that students would often inquire about the background music after just five minutes in the room. Judy's explanation was simple: the music served as a buffer against outside noise, creating an undisturbed environment conducive to meaningful sessions. Over time, the initial need to play lively music at the start of each session diminished as the students became conditioned to the calming effect of entering the group space. Within 4 to 6 weeks, Judy noted that she no longer needed to start with lively music; the children would already be calm by the time they reached her office. If she ever forgot to turn on the music, the students would miss it and ask her to turn it on, showing the enduring impact of this auditory intervention.

Judy's experience highlights the effectiveness of using music as a therapeutic tool in educational settings. Judy facilitated peaceful and productive sessions by incorporating music that resonated with the students' initial emotional states and guided them toward tranquility. Her story shows how music can play an essential role in emotion regulation, providing valuable insights for educators and counselors seeking innovative strategies to support their students' well-being.

Expanding the Reach: Key2MEE® Music App

The Music4Life® Music Medicine Protocol stands at the forefront of therapeutic innovation, extending its benefits beyond traditional clinical settings to impact areas such as education, professional development, and public accessibility. The protocol equips professionals and individuals with the skills and knowledge necessary to harness music's therapeutic potential through educational programs, certification training, and digital platforms.

At the core of Music4life's educational initiatives is the "Music Medicine Boot Camp," an accredited course approved for CEUs by the Nevada State Board of Nursing since 1990. All training is on-demand, online at Music MedicineAcademy.com, with another course at Udemy.com. This global course entitled "Making Music Medicine" opens the door to the therapeutic benefits of 17 mental health strategies through music. All courses and trainings support learners intentionally using music for emotion regulation, mood management, and enhanced well-being. The curriculum ranges from the basics of music therapy and the Music4Life® Music Medicine Protocol to advanced techniques for creating prescriptive playlist Music Medicine Pills®, catering to seasoned music therapy professionals, caregivers, educators, and clinicians new to its therapeutic possibilities.

Furthering professional development, Music4Life's certification training and workshops provide in-depth instruction on integrating music therapy-informed techniques into various practices. These programs cover the protocol's theoretical underpinnings and application strategies and facilitate a community of practice among mental health providers, fostering collaboration and knowledge exchange. The workshop curriculum "6 Habits of Music Medicine for Highly Empowered People" is facilitated by Music4Life Specialists at NAMI-Southern Nevada (National Alliance in Mental Illness) and through innovative collaborations such as a symphony and family support center.

This comprehensive approach to training addresses the shortage of qualified music therapists by broadening the scope of who can apply music therapy-informed principles, thus making its benefits more accessible. The Key2MEE® Music App, a notable patented technological advancement, exemplifies this by offering personalized music prescriptions that empower individuals to engage with music therapy-informed interventions independently. Key2MEE.com reflects a modern approach to healthcare, where digital solutions include the Emotional Profile Quiz, tutorials, tools, prescriptive playlists, and telehealth access to the network of Music4Life® Specialists. Considering all genres, utilizing preferred and pre-selected music increases the accessibility and applicability of therapeutic interventions to regulate emotions for mood mastery. The capacity to monitor adherence and effectiveness will be enhanced by tracking progress and training clinicians to utilize Key2MEE.com with clients (McFerran et al., 2022).

Expanding the Music4Life Music Medicine Protocol into various domains accentuates the growing recognition of music therapy's benefits beyond clinical settings. Music4Life contributes to the scientific understanding and application of music therapy by advocating for increased awareness, research, and funding to ensure its integration into daily wellness practices to regulate emotions.

Music transcends mere entertainment; it serves as a profound conduit for connection, understanding, and healing. The various narratives—from intimate moments with loved ones through music to revolutionary insights into how music impacts our brains—support music's unique role, not just as a form of expression but as a powerful healing tool. Music therapy, blending traditional and innovative practices, emerges not only as a source of comfort and hope but also as an improvement in cognitive functioning, emotional expression, gait training, movement, and pain management.

Reflecting on music therapy's integration of art and science to meet both emotional and physical needs reveals its invaluable impact. Music therapy's extensive applications, from supporting individuals with PTSD to improving group dynamics in schools, demonstrate its versatility and effectiveness. The shift towards personalized music therapy, including Music Medicine Pills®, envisions a future where everyone can access music's therapeutic benefits tailored to their individual needs. Personalized Music Medicine Pills, meticulously developed by trained Music4Life® Practitioners, are fine-tuned to ensure the most beneficial therapeutic outcomes for each individual.

The evolution of music therapy, particularly through approaches like Music4Life's Music Medicine Protocol, represents significant progress in our use of music for healing. This evolution paves the way for more tailored and accessible music therapy-informed strategies. As we continue to innovate with personalized tools for mood mastery, we aim to make the profound benefits of music accessible to everyone, tailored to meet the unique needs and circumstances of each individual.

2

THE JOURNEY OF RECOVERY AND RESILIENCE

M usic is often enjoyed as entertainment, but its purpose extends far beyond when applied thoughtfully. It can support individuals dealing with serious challenges such as illness, addiction, and emotional distress. Given the universal nature of music, it resonates deeply with our emotions, making it an indispensable resource for those facing significant adversities.

Research has shown that music therapy can reduce stress, alleviate pain, and enhance healing. These positive effects often result from music's ability to engage the brain's reward centers, releasing dopamine that reduces pain and boosts pleasure. In recovery, it can help lift spirits and ease anxiety and depression. It also allows individuals to express complex emotions nonverbally, providing an outlet when words are insufficient. Through its rhythms and harmonies, music creates an organized framework that helps individuals manage their emotional experiences, aiding their recovery and healing ("Music Therapy and Addiction Treatment," 2021).

Music offers a dynamic and adaptable presence in addiction treatment, providing a unique blend of therapeutic approaches that cater to a wide range of individuals. By incorporating active music-making and listening, this form of therapy taps into the brain's reward systems in ways that mirror the effects of substances, potentially mitigating cravings and elevating mood. Its application is sensitive to the individual's history and preferences, aiming to avoid any music that could inadvertently trigger negative responses.

The therapeutic process in music therapy is highly personalized, involving an array of musical experiences designed to meet the specific needs of those in recovery. These can include activities like songwriting, engaging in music-assisted creative arts, lyric analysis, music-making, and even music-assisted meditation, all geared towards facilitating emotional expression, managing withdrawal symptoms, and promoting overall mental, emotional, and spiritual health.

While the efficacy of music therapy in addiction treatment continues to be explored, the subjective benefits reported by participants highlight its valuable role in supporting recovery journeys. The versatility and effectiveness of music therapy illustrate its potential as a useful complement to traditional treatment methods across the broad spectrum of addiction recovery (Murphy, 2013; Borling, 2017).

One remarkable case that exemplifies this is Kelly Swan, who, in an unexpected turn, overcame her polysubstance addiction (cocaine, marijuana, and alcohol) 36 years ago through a unique approach to music. Kelly discovered the associative power of music, realizing that certain melodies could trigger specific moods and cravings linked to her addiction. This realization led her to replace pain medication with carefully selected music as a form of therapy.

During the onset of the COVID-19 pandemic, Kelly faced a medical crisis that landed her in the hospital with severe pain due to a perforated bowel. After enduring 16 days of complications, her sister ensured that Kelly had access to Native American flute music in the hospital, knowing her preference for it over her usual piano music, which she found exacerbated her stress and pain levels.

Kelly expressed a deep affinity for the flute's simplicity, noting, "It's un-complicated. I can just follow and ride on the note." This music had a transformative effect, lifting her consciousness above the pain and allowing her to acknowledge it without being overwhelmed. Through mindfulness training, Kelly learned to focus her consciousness like a spotlight, centering her attention on the flute music and letting the pain fade into the backdrop. This approach proved effective beyond her hospital stay; three years later, during another hospitalization, she experienced a faster recovery without pain medication by listening to the same Native American flute music. Even now, when faced with back pain from a past sky-diving accident, she turns to this music instead of medication, finding solace and healing in its melodies. She has grown accustomed to this music through frequent use, making her more responsive to its soothing effects.

Music significantly influences physiological and emotional states, provid-ing therapeutic benefits that enhance psychological relief. When calming music engages the autonomic nervous system, it decreases heart rate and lowers blood pressure, promoting relaxation and recovery for individuals with health issues. It also stimulates the production of dopamine and oxytocin, which enhance mood and overall well-being.

This soothing quality of music makes it a powerful tool for expressing and navigating complex emotions, especially beneficial for those dealing with trauma or mental health challenges. Music evokes a broad spectrum of emotions, providing a crucial outlet for emotional release. Moreover, music's structured and systematic nature brings peace and order, effectively quieting and organizing thoughts, thus fostering mental clarity and emotional stability.

Having instant access to such a wealth of music allows me to curate and utilize prescriptive playlists tailored to specific emotional and physical needs. This capability has proven invaluable, not just in my own recovery from breast cancer but also in my work with clients. The right music is always at my fingertips, whether it's to calm anxiety before a procedure, boost morale during a tough day, or foster deep relaxation after a stressful event. We're fortunate to live in a time when your phone becomes a powerful, portable command center of prescriptive playlists capable of transforming your experience quickly - anywhere.

Finding Harmony Amidst Breast Cancer

Battling breast cancer is a journey through both emotional and physical trials, where the soothing presence of music therapy can make a significant difference. As a form of treatment, it offers solace and potent emotional support, helping to fortify my resilience during challenging times.

Central to my therapeutic approach is the Music4Life® Music Medicine Protocol, developed from evidence-based practice with tailored care. This protocol integrates music into the cancer treatment regimen, adapting to my specific emotional and physical needs. It's more than just listening; it involves carefully chosen melodies and rhythms to foster a healing environment that supports my mind and body throughout recovery.

As my daughter navigated through her turbulent teenage years, my worry for her well-being grew steadily. This concern reached a climax in 2014, the same year I noticed a new, larger lump in my breast. Despite this alarming discovery, I initially dismissed it as just another fibroid, my focus entirely consumed by my daughter's crises.

My daughter's husband sent me distressing texts, abruptly labeling her a drug dealer and expressing his overwhelming frustration. I found myself glued to my phone, anxiously awaiting updates that swung wildly between hope and despair. The situation escalated until suddenly, my daughter disappeared. Desperate, I involved the police and our family in the search, only to find that she had chosen to vanish and was insistent she was "fine." Determined to keep any connection, I contacted her new acquaintances, hoping to remain a part of her life.

By December 2014, the stress manifested physically; the lump in my breast began to hurt. Simultaneously, I was navigating the complexities of changing life insurance policies. A routine screening for the insurance led to a shocking denial due to the results of my lab tests. Concerned, I consulted my doctor in mid-January 2015. He reassured me that insurance denials over health concerns were common and initially seemed unworried. However, when I mentioned the lump, his demeanor changed. He examined it and urgently advised me to seek further medical evaluation as soon as I secured health insurance.

Two months later, with insurance in place, I quickly underwent a mammogram, ultrasound, and biopsy. The results were devastating. As I pulled over to take the call, the nurse's words echoed through me, "You have breast cancer." I immediately phoned my husband, who oddly remarked that this hardship would be brief—a comment he later didn't recall making. Nonetheless, I clung to his words, hoping for a swift journey through treatment.

Despite the overwhelming news, I maintained my professional responsibilities. Just days before my biopsy, I presided over a regional music therapy conference, burdened with heavy duties and speaking before hundreds. During an executive board meeting, a call from my estranged daughter about my health shook me deeply, forcing me to step out and let my vice president take over. My colleagues, unaware of my pending diagnosis, learned only of the family turmoil, which was painful enough to share.

Refusing to let cancer dictate my life, I pushed forward, continuing my extensive work schedule, facilitating music therapy sessions in addiction treatment facilities, and presenting at conferences. I visualized vanquishing cancer, even hosting a healing circle in my music therapy office, where I envisioned the tumor dissolving into light.

As I moved through this journey, I used music to manage my anxiety and pain. I crafted specific playlists for surgery and recovery. This therapeutic strategy allowed me to maintain complete control of my emotional balance within a chaotic situation. In the face of overwhelming stress and uncertainty, it served as a crucial anchor, grounding me and restoring a sense of calm. Even in the face of surgical delays and intense discomfort, I remained tethered to my belief in healing—both emotional and physical.

The Music4Life® Music Medicine Protocol was integral to my treatment and recovery process throughout this arduous journey. This innovative approach to music therapy, which I had developed and refined through years of practice, allowed me to systematically use specific music sequences that aligned with my emotional and physiological states. During moments of high anxiety, such as waiting for surgery or undergoing uncomfortable surgical preparation, the carefully curated playlists provided a much-needed mood mastery focus, helping to modulate my stress responses and enhance my overall resilience. The music acted not just as a distraction but as a therapeutic ally, engaging my mind and body in a healing dialogue that was comforting and empowering.

The rapid progression from the diagnosis of breast cancer on March 24 to its eradication by April 20 was a whirlwind that, under other circumstances, might have left me reeling. However, with the help of the Music4Life Protocol and a robust support system, I navigated this intense period with a focus and determination that surprised even me. Following the successful treatment, I embraced further preventive measures with 15 rounds of radiation, ensuring thorough care. I regained control quickly enough to attend a family wedding and enjoy a memorable 4-day canoe trip with my family, ending at Judith's Landing. This experience symbolized both a literal and figurative journey of recovery and reflection.

The decision to end almost two years of anti-estrogen hormone therapy was made with the full support of my oncologist, reflecting our mutual confidence in the progress I had made. This decision marked a significant milestone in my recovery, affirming my belief in the power of combining conventional medical treatments with holistic approaches like music therapy. The outcome of my treatment—a stark contrast to the grim scenario initially outlined by my physician—is a testament to the effectiveness of integrating music therapy into traditional medical frameworks, reinforcing my life's work and passion for music therapy. This experience has transformed my approach to personal health and resilience and deepened my commitment to helping others heal through the power of music.

During my battle with breast cancer, the unique application of music therapy, specifically through the Music4Life® Music Medicine Protocol, became a cornerstone of my emotional support system. This protocol, which I had meticulously developed, was critical in managing my psychological well-being through meticulously crafted playlists. These playlists were not just music collections but were tailored to resonate with my fluctuating emotional needs, facilitating deep emotion regulation and coping during some of the most challenging moments of my life.

One particularly impactful aspect of my use of music came in the form of visualization techniques before surgery. As I prepared for each medical procedure, I employed music to help focus and calm my nerves, enhancing my visualization of the successful outcomes. For instance, during the March 20, 2015, biopsy, I consciously watched the procedure on the computer monitor while using music to deepen my focus. This setup allowed me to fully visualize the tumor, enhancing the mental imagery where I envisioned it being targeted and obliterated by beams of light. The music's dynamic layers facilitated this visualization. They bolstered my emotional resilience, shifting my mindset from a passive patient to an active participant in my healing process.

The impact of music extended into another profound session on March 29 during a gathering with my prayer team. A dozen practitioners and ministers formed a healing circle around me in the music therapy room at my office. The music played a crucial role. It helped me visualize the tumor being blasted apart by light and ultimately disappearing. This session had a profound effect on my mental state, to the extent that I found myself not checking for the tumor as frequently as before. By the following weekend, when I checked, the large lump was no longer palpable. I excitedly contacted my physician, who emphasized the need for further diagnostics to ensure comprehensive care, reflecting the importance of understanding the tumor's type and stage despite the encouraging physical changes. This sequence of events highlighted how the structured and systematic nature of music prepared me psychologically and endowed me with a renewed sense of control and agency over the healing process.

Reflecting on this intense period, I vividly remember how instrumental music was—as a therapeutic backdrop and as an active participant in my healing journey. "My breast cancer journey was quick because the Music4Life® Music Medicine Protocol works even when you are not listening to music. Today, nine years later, I continue to be cancer-free." This quote encapsulates the profound and enduring impact that music therapy had on my recovery, illustrating its role not just in physical healing but in fostering resilience that has sustained me long after the medical treatments concluded.

Music was a constant and comforting companion throughout the journey, from diagnosis through surgery and into recovery. It provided solace during times of uncertainty and strength during moments of physical and emotional challenge. One playlist featured soothing violin pieces that narrated my journey toward healing. This auditory support was crucial in helping me maintain emotional balance and resilience through the ups and downs of recovery.

The integration of music into each phase of my treatment emphasized its therapeutic potential, transforming a challenging recovery into a journey of profound healing. Music ensured that I never felt isolated, surrounding me with melodies that reinforced my spirit and resilience every step of the way. This comprehensive approach, where emotional healing is prioritized alongside physical recovery, exemplifies the transformative power of music therapy in oncology and overall healthcare settings. The consistent and strategic use of music throughout my treatment not only alleviated physical symptoms but also provided a powerful psychological aid that was instrumental in my swift and successful recovery.

The Music4Life® Music Medicine Protocol stands out for its adaptability and personalization. These aspects tailor music-based interventions to meet the specific emotional and psychological needs of individuals battling cancer. In my own treatment for breast cancer, this personalized approach was meticulously implemented through the creation of two specialized iTunes playlists labeled "Surgery" and "Surgery-Recovery." These playlists, developed following a Mood Sequence Formula™, included 15 selections of soothing music lasting 1 hour and 42 minutes and 14 selections of violin music lasting 1 hour and 21 minutes for recovery, respectively (refer to Appendix A to view the two playlists).

This customization allowed the music to directly address and alleviate the intense emotions and physical discomfort typically experienced during stressful times. I collaborated closely with the nursing staff to effectively integrate music into the surgical process. The nurses helped by taping headphones to my ears and securing my cell phone to my body away from the surgery site, ensuring continuous application of this music medicine-based intervention. This preparation proved essential as the pre-op phase was unexpectedly challenging, marked by significant anxiety, pain, and delays.

Reflecting on the effectiveness of the Music4Life® Music Medicine Protocol, it is clear that the personalized playlists not only helped manage the physical pain and discomfort associated with surgery but also significantly reduced the emotional duress. The calming sequences of the music provided a mental escape from the stressful surgical environment, maintaining a sense of peace and resilience throughout the procedure.

The protocol greatly enhanced my quality of life during one of the most challenging periods of my life, ensuring that I was not just surviving the ordeal but actively engaging in my recovery. Each note and melody was designed to soothe and heal, demonstrating the protocol's capacity to transform the healing journey. The ability of the Music4Life Music Medicine Protocol to adapt to specific patient needs, coupled with the precise personalization of music selections, underscores the profound impact music therapy-informed methods can have on those battling cancer, offering significant emotional relief and fostering a conducive environment for recovery.

Strategies for Recovery

Music offers support and enhancement across various stages of heal-ing—from initial treatment to long-term maintenance. This method cus-tomizes music therapy-informed methods to meet individual needs, mak-ing it equally effective during intense treatment phases and for ongoing wellness. By incorporating music therapy at various stages of recovery, pa-tients receive ongoing support, ideally with a music therapist, who adjusts music to their evolving needs, helping them achieve and maintain their long-term recovery goals.

To effectively incorporate music into recovery processes, it's important to understand how adaptable music therapy can be to individual preferences and specific stages of recovery. For example, selecting genres or pieces a patient connects with can significantly enhance the therapeutic impact, making the experience more personal and practical. Music therapy's role in recovery is substantial—it actively reduces stress, aids in emotion regula-tion, and promotes mental health. By complementing traditional recovery approaches, music therapy offers a holistic method to support healing and foster resilience, making it a valuable component of comprehensive recovery programs.

John's story offers a compelling look at the significant effects of person-alized music therapy. Struggling with severe anxiety and the aftershocks of a traumatic event, John found traditional treatment methods helpful but not wholly transformative. When he began working with a music therapist who tailored sessions to his musical tastes and emotional needs, John discovered a powerful new dimension to his healing process. The music soothed him and helped him access and articulate feelings that had been locked away, facilitating a deeper and more enduring recovery.

John found himself grappling with the long shadows cast by a childhood marred by mental abuse. Traditional therapy sessions offered him some relief, but the deep-seated trauma of his past created barriers in his mind that seemed impenetrable. That was until he encountered the transformative potential of music therapy under my guidance, introducing him to a form of healing that resonated with the very core of his being.

John vividly recalls the moment music therapy began to make a difference, "Music therapy that Judith Pinkerton did, was the only therapy that could bust through a wall that I'd built in my head from mental abuse when I was a child." These sessions weren't just about listening to music but an active engagement with a sound that beckoned him toward healing. The unique strategies I taught him were explicitly designed to address his PTSD symptoms, and they empowered him to take control of his emotional and psychological well-being.

The impact of these sessions extended beyond the confines of the therapy room. I equipped John with tools and techniques he could use at home, ensuring that his journey toward healing didn't pause when he stepped outside my treatment room. His testimony speaks volumes about the efficacy of music therapy, "My PTSD has decreased dramatically using music therapy-informed strategies that she taught me. She showed us how we could do it at home."

Through music, John learned how to tap into deeply buried emotions and gradually dismantle the psychological barriers erected during his childhood. The therapeutic sessions provided him with a safe space to explore his trauma and begin the process of healing, offering a unique breakthrough that traditional therapies had failed to achieve. As John continues to use these music therapy-informed strategies at home, he finds not just relief but a hopeful pathway leading away from the shadows of his past towards a brighter, more serene future.

Similarly, Sonny, grappling with the challenges of addiction treatment, found himself at a turning point during my music therapy sessions. Having always felt a profound emotional impact from music, Sonny began to understand its potential as a deliberate therapeutic tool, an insight that would profoundly influence his approach to recovery.

"I've known for a long time that music has a great emotional effect on me," Sonny reflected, sharing his initial understanding of music's influence. However, with my guidance, he opened his eyes to the possibilities of using music intentionally. He learned to first select music that mirrored his current emotional state, a crucial step that allowed him to fully 'tune in' and synchronize his feelings with the rhythm and melodies. This alignment was just the beginning.

Once in sync with the music, Sonny discovered he could take control, steering his emotions in a direction that fostered healing and empowerment. "I can take that music and shift my mood and the emotion of the music into the direction that I want to go, which is loving and powerful," he explained. This process of intentional music listening became a vital tool in his recovery, providing him with a dynamic way to manage his emotional landscape.

Sonny emphasized that the beauty of this approach lies in its versatility—music therapy isn't confined to any specific genre or style. Whether it involves the soothing tones of a classical piece or the upbeat rhythms of rock, music therapy actively engages participants in their emotional journey, allowing them to tailor the experience to their needs. "It doesn't have to be any particular style of music or band. It doesn't have to be Native American chanting or mystic drums," Sonny noted. This realization was liberating, highlighting the vast musical choices available to aid emotion regulation and personal growth.

The insight Sonny gained from the music therapy sessions I facilitated significantly changed his approach to recovery and emotional self-regulation, empowering him to actively shape his emotional responses and path to healing (The Music4Life® USA, 2021).

Scan this QR code to hear Sonny discuss his entire story.

The narratives of John and Sonny beautifully illustrate the impact of music therapy on recovery. They highlight its role in unlocking emotional expression, fostering self-awareness, and catalyzing personal transformation. Each story showcases the adaptability of music therapy to individual needs and recovery stages, making it a pivotal tool in therapeutic practices.

These stories emphasize that music therapy is a core component of effective therapeutic interventions, not just a supplementary aid. By incorporating music therapy into recovery programs, practitioners deliver a holistic approach that actively utilizes music's therapeutic potential to address complex emotional and psychological challenges. John and Sonny's experiences demonstrate how music therapy provides lasting change and equips individuals with tools for ongoing mood management and recovery.

Family Dynamics and Music

Navigating the intricate connections between family dynamics, trauma, and recovery can be deeply challenging, especially when words fail to capture the full spectrum of emotions involved. For many families, common issues like misunderstandings and unresolved conflicts can create persistent tension that complicates the healing process. Music therapy offers a vital non-verbal way to bridge these gaps, providing a means of communication that enhances empathy, aids in emotional processing, and strengthens relationships (Jackson, 2015). This is particularly important when expressing feelings verbally can be too painful or when members are at different stages of emotional readiness. By weaving music into the healing journey, families can address deep-rooted issues and traumas more effectively, paving the way for recovery and nurturing a deeper mutual understanding.

In family dynamics, mainly where addiction is involved, reintegrating a family member post-rehabilitation can create a tense environment, with everyone on high alert for signs of relapse. This sensitivity can lead to strained relations, as actions reminiscent of past addictive behaviors are closely monitored. Music therapy can help maintain a balanced dynamic during this delicate transition, easing collective anxieties and promoting a supportive home environment.

A practical application of music therapy in these settings involves the creation of personalized Music Medicine Pills®. These are customized playlists designed to manage specific emotional states associated with the potential for relapse. For example, a recovering addict might use a specially curated playlist to shift feelings of anxiety, depression, anger, or mood swings, which are common relapse triggers. This proactive approach helps the individual maintain emotional equilibrium, reassure family members, and reduce tension and misunderstandings.

Moreover, regular prescriptive music listening sessions can be therapeutic and preventive. These sessions allow for cleansing emotional disturbances and reinforcing positive emotional states, aiding the recovery process. They also present opportunities for family members to engage in meaningful interactions about the effects of the music, enhancing empathy and understanding among them. Questions like, "Did your music listening help you feel better?" encourage communication and provide feedback to reinforce the recovery journey.

By incorporating music therapy-informed strategies into the family setting, it becomes possible to address and mitigate the emotional and psychological challenges that often accompany family trauma and addiction. Music therapy not only supports the individual in recovery but may also strengthen familial bonds, making it an invaluable component of the healing process for the entire family. Families can experience deeper emotional connections through these music-based interventions and develop a more resilient framework for dealing with future challenges.

A case in point involves a music therapy client who creatively adapted his use of a music-based intervention to ease family tensions. Aware of his family's reaction whenever he reached for his Music Medicine CD—immediate concern and heightened alert—he switched to a more discreet method, creating a personalized Music Medicine Pill® via Pandora. This adjustment helped to mitigate the family's anxiety, as there was no longer a conspicuous trigger to signal distress.

The strategy was twofold: "I am trapped in an unsettled mood with relapse close by, so therefore I am treating this trigger mood to shift out of it and avoid relapse," he explained. The music acted as a direct intervention to counteract potential emotional spirals that could lead to a relapse. His family played a supportive role, occasionally offering gentle reminders to engage with his prescriptive playlist when they sensed he was struggling.

On the preventative side, he made it a routine to listen to prescriptive music almost daily, which he described as a way to "cleanse my emotions for optimal recovery and to prevent being trapped in an unsettled mood that triggers my relapse." This regular engagement with music was crucial for maintaining his emotional balance and was designed not to alarm his family. They learned to observe the benefits subtly, noting the positive changes in his mood and sometimes asking, "Did your music listening help you feel better?"

This approach supported his ongoing recovery and educated his family on how music could serve as a powerful ally in the process. It transformed the role of music from a potential sign of crisis to a routine part of healing and mood management, along with a more supportive and understanding family environment. Through music, the family found a common language for navigating the challenges of recovery, enhancing trust and empathy among its members.

While music therapy-informed strategies provided a transformative tool for one family navigating recovery challenges, enhancing their ability to communicate and empathize through a shared musical language, it has also proven vital in individual contexts outside of addiction. Take, for instance, the story of Mallory. Her adolescence was overshadowed by intense emotional turmoil and isolation, exacerbated by bullying at school and complicated family dynamics at home. Music therapy was introduced into Mallory's life when she was 13 as a method to manage her overwhelming emotions and the strained relationships within her blended family. Though initially skeptical, she discovered that music offered a unique way to express herself and connect with her family members, who were also dealing with their own grief and challenges.

Mallory's journey through adolescence was marked by intense emotional turmoil and isolation. Tall and overweight, she was often the target of cruel taunts at school, which only compounded the grief and anger she felt following her father's death when she was just eight years old. Home was her only refuge, where she could be alone with her sorrow. Yet, even there, the dynamics were complex with the introduction of a stepfather and step-siblings who brought their own shadows to the family picture.

Music therapy entered Mallory's life when she was 13, introduced as a tool to cope with her sprawling, tangled emotions and the fraught family

dynamics. Initially skeptical, Mallory found that the therapy sessions o-
ffered a novel way to communicate and process her feelings without words,
which had often failed her. The music became a conduit for expression and
a bridge to understanding between her and her family members, who were
also struggling to navigate their collective grief and frustration.

Mallory learned to use the MEE^{TM} tape—a personalized music therapy tool
that predated the Music Medicine Pill$^{®}$ to cope with her emotions and
actively reshape them. "Music was just music for entertainment before,"
she reflects, "but now, it's everything—therapy and entertainment, a part
of me." This shift wasn't just internal; it manifested in her interactions with
her family. As she navigated her feelings through music, her family began to
understand her better, helping to ease the tension and misunderstandings
that had once seemed impossible.

Therapy also empowered her to confront and begin healing from her
father's death. This subject had once been too painful to touch. Music
allowed her to process her grief in layers at her own pace, making it less
overwhelming. Her ability to articulate her emotions improved, enhancing
her interactions with her stepfamily and helping to foster a more empathetic, supportive home environment. The shared experience of music
therapy sessions occasionally included her family members, further aiding
in healing old wounds and building a new, stronger foundation of mutual
respect and understanding.

As she grew older, her relationship with music evolved. Once a passive listener, she became an active participant, choosing tracks that mirrored her
feelings to help shift her mood or comfort herself. Her music preferences
matured; she moved away from the angst-ridden tracks of her early teens

to more diverse genres that reflected her broader emotional landscape. "I can pick songs that make me feel exactly how I feel, then by the end of the CD feel better," she says about the power of her MEE™ tape (and with technological advances, now her MEE CD, both predecessors of the Music Medicine Pill®).

Now 33, Mallory no longer sees herself as a victim of her circumstances but as a proactive agent in her own life. Music therapy taught her that change is possible, and it equipped her with the tools to maintain her mental health and forge deeper connections with those around her. It also prepared her to extend her therapeutic journey beyond music, opening her up to other forms of treatment and self-expression. Her journey is a testament to the capacity of music therapy not just to heal an individual but to transform family dynamics, bringing members closer through the shared language of music.

Mallory's experience demonstrates the transformative power of music therapy in reshaping personal crises and enhancing family bonds. Similarly impactful is the story of Sara, who encountered severe emotional distress following her husband's death and her own cancer diagnosis. Traditional therapeutic methods fell short in addressing her profound anxiety and grief.

Sara, a pseudonym, a personnel analyst overwhelmed by panic attacks after her husband's death from cancer, sought my help during a particularly challenging emotional period. Her distress intensified six months later with the diagnosis of a cancerous polyp in her colon. At that time, traditional treatment methods had failed to alleviate her suffering.

In her quest for relief, I introduced Sara to a personalized therapeutic approach—a specially crafted MEE™ tape designed to meet her unique emotional needs. This tailored music therapy intervention proved transformative. Remarkably, within just three weeks of daily listening, Sara's panic attacks ceased, and she was able to stop using Xanax, a medication she had previously relied on to manage her anxiety.

This music therapy approach not only halted her symptoms but also showed preventive potential. Sara acknowledged the importance of the intervention, noting, "I know that if I don't listen to the tape, the attacks will start again." Her ongoing engagement with music therapy has provided a sustained space for emotional processing and stability, which has been crucial in supporting her through the aftermath of her trauma.

Sara's experience demonstrates the healing capacity of music therapy and its ability to nurture a space for ongoing emotional expression and support. Dealing with trauma through such therapeutic interventions can offer a vital resource for individuals and families alike, creating a shared space where emotions can be expressed and managed collectively, enhancing mutual support within the family.

Music therapy does more than soothe individuals; it harmonizes the family, turning areas of discord into understanding and fear into resilience. Providing a non-verbal means of communication enables family members to safely express and manage complex emotions, deepening connections without the need for words. This approach transforms music into a bridge that helps to mend relational gaps, allowing empathy and understanding to grow organically. Engaging in music therapy together not only aids in individual healing but also solidifies family bonds, creating a supportive and cohesive environment where each member can feel genuinely supported and understood.

Testimonials and Concluding Remarks

The transformative journey through the Music4Life® Music Medicine Protocol encompasses a spectrum of personal experiences that reveal its profound impact on recovery. Individuals from various walks of life have turned to music therapy as a lifeline, navigating through intense physical pain, emotional turmoil, and psychological distress with remarkable outcomes. These testimonials highlight true stories of individual triumphs and illustrate the universal appeal and effectiveness of music therapy in fostering deep emotional healing and enhanced well-being. Through the power of music, those facing daunting challenges have found relief and a renewed sense of hope and resilience, reshaping their lives in ways they never imagined possible.

The personal accounts and testimonials discussed in this book originate from my own experiences as a licensed certified music therapist, the creator of the Music4Life Music Medicine Protocol, and a thriver of breast cancer. This narrative is based on firsthand experiences with the protocol during my journey through diagnosis, treatment, and recovery, providing a practical application of the protocol in a real-world setting. The effectiveness of the protocol in managing the complexities and challenges of undergoing cancer treatment is reinforced by the tangible outcomes observed and documented throughout my recovery. The authenticity of this account, alongside those of a few clients (selected from thousands of participants), underscores the impact and practicality of this music therapy approach in clinical practice, serving as a valuable example for those considering similar therapeutic approaches.

The journey of "Anna," a pseudonym with the Music Medicine Protocol, illustrates a transformative path from enduring chronic clinical depression and anxiety to finding profound relief and a revitalized quality of life. For over 30 years, Anna reported struggling with mental health challenges, supported by medications like Prozac, Wellbutrin, and Xanax, which offered minimal comfort. Her challenges were exacerbated by sleepless nights and migraine headaches, adding to her distress.

A significant change occurred in February 2005 when Anna attended one of my presentations. Intrigued by the concept of music as medicine, she purchased two Music4Life® CDs—the "MEE™" Concert" and "MEE in the Key of Peace." Initially skeptical, Anna found the impact of these CDs to be immediate and profound. While listening to the "feel good" CD for the first time, she experienced an intense emotional release that brought her to tears on her drive home. This reaction underscored the deep emotions she had long suppressed.

Incorporating this music into her daily routine, Anna discovered that consistent listening markedly alleviated her symptoms. She noted that the music not only eased her depression and anxiety but also enhanced her sleep quality, which had been poor for years. Remarkably, since starting her Music Medicine Regimen, Anna reported no longer needing medication for her condition (note: Anna did not report a physician's advisement). She describes the CDs as transformative, capable of lifting the "heavy black cloud" that had lingered over her for decades.

Her experience demonstrates the therapeutic power of music, transforming Anna's approach to managing her mental health. She moved from relying on pharmaceuticals to embracing a holistic and enjoyable therapy that she could control and personalize. This shift not only improved her mental health but also her overall lifestyle, empowering her to run two businesses and plan for a third.

Anna's story as a workshop participant is a compelling example of how music applied as medicine may serve as a powerful alternative to traditional medical treatments, providing mental health relief and enabling personal and professional growth. When working with clients, I always recommend physician-directed reduction, prescription, or cessation of medication with documented reports of clients who refused medication becoming compliant and agreeing to finally use medication because of their experience with this protocol.

The story of Claire, a pseudonym used for confidentiality, illustrates the immediate and impactful nature of the Music Medicine Protocol in crisis situations. After a traumatic car accident, Claire found solace and stabilization in the same kind of music-based intervention, using the MEE™ Concert to significantly ease her initial panic and physical symptoms, showcasing the versatility and immediacy of Music Medicine Protocol in both chronic and acute settings.

After a distressing car accident, Claire, a business executive whose office was just down the hall from mine, came to me visibly shaken and in shock, recounting the traumatic event. In an effort to offer her some relief, I suggested she try the Music Medicine CD known as the MEE™ Concert. Shortly after listening, Claire experienced the profound calming effects of the music. The first two songs on the CD were particularly impactful, helping her transition from a state of turmoil to one of tranquility, offering immediate relief from her anxiety and physical discomfort.

Claire described the sensation as feeling like she was "floating," an expression that captures the profound sense of detachment from the immediate stress and discomfort caused by the accident. She also noted a noticeable change in her physical sensations; her blood flow and heartbeat reached a steadier, more relaxed rhythm, guiding her into a deeper state of relaxation.

This experience alleviated her immediate symptoms of shock and enabled her to regain her focus and composure, essential for her demanding role as an executive. Claire's account highlights the MEE Concert's ability to provide immediate therapeutic benefits, enhancing her ability to function and continue with her professional responsibilities. The impactful experience led her to plan on continuing this type of therapy, indicating the lasting impression of the music's soothing capabilities. Her story demonstrates the potential of the Music Medicine Protocol to provide rapid, effective relief in acutely stressful situations, underscoring its value as a tool for emotional and physical recovery.

I have worked with thousands of clients, each presenting a unique set of challenges that showcase the versatility and profound impact of music therapy across various conditions. One client, a vocational rehabilitation counselor who I will refer to as "Rachel" to maintain confidentiality, found the Music Medicine Protocol integral in managing her stress levels and maintaining her health. Before incorporating the MEE™ Concert CD into her routine, she avoided exercise due to spikes in blood pressure. This prescriptive music listening approach allowed her to engage in physical activities like biking and weightlifting without the health risks, demonstrating the effectiveness of this approach in physiological regulation.

A retired airline pilot, referred to here as "Tom," experienced a significant physical reaction during a Music4Life® Music Medicine demonstration. He described feeling what seemed like a heart chakra opening. This unexpected physical sensation occurred alongside the alleviation of chronic pain from a slipped disk and leg pain that he had endured since 1956. This instance underscores the potential of the Music Medicine Protocol to address long-standing physical ailments, highlighting its profound impact on chronic conditions.

Poco, a cancer survivor, found this music therapy approach instrumental in breaking through denial and restoring self-esteem, illustrating the emotional depth that music therapy can reach. The treatment provided not just a coping mechanism but a profound emotional release that facilitated a deeper healing process.

A retired chemical engineer, who I'll refer to as "Martin" to maintain confidentiality, described how his regular prescriptive music listening profoundly impacted his emotional state. He shared that this approach helped alleviate physical feelings of depression and replaced them with a sense of peace. Martin's experience demonstrates the capability of this approach to complement existing medication, providing 24-hour relief using prescriptive music listening in the evening when medication cannot be repeated.

A therapist, whom we'll refer to as "Danielle" to maintain confidentiality, utilized a custom Music Medicine Pill® to address her grief and chronic pain from lupus. This personalized prescriptive playlist helped her achieve a level of deep relaxation through the release of emotional tension, which enhanced the effectiveness of her pain medication, further demonstrating how music therapy serves as a complementary treatment alongside traditional medical approaches.

The testimonials from diverse individuals underscore the wide-reaching impact of the Music4Life® Music Medicine Protocol in healing and emotion regulation. It effectively manages both physical improvements and emotional states across various life challenges. For instance, Rachel could exercise without health risks. Tom found relief from chronic pain. Emotional breakthroughs are also significant, as seen in Poco's regained self-esteem and Martin's reduction of depression. These stories further illustrate the Music Medicine Protocol role as a catalyst for psychological growth and a tool for handling life's stresses.

These Music Medicine stories not only address immediate needs but also provide preventative benefits, crucial for maintaining long-term emotional stability and averting negative mental health spirals. This aspect is vital for sustained health management, making the Music Medicine Protocol an indispensable part of wellness strategies.

One compelling testimonial comes from a client, referred to here as Lynn, who shared her positive experience with the Music4Life MEE™ Concert CD. Lynn, a taxi driver, explained, "Music4Life's MEE™ Concert CD really worked for me and still does! After my 12-hour shifts driving on the strip, I was usually exhausted and my nerves were frazzled. It was tough to relax and get a good night's sleep. But once I started listening to CDs specifically designed to calm the body and mind, I woke up feeling great—well-rested, revitalized, and with improved clarity and focus. This

71

has been a game changer for me; I've had no accidents and fewer speeding tickets. I also have more energy throughout the day and feel much more relaxed. Music4Life has helped me overcome any discomfort and perform better at my job, allowing me to make more trips, improve my earnings, and increase my tips! Regularly listening to the CD has greatly reduced my stress levels and positively impacted my life." Lynn continues to rely on Music4Life® for relaxation and sleep, and it has even helped manage her slightly elevated blood pressure and supported her recent educational achievements, launching her new career as a Forensic Care Nurse Assistant. Her story highlights how integrating Music Medicine into daily routines can significantly enhance the quality of life and occupational performance.

Reflecting on the transformative power of music, I am constantly reminded of its profound impact, particularly in stories that demonstrate its ability to transcend traditional therapy. The music therapy-informed strategies we use can be accessed anytime through our digital devices. I often say, "We're really lucky to live in a time when your phone becomes a powerful, portable command center of prescriptive playlists capable of transforming your experience quickly - anywhere." From alleviating physical pain and soothing emotional distress to enhancing mental clarity, music therapy-infused strategies within Music4Life's Music Medicine Protocol emerge as a dynamic force in healing. It challenges us to integrate prescriptive music into our own or our loved ones' recovery processes, offering a tool that uniquely adapts to individual healing journeys. More than a temporary escape, this protocol offers a pathway to lasting transformation, enriching our lives and fortifying us against challenges.

3

THE MUSIC4LIFE® APPROACH TO MOOD MASTERY

Welcome to the Music4Life® Music Medicine Protocol, a music therapy approach I've developed to enhance emotion regulation and resilience. Central to this innovative protocol is the U.S.E. M.E. E.™—Music.Exercising.Emotions Model. This model is specifically designed to support music-based interventions by ensuring they are precisely aligned with each individual's unique emotional needs. The protocol engages participants in three strategic steps with an individualized approach, each crafted to facilitate deeper emotional connections and therapeutic benefits through music.

The Music4Life Music Medicine Protocol is built on three foundational principles: the Iso Principle, Vectoring, and Entrainment. Each is essential in guiding the therapeutic process through music.

The **Iso Principle** chooses music that mirrors the listener's current emotional state (Heiderscheit et al., 2015; Altshuler, 1948). This method acts like an acoustic reflection, echoing your present feelings, whether they are anxiety, sadness, apathy, or excitement. Such alignment fosters a significant connection with the music, turning it into an effective catalyst through emotional engagement.

Vectoring then guides the transition by methodically shifting the music from mirroring the current emotional state to leading the listener toward a more desirable one (Shatin, 1970). For instance, if someone starts off feeling anxious, the music will gradually shift from matching an anxious state to calmer, soothing melodies, effectively guiding the listener from anxiety to a state of calm.

Lastly, **Entrainment** aligns the listener's emotional, behavioral, and physiological responses—such as heartbeat and breathing—with the rhythms, beats, harmony, and other musical elements (Rider, 1985). This synchronization maintains the listener's engagement with the music to enhance the emotional impact, carefully constructing a gradual transition to more positive emotional, behavioral, and physiological states.

Through these three principles, the Music4Life® Music Medicine Protocol leverages music as a dynamic force for emotional catharsis, transforming music listening into a dynamic, engaging, and therapeutic journey. It validates and then shifts listeners from their current emotional realities to their desired states of well-being. This comprehensive protocol is structured into three interconnected stages, each designed to elicit the listener's emotional states through a carefully selected and timed classification and sequencing system known as the USE MEE™ Model.

The USE MEE™ Model

1989

JUDITH PINKERTON
SEMINAR CONCERT

SOLO VIOLIN CONCERT SELECTIONS*

MOVEMENT I: STIMULATION   (select one other)
___ Carnival of Venice   Ambrioso
___ Gavotte en Rondeau   Bach
___ Gypsy Medley   Brahms/Liszt/Bizet
___ Humoreske   Dvorak
_I_ Partita E Major: Preludio   Bach
_X_ Scheherezade   Rimsky-Korsakoff

MOVEMENT II: EXPRESSION   (select one)
___ Londonderry Air   Irish Traditional
___ Lullaby   Brahms
___ Sunrise Sunset   Fiddler on the Roof
_X_ The Swan   Saint-Saens

MOVEMENT III: INTERNALIZE   (select one)
___ Canzonetta   Tschaikovsky
___ Greensleeves   English Traditional
___ Pavane   Ravel
_X_ Serenade   Schubert

MOVEMENT IV: INTROSPECTION   (select one)
___ Cadenza   Mozart
___ Caprice No 1   Saint-Lubin
___ Passacaglia   Von Biber
_X_ Sonata in G minor: Adagio   Bach

MOVEMENT V: PEACE   (select one other)
_I_ Andante   Mendelssohn
___ Ave Maria Medley   Schubert/Bach-Gounod
___ Jesu, Joy/Lord's Prayer   Bach/Traditional
_X_ Christmas Medley   Traditional

*excerpts are from *Judith's* concert repertoire. If you would like a customized tape of your favorite music selections performed by solo violin or violin with other instruments, contact *Judith* for more information: P.O. Box 12627, Las Vegas, NV, (702) 798 1530.

1989 Seminar Concert Program

The early mood classification and sequencing framework of the Music Medicine Protocol began intuitively with a creative solo violin concert

(1989), recognizing the need for people to choose their preferred music. During my seminar lecture, people would vote for the music they wanted to experience within each of the five movements. Then, I would spontaneously perform in concert the five preferred pieces following this movement sequence: Stimulation → Expression → Internalize → Introspection → Peace.

This five-part music classification and sequencing framework quickly evolved into three parts, based on the findings of Sentic Cycles research (Clynes et al., 1988), which was introduced to me by a therapist attending one SeminarConcert. Music therapy research, however, generally categorizes music into two parts: stimulative and sedative (Hodges, 2020). The USE MEE™ Model's three-part mood music classification and sequencing framework discerns the difference between stimulative music that unsettles (i.e., anxiety, anger, depression, grief) and stimulative music that positively energizes (optimism, happiness, excitement, enthusiasm). This delineation represents the core of the Music Medicine Protocol, originally labeled as three mood classifications: Negative, Neutral, and Positive (Pinkerton, 1990, 1993). These mood labels evolved into the current interactive system of mood music classification and sequencing that is foundational to the Music Medicine Protocol: Unsettled, Soothed, and Energized (Pinkerton, 1996, 2003, 2010, 2014, 2019, 2021; Wellman et al., 2015).

"U.S.E. M.E.E." is a user-friendly acronym that identifies the framework of our broad spectrum of emotions, categorized into three mood classifications of U.S.E.–how to use music for health: U-Unsettled, S-Soothed, and E-Energized. Each mood classification is populated with specific mood-related emotions. Then mood music is selected to correspond to each emotion, chosen for "me": M.E.E.-Music.Exercising.Emotions. The "MEE" acronym was inspired by one subject describing her experience of the Sentic Cycle, where emotions look forward to getting exercised (Clynes et al., 1988). Music4Life® applies the concept of sequencing emotions to include corresponding mood music, which is different from the application of Sentic Cycles, which uses no music, just sequenced emotions.

The USE MEE™ Model is the interactive system of the Music Medicine Protocol that supports the method of assigning emotions into classifications and positions within a sequence to support a fluid emotional process identified as a Mood Sequence Formula™ (Wellman et al., 2015). The Mood Sequence Formula provides the basis for ordering selected mood music from the classification system to generate a Mood Exercise Regimen® or Music Medicine Pill®, depending on individualized goals. This proprietary process of selecting music utilizes a mood music analysis to pre-qualify music as medicinal (culled from a variety of genres) and then populates those music selections into the pre-identified Mood Sequence Formula to optimize "me" through my emotionally cathartic M.E.E.- Music.Exercising.Emotions Journey.

These three mood classifications, U.S.E., become three specialized mood music playlists.

Unsettled (i.e., negative stimulating emotions): The mood sequence may begin by acknowledging and engaging with the listener's current negative emotional state, selecting music that matches or resonates with specific unsettled emotions. This engages the "iso-principle." This step isn't about exacerbating negative feelings but validating and acknowledging them, allowing the listener to feel understood at the beginning of this cathartic, emotional processing journey.

Soothed (i.e., neutral sedative emotions): After engaging with the negative emotions, the listener transitions immediately to music that embodies a neutral emotional state. This music acts as a bridge, reducing the intensity of negative emotions and preparing the mind and body for a positive shift. This neutral phase is crucial for creating calm and balance, reaching a deeper state of spiritual well-being, whereby the listener is able to reduce, or disengage from, distress.

Energized (i.e., positive stimulating emotions): Finally, the sequence moves nonstop into music that expresses positive emotions, chosen to uplift the listener, foster positive feelings, and encourage an optimistic outlook. This stage aims to enhance emotional well-being by increasing joy and meaningful engagement with life.

All genres are referenced for possible inclusion in these specialized mood music playlists. Along with that inclusion are inherent danger zones to address during the practice of this integrative protocol to offer a clear, evidence-based strategy for emotion regulation. The USE MEE™ Model enhances the anticipated emotional catharsis during the acknowledgment stage, eases the transition to a neutral state with a deeper connection to the inner spirit, and then optimizes the upliftment phase with music assessed to foster positive emotions. This theoretically sound and practical approach offers therapists and individuals a structured yet flexible framework. It stands out by marrying music therapy's intuitive, personal touch with the rigor of cognitive neuroscience, making it a potent tool for emotional healing and well-being.

Ludwig van Beethoven's words, "Music is the mediator between the life of the senses and the life of the spirit," echo profoundly within me, capturing the essence of what I've aimed to achieve with the Music Medicine Protocol. It's this concept of music acting as a bridge, connecting our sensory experiences to our deepest emotional and spiritual selves, that the protocol embraces and seeks to harness for healing. It is this mediation, at the heart of the journey toward healing, that the protocol offers—a journey that is as nuanced as it is deeply human.

My development of the Music Medicine Protocol is a tribute to the incredible potential at the intersection of personal experience and scientific exploration. By intertwining my life-changing encounters with music with the rich insights derived from evidence-based research and clinical practice, I've created a protocol that navigates the complexities of emotion regulation and pays homage to the profound depths of the human spirit. Following are the three strategic steps of this tailored approach, each step crafted to facilitate deeper emotional connections and therapeutic benefits through music.

Step 1: The Correct Music

While music is an incredibly healing tool, its effectiveness hinges on selecting the correct music, which depends heavily on an individual's mood, personal tastes, and specific emotional needs. This precision is central to the USE MEE™ Model, which tailors music-based interventions to match each person's unique emotional state.

At this stage, music is meticulously selected based on three mood classifications that encapsulate all emotions which are biological: Unsettled

(U), Soothed (S), and Energized (E). Each classification aligns with specific emotional states: 'U' for feelings like anxiety, anger, depression, and grief; 'S' for peace, relaxation, contentment, and tranquility; and 'E' for emotions like happiness, optimism, playfulness, and enthusiasm. The music chosen precisely matches select emotions, referencing 45 emotions, resulting in a specialized playlist for each mood classification. Each specialized playlist is a purposefully selected set of songs that meet the rigor of a mood music analysis and are meaningful to an individual in addressing a therapeutic goal (McFerran et al., 2022). Typical playlists are part of the curriculum offered through training at MusicMedicineAcademy.com.

MusicMedicineAcademy.com is a resource where individuals and health professionals can effectively learn how to select and integrate music into therapeutic practices or self-care and clinical settings. The academy offers comprehensive training that covers the theories behind Music4Life's Music Medicine Protocol, practical applications of Music Medicine playlists, and guidance on how to customize music therapy-informed strategies to individual needs. By participating in these courses, users gain knowledge about the therapeutic benefits of music to more competently evaluate each music selection for the desired emotional response to aid overall emotion regulation and healing.

Step 2: At the Right Moment

This stage of the process is all about timing—determining the optimal moment to introduce music for the most beneficial impact. It hinges on a detailed understanding of the listener's current physiological, behavioral, and emotional states. This ensures that the music introduced perfectly aligns with the listener's needs at that exact moment.

Interconnected with this is the Iso Principle, which focuses on syncing the music with the listener's current state to enhance therapeutic effectiveness. The Iso Principle supports a transformative healing process by ensuring the music matches the listener's immediate emotional, behavioral, and physical conditions. This allows for real-time emotional adjustments and may foster long-term resilience against stress.

The concept of "the right moment" is always rooted in the present moment, the point at which the listener's immediate feelings and conditions intersect optimally with the therapeutic intentions of the music. To implement this effectively, enhancing awareness of how one responds to music in real time is important. Listeners are encouraged to become deeply attuned to how different music elements influence their physiological responses (how their bodies react), their behavioral responses (how they act), and their emotional responses (how they feel). This heightened awareness is key in pinpointing the exact type of music that will be most effective at any given time.

Once the listener's current state is understood, the next step is to apply 'the correct music' from the U.S.E. mood classifications—Unsettled (U), Soothed (S), and Energized (E)—that best matches their current mood, behavior, or physiological condition. For example, if a listener is agitated, a track from the 'Unsettled' classification is introduced to validate the agitation and allow the listener to feel heard. The timing of this intervention is carefully considered: introducing soothing music thereafter to prevent a negative emotional spiral, easing them into a state of calm.

By aligning the introduction of music with these pivotal moments, the Music4Life® Protocol maximizes music's therapeutic impact, making it an effective tool for emotion regulation. This precise timing ensures that music actively transforms the listener's mood state rather than just serving as background noise.

Careful selection of music to match the current emotion, based on the Iso Principle, customizes each listening session to the listener's immediate needs, optimizing the therapeutic potential. Through this approach, music acts as a dynamic and responsive support system that addresses complex emotional and psychological challenges in real-time.

Step 3: In the Best Sequence

The third and final step of the Music4Life® Music Medicine Protocol, "In the Best Sequence," features the Mood Sequence Formula™. This formula guides the listener through a structured progression of mood states, with these three phases as the typical sequence: begin with an unsettled state (U), transition through a soothed state (S), and culminate in an energized state (E). Each phase in this typical sequence is meticulously crafted to transform the listener's emotional condition methodically. There are other variations to this typical "U → S → E" Mood Sequence Formula, described in greater detail within MusicMedicineAcademy.com trainings.

Vectoring and entrainment are foundational principles with techniques to optimize the sequence. Vectoring directs the emotional journey which incorporates the entrainment mechanism to ensure optimal transitions between music selections to shift the listener's mood. Starting with music that matches the listener's initial unsettled emotion, such as anxiety or anger, the sequence gradually introduces soothing tracks to mitigate the unsettled feelings, shifting the listener into a calmer state.

The journey then progresses to uplifting, vibrant, energized music, creating a sense of enthusiasm and positivity. This phase leverages the energy of the music, evolving the listener into a positive, invigorated emotional state. Entrainment synchronizes the music elements with the listener's emotional, behavioral, and physiological responses, facilitating a psychologically supportive transformation.

More than merely altering a mood momentarily, this structured emotional process, called the M.E.E.™- Music Exercising Emotions Journey, is designed to cultivate the listener's emotional responses over time. Once the Mood Sequence Formula™ is determined to process emotions, the music is culled from the U.S.E. specialized playlists and placed in the prescriptive playlist called the Music Medicine Pill® for therapeutic outcomes and the Mood Exercise Regimen® for peak performance outcomes. The prescriptive playlist may enhance emotional resilience, agility, and flexibility by compelling repeated change between emotional states, with outcomes that empower individuals to manage moods optimally and develop mood mastery.

Case Story: Application of the Music Medicine Protocol

In a specialized residential treatment center designed to address the complexities of addiction and psychological trauma, each participant arrives with a unique story. Among them is "Casey," a pseudonym used to protect the privacy of a veteran who carries the deep scars of PTSD from his military service, compounded by multiple unsuccessful rehab attempts. His entrance into the center, cautious and constantly alert to his surroundings, underscores a life shaped by prolonged exposure to combat environments.

Recognized early by the center's psychologist as a prime candidate for specialized intervention, Casey's demeanor and vigilant eyes—constantly scanning for potential threats, referred to as 'danger zones'—made it clear that a conventional approach might not suffice. He was swiftly referred for an individual music therapy session, introducing him to a nuanced treatment method that promised to resonate more deeply with his specific needs.

During his initial assessment, Casey actively engaged in a listening assessment to address his treatment goals, focusing on emotion regulation and enhancing his self-soothing capabilities. This process unearthed four problematic emotions he was grappling with, alongside eight he aimed to cultivate. In response to his feedback, I meticulously selected sixteen tracks aligned with his emotional needs. These tracks were then compiled into a one-hour music therapy treatment CD called a Music Medicine Pill®, personalized to facilitate his healing journey during his residence at the treatment center.

Casey was prescribed a detailed listening regimen and encouraged to journal his experiences as part of his therapy. Remarkably, just two weeks into following his listening schedule, Casey began to witness a profound shift in his emotional landscape. His journal entries and subsequent assessments reflected a significant increase in feelings of peace and happiness and a notable reduction in unrest. This remarkable transformation was also observed by the treatment team and highlights the effectiveness of the Music4Life® Music Medicine Protocol, demonstrating its capacity to actively ameliorate deep-seated emotional disturbances and pave the way for a more stable and joyful existence.

The Problem and Solution: Empowered Emotion Regulation

The impact of unmanaged emotions extends deeply into our communities, manifesting in profound and often painful ways. Issues such as mental distress, self-harm, and various forms of aggression, including bullying and domestic violence, can arise when feelings like anger, depression, grief, and anxiety remain unchecked. These emotional states don't just affect the individuals experiencing them but ripple out to touch families and communities, challenging our collective ability to foster a nurturing environment. One compelling example is Tiffany's story. Tiffany first met me in a girls' group home as a teenager in 1999. She experienced significant anger from a dysfunctional home environment. Because she loved music, Tiffany agreed to work with me to create her "M.E.E.™ tape."

Tiffany described her healing process as unparalleled. "My experience on the M.E.E. tape was a great one that I've never experienced anything like before, and nothing in mind can compare to it. I learned that the music everybody listens to has a great deal of influence on how they act, feel, and who they are. And the way people listen to music is very important. I learned the different ways you can listen to music, and how affecting it is once you find the right music. This M.E.E. tape is designed to exercise your emotions through music. It starts out with unsettled music that triggers you, then it moves into soothing music to relax you and allows you to let your feelings show and come to the surface in a positive way. Then I was exercised to go into energetic music, and that was the state where I was headed. At first, I didn't think it would work, but I have to say it made a big difference in how I dealt with my feelings and emotions. I'm thankful for this tape and Judith's capability of knowing music."

Echoing Tiffany's transformative experience, music therapy offers a gentle yet powerful avenue for healing. By embracing music as a tool for emotion regulation, individuals can begin to recognize, accept, and manage their feelings more effectively. This process helps improve personal mood states and may build resilience, empowering people to navigate life's challenges with greater ease and less distress.

Furthermore, music therapy holds promise in addressing specific, acute societal challenges. It can help soothe the turmoil within those in abusive relationships, diminish aggressive behaviors, and potentially reduce the frequency of heartbreaking events like active shooter incidents. Remembering tragedies such as those at Columbine, Virginia Tech, Aurora Theater, and Sandy Hook, we see the critical need for strategies that manage emotions constructively.

Integrating music as a therapeutic intervention may significantly alleviate these profound societal issues. More than just a source of entertainment, music becomes a critical element of emotional wellness and public health strategies, helping to cultivate a more supportive, resilient community.

Music, when applied like medicine, holds transformative power to address severe societal issues such as abusive relationships, animal abuse, and active shooter incidents. The Music Medicine Protocol advocates for addressing the root causes of explosive and implosive moods, rather than just the symptoms, to significantly reduce the violence and self-harm that are currently rampant.

In the United States alone, approximately 40 million people suffer from anxiety disorders, with countless others trapped in cycles of anger, depression, grief, and the most pervasive issue of all—stress. Suicide has become a leading cause of death. These negative emotions contribute to societal unrest, feeding into destructive behaviors and attitudes that harm individuals and their communities. Only by moving beyond our old ways of thinking about music, introducing fresh perspectives for mood management, and taking bold, disruptive actions with Mood Sequence Formulas™ can we truly hope to mitigate mood problems, create new possibilities for recovering mental health, and achieve remarkable outcomes in mood mastery. A powerful pattern for disruption is warranted in music listening habits ("The Power of Pattern Disruption," 2024).

Music has a unique ability to penetrate our central nervous system, directly influencing our state of mind and mood. People often choose music that mirrors their current mood state. When individuals are trapped in negative cycles, they tend to select music that resonates with their feelings of unrest, which may inadvertently reinforce these negative emotions. However, the strategic use of the USE MEE™ Model may alter this dynamic.

By consistently applying these powerful prescriptive playlists, the medicinal qualities of music can be harnessed, leading to significant changes in emotional states. The Music4Life® Music Medicine Protocol is designed with music therapy strategies to reduce feelings of unrest while enhancing emotions of peace and happiness. As a result, individuals experience profound transformations in their emotional well-being, which may ripple out to positively impact broader social issues related to violence and self-harm.

Music therapy significantly aids emotion regulation by engaging brain activity (Moore, 2013). The strategic use of music through the Music4Life Music Medicine Protocol involves selecting tracks reflecting the listener's current emotions and guiding them through desired emotional states by synchronizing music with emotional, behavioral, and physiological responses to reduce distress and improve positive emotions. This approach helps acknowledge and transform problem mood states. Music strengthens neural pathways associated with positive emotions, making them more accessible during stress (Zaatar, 2024). Regular music therapy sessions also encourage the development of coping skills and foster community among participants. Empirical studies support music therapy's effectiveness, showing notable improvements in emotional well-being and social cohesion, proving it to be a dynamic tool for psychological healing and community building (Bronson et al., 2018).

There is growing interest in music therapy's effectiveness in improving resilience ("The Use of Music for Resilience-Building," 2021). Revisiting clients over the past decade will increase documented clinical evidence of music therapy's capability to enhance resilience. Music4Life partnered with a hospital and music therapist, Dr. Annie Heiderscheit, to create an IRB-approved study with employees planned for future utilization, studying the effects of the Music Medicine Protocol on stress, anxiety, and resilience.

The Music Medicine Curriculum

The Music Medicine curriculum explores the transformative potential of music in healing and emotion regulation and targets the root causes of behaviors associated with poorly managed moods. Anxiety disorders, anger, depression, grief, and stress are primary contributors to emotional unrest. Typically, people choose music that reflects their current emotional state, which may perpetuate feelings of unrest if the music is unsettling. However, through the consistent application of the USE MEE™ Model, music's medicinal qualities may effectively transform these emotional states and profoundly influence our central nervous system and mood at a cellular level. This approach not only alleviates symptoms of unrest but also enhances feelings of peace and happiness, potentially promoting long-term mood mastery and resilience.

The therapeutic use of music also has significant implications for the music industry and healthcare. As individuals increasingly seek music that promotes peace and happiness, the industry will shift to meet this new demand, potentially reshaping the market to prioritize music that supports mental health and well-being. This trend is exemplified by the experience of a veteran with road rage issues who, after a two-week regimen of targeted music listening, shifted his preferences from metal/alternative music to more soothing and happy tunes that helped him manage his road rage. Such changes in consumer behavior could dramatically alter the music landscape.

Moreover, effective stress management through music therapy-informed strategies could result in considerable savings in healthcare costs. By managing stress, which is a significant health hazard, through prescribed music listening routines, there could be a significant impact on medication use, including physician-directed reductions and cessation (Wellman et al., 2015). Promoting the USE MEE™ Model with integrative prescriptive playlists could revolutionize current healthcare practices, influence the use of medications, and foster a healthier society through the proactive use of music. This innovative approach highlights music's role not only as a source of entertainment but a helpful tool in health management through emotion regulation.

What do we mean when we speak about using music as medicine? My journey as a professional musician for more than 50 years and a certified music therapist for 22 years has culminated in a profound understanding of this protocol. I invite you to explore this through the evidence-based curriculum "6 Habits of Music Medicine for Highly Empowered People" (Pinkerton, 2022). This curriculum transforms six familiar music listening practices into highly empowered processes that make music work like medicine, encapsulating the Music4Life® Music Medicine Protocol. It is designed for individuals to self-instruct and for trained facilitators to implement varied group offerings.

The program is structured around 30 specific goals supported by 30 therapeutic activities to enhance mental and emotional health through music. These goals start with foundational tasks such as identifying keywords that represent your music listening habits and observing the health zones impacted by your music choices. The program deepens this engagement by encouraging participants to recognize and understand three distinct mood zones and note how music influences these zones.

Participants in the program learn to navigate their emotional landscape more effectively by identifying Chronic Comfort Zones™, which are classified as Unsettled, Soothed, and Energized. They link emotional awareness with life conditions, enhancing their understanding of how these states interact. The curriculum emphasizes developing skills for active music listening, seeking to strengthen mental resilience against negativity, and using music strategically throughout the day to maintain balance and focus.

The program also aims to help participants understand the impact of a changing world on mood control, reduce negative influences through strategic music choices, and gain deeper insights into how life themes and "earworms" affect moods. Participants are encouraged to daily recognize the influence of music on their feelings, improving their mental hygiene by understanding how two states of consciousness relate to their music diet.

Advanced goals involve creating specific Music Medicine playlists to enhance music hygiene, creating U.S.E. mood playlists for targeted listening, and learning to transition between mood states optimally. Additionally, the program fosters the development of emotional fluidity and resilience through prescriptive music application.

Finally, the "6 Habits of Music Medicine for Highly Empowered People" supports participants in gaining control over their personal environments, enhancing their cognitive, emotional, and mental health, and building supportive social networks. This comprehensive approach empowers participants to re-categorize their music preferences and create playlists based on this music therapy-informed formulaic system, potentially boosting resilience and supporting their overall mental and emotional well-being.

Discover the Music4Life® Music Medicine Protocol through this engaging curriculum, designed for trained facilitators who are Music4Life Specialists. This comprehensive program is delivered in a series of six weekly classes, each lasting 2½ hours, or presented in continuing education workshops. Originally launched at NAMI-Southern Nevada in 2023, the curriculum has since expanded through partnerships with trained mental health facilitators, symphony musicians, and family support organizations. Whether you want to deepen your understanding of Music Medicine or seek new ways to support emotional wellness, this curriculum offers valuable tools and insights in an accessible format.

Building upon the strong foundation of Music4Life's Music Medicine Protocol, the curriculum introduces the "6 Habits of Music Medicine" as a structured approach, starting with the first vital music listening habit, Zone Recognition. This initial step teaches participants to identify and categorize their emotional states—what we refer to as "mood zones"—and how different types of music may significantly influence health zones. Through a combination of theoretical knowledge and practical activities, such as journaling and completing the Emotional Profile Quiz in the Key2MEE® Music App, this habit helps participants gain a deeper understanding of their mood triggers and the transformative power of music. This insightful process sets the stage for the subsequent five habits, each designed to further empower individuals through the strategic use of music.

Habit #1 - Zone Recognition

Understanding music's profound impact on our emotional and physiological states begins with recognizing our "mood zones" and how various types of music affect them. Instead of merely tolerating our feelings, a more empowered approach encourages us to actively engage with and categorize these emotional states, exploring the connections between our health, moods, and the music we listen to. This process involves deepening our awareness of how we might be entrapped in repetitive and possibly unhelpful music listening habits, commonly called the "Chronic Comfort Zone™."

Through five educational activities, including journaling tasks and self-assessments, individuals gain new insights into their different zones and how these relate to their music-listening habits. Reviewing these activities comprehensively is essential to determining potential traps within habitual listening patterns.

In my blog article entitled "Music Powers Potential," I explore what I call the "cycle of connectedness" that clarifies this relationship (Pinkerton, 2023). For instance, when we instinctively select music—what I call the "savage" response—we are often driven by an immediate emotional appeal that the music holds, regardless of our current mood. The 'breast' represents our hearts or emotions, influencing music choices that resonate with or seek to alter our feelings. The "beast" pertains to physiological reactions; for example, music may modify our heart rate or blood pressure, supporting physical activities or calming us down. Lastly, the "mindset" involves the cognitive impacts of music, where our thoughts—and behaviors—are influenced by the music we listen to.

This deeper understanding serves as a foundational element in using music deliberately to enhance our lives, suggesting a more conscious engagement with the music we choose and its effects on our overall well-being.

Habit #2 - Emotional Awareness

The "6 Habits of Music Medicine for Highly Empowered People" is also a boxed card set I developed for Music4Life® that is instrumental in helping individuals leverage music as a therapeutic tool by increasing emotional awareness to actively manage mood through music. Habit 2, "Emotional Awareness," stands out in this set for its practical approach to using music intentionally to foster well-being.

This habit incorporates five therapeutic music-listening activities. These activities guide users to identify three Chronic Comfort Zones™, where one might be emotionally trapped, engage in the Emotional Profile Quiz to connect deeply with their emotions, learn strategies for active music listening to deliberately influence moods, gain emotional literacy through various approaches to strengthen their mindset, and strategically use music to enhance their emotional health.

Feedback from participants in various programs underscores the impact of these practices. One Recovery Class participant noted the transformative insight gained through these activities: "I realized that my music choices were self-destructive, and that made me take a step back and re-evaluate my listening choices." This realization highlights the power of intentional music listening in identifying and altering unhelpful emotional patterns.

Additionally, a military class participant shared their enhanced self-awareness and the therapeutic benefits of changing music listening habits: "I am more aware of the music I am listening to depending on my mood. I would recommend Music4Life® to people who are pretty sad or angry because it will help them change their music type to improve their life."

This testimony reflects the program's effectiveness in helping individuals understand the profound connection between their emotional states and music choices.

These insights and experiences are fundamental to the design of the "Power Up 365" program, another component of Music4Life's offerings. This program provides daily motivational quotes paired with a beautiful image and specific Music Medicine recommendations. This regular engagement helps participants maintain a positive and reflective mindset, further supporting their journey toward emotional empowerment and stability.

These resources, available through theMusic4Life.com, offer structured and supportive approaches to harnessing music's therapeutic potential. They make every listening experience an opportunity for emotional growth and improved well-being.

Habit #3 - Mood Control

There's a marked difference in emotion regulation between the common practice of letting one's environment dictate mood and the more empowered approach of intentionally using music to shape one's emotional landscape. This shift involves not just reacting to emotional triggers but actively managing them through music, thus empowering oneself to control the mood of the day.

Participants in our programs learn to distinguish between suppressed and repressed emotions and how these subconscious processes drive their behaviors. They also explore how life themes, earworms (songs that repeat in one's mind), and memories relate to the music they love, gaining new insights that may profoundly influence their emotional well-being.

One military class participant shared a poignant example of how an ear-worm influenced his mood. He often listened to the Indie pop song "Pumped Up Kicks" by Foster the People, which brought back memories of good times with friends from high school. Despite the nostalgia, he felt melancholy upon hearing it, not realizing the song's lyrics discuss a troubling subject matter. This mismatch—the unsettling themes of the lyrics against the backdrop of energizing music—typically could cause confusion by unconsciously aligning feelings of happiness with a traumatic narrative. However, in his case, the melancholy stemmed from missing his friends and a yearning for past times that could not be replicated, especially as he faced new challenges and environments in his military training.

In addressing this, I introduced the USE MEE™ Model, classifying the song as U/E—unsettled lyric content paired with energizing music. Recognizing this helped the participant understand his feelings and prompted the creation of a prescriptive playlist to address and navigate his sadness more effectively.

The flexibility of the USE MEE™ Model, which doesn't push a specific genre but tailors the musical experience to individual emotional needs, has resonated well with many. Another student from the Udemy.com class, "Making Music Medicine," expressed her appreciation, noting how this approach led to many "aha moments" and made a lot of sense in understanding the deep impact of music on emotional states. This method underscores the profound capability of music to act as a therapeutic tool, offering significant control over one's emotional health and daily mood.

Habit #4 - Music Hygiene

In Music Hygiene, many people treat music as a drug, listening only to what immediately makes them feel better. This approach is quite different from a more strategic and empowered method, which involves creating a "music diet" that cleanses emotions and enhances desired moods, facilitating balanced and healthy management of all mood states.

This proactive strategy goes beyond mere preference to a comprehensive understanding of how music impacts states of consciousness, emotions, physiology, and behavior. By developing prescriptive playlists, individuals can harness the therapeutic benefits of music to address specific needs and situations, transforming their music listening into a proactive tool for emotional and psychological health.

For example, another military class participant described the transformative effect of this approach: "I learned how to curate my music library in a way that is productive." This highlights a shift from passive to active engagement with music, where the curated library serves as a tool for personal growth and emotion regulation.

Furthermore, a recovery class participant emphasized the necessity of mindful music selection: "I like unsettling music which is fine and okay but I need to listen to settling music so I don't make the pissed off pessimism a comfort zone. I need to comfort and calm down so I don't feel that anger which can cause a relapse." This insight shows a critical aspect of music hygiene—recognizing and modifying music choices to prevent detrimental emotional states and promote a more stable, healthy emotional environment.

A music diet stresses the strategic use of music as a powerful tool to cleanse and refine one's emotional landscape. It provides a systematic approach to achieving emotional balance and enhancing well-being through carefully selected musical experiences.

Habit #5 - Emotional Fluidity

Emotional Fluidity is the ability to adapt flexibly to events and interactions, navigating life with ease and openness rather than being rigid and stuck. It involves the intentional use of music to navigate and manage one's emotional states by incorporating prescriptive listening techniques to achieve a flow state on demand, allowing for positive transitions between various moods.

A common practice of Emotional Fluidity is the simple act of listening to music to change moods. In contrast, a highly empowered process involves using music with prescriptive listening techniques to train the brain to manage transitions between mood states. Then, one may achieve the flow state on demand, thereby enhancing emotion regulation and fostering new insights into the frequency and sequencing of music listening to maximize its benefits.

During my initial introduction of Music4Life® to military troops on October 25, 2007, the impact of this approach was vividly demonstrated. The mental healthcare stigma was absent during this unprecedented training. Fifty-seven troops learned about minimizing the negative effects of war by using the one thing they would not forget to take with them: music. Originally scheduled for 20 minutes, the session extended to 75 minutes as Security Forces troops sought to understand how they could use their music differently to stay balanced and ward off combat stress. At the end of the M4L training, the Unit Deployment Manager required all his troops to complete the M4L health assessment and turn it in. Remarkably, 50 out of 57 troops (87%) complied, with more than 50% reporting feeling stressed, frustrated, anxious, exhausted, and angry.

This compliance was significant because the Department of Defense reported that 38-98% of Army and Air Force troops failed to complete pre-/post-deployment health assessments. I had the opportunity to observe the deployers during the break-out session, choosing to sit in the front to watch their reactions closely. To my surprise, the troops' engagement level was remarkably high. Except for a couple, all participants were deeply involved, discussing the neuroscience, psychological and music therapy theories presented and how these related to their personal experiences and upcoming deployments. My presentation was particularly effective as I tailored the material to incorporate military language and concepts, making it relevant and accessible to the audience discussing the adapted "My War" playlist for a positive mindset, listed in Appendix B. My ability to "AFize" the content—adapting it to the specific context of the Air Force—resonated well with the troops, helping them see the practical benefits of Music4Life® for their mental resilience and mood management during deployment.

Susan B. Robinson from the Airman and Family Readiness Center at Nellis A.F.B. reflected on this session, noting her initial skepticism about how the troops would receive the concept. However, once the presentation began, her doubts dissipated as she observed the troops' genuine interest and engagement. She expressed excitement about the potential of using this tool extensively at Nellis and potentially expanding its use across the Air Force, indicating the successful integration of music-based emotional training in a military setting. Unfortunately, the Community Resilience Program submitted by Nellis Air Force Base during 2007-08 to support Music4Life's work with military members was twice denied as it preceded the 2009 Armed Forces recognition of "invisible wounds" (Conan, 2009). Today, the armed forces recommend music therapy for mind-body practice ("Holistic Health and Fitness," 2020).

Habit #6 - Environment Consciousness

In the area of environmental consciousness, transitioning from using music merely as personal entertainment or as a means to isolate oneself from others to a more thoughtful approach that creates harmonious environments represents a significant evolution in music listening habits. This empowered process involves intentionally designing environments with music that honors oneself and respects others around us. It's about expanding consciousness to foster environments that thrive mentally, emotionally, behaviorally, physiologically, and socially through strategic music selection.

Various participants have experienced the benefits of this approach. Another military class participant highlighted the role of music in personal development: "I can use music to improve my physical, motivational, emotional goals. All to become the best Airman I can be." This statement underscores how music can be a powerful tool for achieving personal and professional aspirations and enhancing overall effectiveness and well-being.

One Udemy.com class participant who works in a care home shared insights from the Music4Life® "Making Music Medicine" course. She found it particularly relevant as it affirmed her experiences with music's impact on individuals with dementia and learning disabilities. The course boosted her confidence in implementing personalized music interventions like MP3 players and Alexa devices for residents, facilitating emotional connection through their favorite songs.

Additionally, a recovery class participant expressed a sentiment about the social value of music: "I like sharing music that matters to me with others." This emphasizes music's role in fostering connections and communal healing.

The "6 Habits of Music Medicine for Highly Empowered People" boxed card set integrates these principles within the framework of Music4Life's evidence-based practice. Each of the six habits includes eight types of therapeutic activities—investigative, learning, listening, journaling, assessment, mindfulness, playlist creation, and outreach—for a total of 30 activities. After completing a 30-day regimen, users are encouraged to continue interacting with the cards randomly to reinforce and practice the acquired skills, ensuring a lasting impact on their ability to create and maintain enriching music environments.

Joining Forces with Music4Life®

Music4Life® uses music as a potent tool for creating a healthier, more productive society. This organization emphasizes respecting individual music preferences, recognizing that each genre may offer therapeutic value when used responsibly. A personalized approach to music therapy is essential, as demonstrated by a case shared by music therapist Lillieth Grand. She recalls a young man in a coma who showed significant improvement with high blood pressure and low oxygenation, returning to normal range within minutes of listening to gangsta rap, his favorite genre. Whereas, listening to his mother's well-intentioned choice of classical music exacerbated his medical issues. This example highlights the necessity of aligning music therapy with individual tastes to ensure its effectiveness, advocating for validating the person with familiar, preferred music as a foundational element of therapeutic interventions.

Educational programs like Music4Life's Music Medicine Boot Camp further illustrate the practical application of music therapy. Darlene R., R.N., MHA, expressed that the skills and knowledge acquired from the boot camp would enhance the care she provides to her patients. Such initiatives show the adaptability of music therapy across various settings, enriching professional practices in healthcare and beyond.

The role of music in wellness spans from historical applications to contemporary needs. In my article in Corporate Wellness Magazine (Pinkerton, n.d.), I noted that the Muzak Corporation initially used music to calm elevator fears. However, today's applications are much broader, addressing everyday stresses from work, family conflicts, and financial issues to the impacts of natural disasters. Music Wellness Programs encourage the integration of music into self-care strategies, enhancing emotional and psychological well-being in both corporate and personal environments.

By integrating the principles and strategies of Music4Life®, significant improvements can be made in addressing the emotional and psychological challenges many face today. Music4Life converts the practice of music therapy into music therapy-informed strategies for DIY (Do-It-Yourself) approaches. These strategies help manage stress and other symptoms, enhancing the quality of life and productivity for individuals nationwide, proving that music's impact extends far beyond entertainment.

Testimonials and Success Stories

The transformative impact of the Music Medicine Protocol is vividly demonstrated through a collection of testimonials and success stories from various settings. These narratives emphasize significant personal changes and offer insights into the protocol's application in professional contexts, highlighting its effectiveness in promoting personal growth and enhancing professional practices.

The therapeutic use of music also has significant implications for the music industry and healthcare. As individuals increasingly seek music that promotes peace and happiness, the industry will shift to meet this new demand, potentially reshaping the market to prioritize genres that support mental health and well-being. This trend is exemplified by the earlier story of the veteran with road rage issues, who, after a two-week regimen of targeted music listening, shifted his preferences from metal/alternative music to more soothing and happy tunes that helped him manage his emotions. Such changes in consumer behavior could dramatically alter the music landscape.

Past clients are continually reaching out to me to inform me of new mood music preferences and how they continue to use the Mood Sequence

Formula™ successfully. Similarly, a patient in a treatment facility made a conscious effort to shift music preferences after noticing that certain genres worsened their mood. This simple yet impactful change greatly improved their daily emotional well-being.

In educational settings, the protocol has proven equally transformative. Eden, a U.O.P. Music Therapy Student, described how the training enhanced their ability to think critically about using music elements in therapy sessions. The program encouraged them to adapt their music interventions to better match the present mood of their clients before transitioning to the target mood. It also broadened their personal music exploration, helping them connect more deeply with their emotions and those of their clients.

An elementary school teacher plans to incorporate the U.S.E. playlist and Mood Sequence Formula into her classroom to aid students affected by trauma and enhance the overall classroom environment. She also intends to develop lessons that allow students to create their own U.S.E. playlists, empowering them to manage their emotions effectively. For herself, maintaining a personal U.S.E. playlist has become a tool for better managing her moods, ultimately making her a more effective educator.

Clinicians have also found significant benefits from incorporating the Music Medicine Protocol into their practices. Donnie Lee III, MT-BC, LPMT, a music therapist and Music4Life® Practitioner, shares, "Adolescents in alternative learning settings due to behavior often have challenges managing their emotions. This is due in part to the developmental process of the brain, and also due to toxicity and trauma in the child's environment. The *6 Habits of Music Medicine for Highly Empowered*

People have helped my students to identify their emotional challenges and communicate these challenges more efficiently, which allows me to enlarge their perspective about using music differently to bring different results."

Chris Cummins, LMFT, LCADC, ACS, describes a personal and professional transformation, saying, "Every day, I used music as a way to numb myself. You could say it was similar to a drug or alcohol fix to escape my mental state. The 6 Habits Music Medicine card set helped me to realize how I was using music and how to use it intentionally instead. The moment I began using these cards, I changed the music I was listening to and was immediately positively impacted. I plan to use this card set as an intervention with the patients I serve for that revelation-type session that us therapists strive for in our clinical practice."

These testimonials from individuals in treatment, students, therapists, and educators illustrate the profound and versatile impact of the Music Medicine Protocol. By providing tools for mood management and behavioral adjustment, the protocol not only facilitates personal transformation but also enhances professional capabilities, making a significant positive impact on individuals and communities alike.

Implementing the Music Medicine Protocol

This section offers practical tips and strategies for individuals and professionals to effectively utilize the Music Medicine Protocol, facilitating its integration into daily routines and therapeutic settings for improved emotion regulation.

When creating personal U.S.E. (Unsettled, Soothed, Energized) playlists, it is foundational for individuals looking to harness the protocol. These playlists should be thoughtfully curated to reflect the user's specific emotional needs, beginning with music that matches their current state and gradually transitioning to tracks that promote more desired mood states. For instance, someone feeling anxious might start with music that captures this feeling, then move to calming melodies, eventually shifting to uplifting and energizing songs. Integrating these playlists into daily activities helps manage stress and improve mood with the goal of building emotional resilience. Individuals are encouraged to explore various music genres with peers to find what best resonates with their emotional landscape, ensuring that the music aligns with their needs and enhances its therapeutic effects.

Professionals in therapeutic fields, such as therapy or counseling, can enhance their practice by incorporating the Music Medicine Protocol. These professionals need specialized training, like the Music Medicine Clinical Specialist certification, to better understand how to select and utilize music effectively in therapy sessions. This training helps professionals tailor music selections to fit their clients' emotional states and needs, facilitating smoother transitions from negative to more positive moods. Maintaining access to ongoing resources and support, such as subscribing to professional journals, attending workshops, and engaging with music therapy networks, is crucial. Available through MusicMedicineClub.com, these resources provide valuable insights and updates that help professionals stay informed about new techniques and tools in music therapy.

By adopting these approaches, individuals and professionals can fully leverage the Music Medicine Protocol to enhance personal mood management and enrich their therapeutic support.

Expanding the Reach and Future Directions

The Music4Life® Music Medicine Protocol is rapidly evolving with the Key2MEE® Music App. It extends its influence beyond traditional settings into community centers and schools while embracing cutting-edge technological innovations like virtual and augmented reality (V.R. and A.R.). This broadening scope enhances the protocol's effectiveness, accessibility, and adaptability to contemporary emotional and psychological needs.

In educational environments, integrating music therapy into curricula transforms student engagement and emotion regulation. Teachers employ U.S.E. playlists and Mood Sequence Formulas™ to help students manage stress and trauma, hoping to build long-term resilience and emotional intelligence. For instance, "Sawyer" (pseudonym), an innovative teacher, utilizes these tools to create a supportive classroom atmosphere that aids in emotional recovery and stability.

Community centers have also recognized the benefits of music therapy, implementing programs that cater to diverse groups, including the elderly and at-risk youth. These initiatives foster social cohesion and emotional well-being, creating inclusive spaces where participants can express and explore their emotions through music. The positive feedback from these programs indicates a growing appreciation for the role of music therapy in enhancing community life.

Technologically, music therapy is witnessing a revolution with the adoption of V.R. and A.R., which provide immersive, customizable therapeutic experiences. V.R. transports patients into calming, controlled environments, optimizing the therapeutic effects of music by combining it with visual stimuli. Meanwhile, AR brings an interactive dimension to therapy, allowing real-world engagement that enhances the music's impact. These technologies make therapy sessions more engaging and allow for tailored therapeutic interventions to individual needs, broadening access to those unable to attend in-person sessions.

As the Music4Life® Music Medicine Protocol continues to evolve in the Key2MEE® Music App, it sets new standards in therapy. By reaching new audiences and incorporating innovative tools, it offers fresh pathways to healing and underscores the dynamic potential of music as a therapeutic modality. This ongoing expansion reflects the protocol's commitment to adapt and respond to the shifting landscapes of societal needs, paving the way for future advancements in the field.

The Transformative Power of Music

As we reflect on the insights and narratives shared in this chapter, it's clear that the Music4Life® Music Medicine Protocol is more than a mere therapeutic tool; it's a gateway to profound personal transformation and professional enhancement. We've explored how this protocol, rooted in the USE MEE™ Model, meticulously selects, times, and sequences music to address and harmonize individual emotional states precisely. This approach has provided relief and new pathways for individuals like Casey and offered a new lens through which professionals across various fields can refine and apply their practices.

Through stories like Casey's—a veteran who reshaped his emotional landscape through personalized music therapy—we've seen firsthand the capacity of music to foster significant emotional shifts, enhancing feelings of peace while reducing unrest. This chapter has also highlighted how the protocol extends beyond individual treatment, influencing educational settings and professional environments through strategic music integration.

In educational realms, teachers and counselors are incorporating U.S. E. specialized playlists and Mood Sequence Formulas™ in prescriptive playlists to support student environments and those affected by trauma, illustrating music's role in shaping a conducive learning environment. In business realms, Tony Robbins, named one of 200 Top Business Gurus by Harvard Business Press, states, "By harnessing the power of our emotions, we become architects of our destiny. ... When you change your mood, you change your life" (Team Tony, n.d.). Similarly, therapists and healthcare providers use Music4Life® tools in professional settings to enhance critical thinking about session structures that optimize client engagement, underscoring the broad applicability of the Music4Life principles in mastering the ability to control moods.

The overarching message is clear: when applied with intention and expertise, music holds a transformative power that transcends traditional therapy. It not only aids in emotion regulation and potential resilience but also acts as a holistic force for enhancing personal development and well-being across communities. As we move forward, we must continue exploring and embracing music's role in public health strategies and individual healing journeys, ensuring its benefits reach those in dire need of innovative and empathetic care solutions progressing toward mood mastery.

4

MUSIC DIETS FOR MOOD CONTROL

E xploring the relationship between music, mood control, and emotional health reveals music's significant and often unnoticed impact
on our mental well-being. Music transforms our emotions, regulates our
moods, and ultimately contributes to a healthier emotional condition.
According to the National Center for Complementary and Integrative
Health, music activates various brain regions involved in cognition, sensation, movement, and emotions, leading to significant physical and psychological benefits (National Center for Complementary and Integrative
Health, 2024). For example, children with musical training have a larger
corpus callosum, improving communication between the brain's hemi-
spheres and enhancing cognitive functions like memory and attention
(Schlaug et al., 1995). These benefits arise from the complex mental engagement required in musical practice, which continuously strengthens
the brain (Hyde et al., 2009).

Reflecting on my personal experiences, I often ponder how different my life could have been without my early violin training - a personalized music diet. Throughout those early years, my parents made many decisions for me, nudging me towards becoming a violinist rather than a ballet dancer, a path that was natural and cost-effective to them. My father, an Eastman School of Music graduate, was my violin teacher and orchestra conductor. At the same time, my mother, a talented pianist, violist, and vocalist, sang softly to us, careful not to disturb the quiet environment my father valued unless it involved rehearsals or performances. Managing a household where each of my four siblings and I learned to play stringed instruments proved incredibly challenging for her. My venture into playing alto saxophone in the high school jazz band marked one of the few times my father intervened differently, requesting that I stop my practice several times.

This background gives me a unique perspective on the benefits of music education, especially as I observe its impact on my (grand)daughter. Today, as I consider the possibility that my adopted (grand)daughter may have ADHD, I am reminded of the power of music—not only as a personal sanctuary but also as an essential tool for emotional expression and coping. Her natural athletic abilities and artistic inclinations, while not my primary interests, have led us to incorporate a diverse range of musical instruments into her life, harnessing music's transformative potential to bolster her development.

Transitioning from the nurturing aspects of music in a familial setting to a broader societal impact, my professional engagements, such as those with the Music4Life® Music Medicine Boot Camp and presentations at the International Women's Forum World Conference in Jamaica, delve into more complex interactions between music and mood. While celebrating cultural icons like Bob Marley is expected, I also address the darker legacy of specific music genres, notably dancehall music, which has been dubbed 'murder music' due to its associations with violence. This term evolved as dancehall music, characterized by its powerful rhythms and often aggressive lyrics, which became linked with an alarming spike in violent crime in Jamaica, once recording the world's highest murder rate.

This connection between music and violence highlights the pressing need to scrutinize our music listening habits. Identifying potential "danger zones" in music—such as problematic lyrics, repetitive, intense beats, and high volumes—is essential in understanding how these elements can provoke harmful behaviors. For instance, community disputes over loud music have shown how such elements can exacerbate conflicts.

Exploring the impact of dancehall music on societal violence illustrates the significant influence of music on human behavior. Dancehall's association with violent crime reflects how deeply music can affect our actions and mood states, necessitating careful consideration of the music we engage with.

Moreover, the historical use of music during wartime or the repeated playing of melancholic tracks like "Gloomy Sunday" further reveals the extensive psychological effects music can have. Often referred to as the "Hungarian Suicide Song," "Gloomy Sunday" is notorious for its sorrowful melody and despairing lyrics, which have been linked to depression and, in some cases, suicide among listeners. Billie Holiday's 1941 rendition of this haunting ballad expanded its reach, embedding it deeply in the cultural consciousness of the United States. The song's opening lines, "Sunday is gloomy, my hours are slumberless," evoke a pervasive sense of sorrow that deeply resonates with listeners (Miller, 2008).

This particular song demonstrates the significant impact that music can have on mood and mental states, serving as a powerful reminder of the importance of understanding and respecting the emotional effects of musical compositions. Beyond its anecdotal association with increased rates of suicide, "Gloomy Sunday" highlights music's ability to access and intensify the darker aspects of human emotion, thereby significantly influencing behavior and mood. The historical context provided by Stephen Miller in "The Peculiar Life of Sundays" discusses how Billie Holiday's version emphasized the despair and hopelessness intertwined with the song's narrative, illustrating music's broader social and psychological functions (Miller, 2008).

Through these observations, I aim to equip individuals with the knowledge to make informed choices about their music environment. I want to promote a safer, more mindful engagement with music that enhances rather than endangers communal and familial well-being. This holistic approach helps mitigate potential negative impacts. It enriches our lives by strengthening bonds through shared music experiences and thoughtful, supportive interactions.

For those interested in exploring further how music can influence behavior, sometimes with severe consequences, I invite you to examine my publication, "CAUTION: Music May Murder," a comprehensive four-page document that is part of the Music Medicine training at MusicMedicineAcademy.com. This publication provides extensive insights into the

Power of music to incite violence and killing and is available through the Music4Life® program materials.

Considering the dual nature of music's influence, it is essential to acknowledge its potential risks and its profound ability to enrich and transform lives positively. Engaging actively with music enhances our understanding of its impact on mood, empowering us to use it intentionally for emotion regulation. The selection of music across genres influences our mood states through varying beats per minute (BPM), facilitating transitions from calm to exhilaration. Research confirms these benefits, showing that listening to music can regulate arousal and mood, boost self-awareness, and strengthen social connections. It also triggers physiological responses such as dopamine release, improving mood, motivation, and emotional experiences while contributing to physical health improvements like lower blood pressure and enhanced heart function. This comprehensive influence underscores music's integral role in mental and physical wellness.

In my article, "The Art of Overcoming PTSD: Building Resiliency Via Music Therapy," (Pinkerton, 2022), Madison's story vividly illustrates the therapeutic potential of music. He views his customized Music Medicine Pill® as crucial to his PTSD treatment and overall recovery process. Before adopting music therapy, Madison utilized metal music to manifest and justify his intense feelings of anger following his best friend's tragic suicide. Music therapy opened a pathway for him to connect with a spectrum of emotions and begin healing. He reflects, "Music therapy finally helped me deal with the emotional triggers of that trauma breaking me down daily. I opened up to different kinds of music, beyond metal, to feel different emotions. It helped me get in tune with feeling sad and happy, and not just rage, with key ways to feel it, accept it, and not deny it or push it down or get violent towards myself." Thanks to this therapeutic approach, Madison now views his friend's memory without the accompanying rage, allowing him to find peace and maintain sobriety (Pinkerton, 2022).

Before this treatment, he used metal music to express and justify his feelings of rage following his best friend's suicide. Madison shares, "Music therapy finally helped me deal with the emotional triggers of that trauma breaking me down daily. I explored various music genres beyond metal, allowing me to experience a range of emotions beyond anger. This broadened my emotional awareness, helping me to genuinely feel sadness and happiness. It taught me how to acknowledge these emotions, accept them without suppression or aggression towards myself.Because of music therapy, I can think about Chandler now with the emotional trigger gone, no longer sparking the rage about half my world being ripped away from me. Three years later, I still use a variety of music for sobriety and healing my PTSD" (Pinkerton, 2022).

Rocko's journey also reveals the significant impact of music therapy. During a group music therapy session at a residential addiction treatment center, Rocko revisited a song that had previously been denied due to its intense lyrics. Initially, when I first met him more than three years earlier, he had requested to play this same song. At that time, I had decided against it after reviewing the lyrics, concerned about the potential difficulty in managing the emotional responses it could elicit among his peers in a drug court music therapy session. Rocko protested, asserting, "My pick of songs matters, not your opinion." This experience highlights the importance for therapists to regularly engage with the Music Medicine Protocol, which helps them develop a refined ability to navigate and respond to the complex emotional dynamics that can arise during therapy sessions.

Later, in a different setting at the residential addiction treatment facility, the clinical director informed me of a change in session scheduling due to a new patient's death that morning, which positioned my music therapy session early in the afternoon following the cognitive therapy debriefing. Thirty-three adult male patients and four visiting university students participated in the session. They overwhelmingly chose to engage in their favorite session called "FAVES." Utilizing the Music Medicine Protocol, I spontaneously incorporated the Mood Sequence Formula to shift negative moods, respecting the details shared by patients about their preferred music (reference Resources about "FAVES" session plan).

Rocko was the second patient in the lineup, and he requested that I play his preferred music, which I had previously refused more than three years ago. I could not refuse him this time. I asked him and everyone else to select a word from a list of 60 core values to focus the session positively. His song, "Dance with the Devil" by Immortal Technique, was played second after Creed's "One Last Breath." Halfway through, I paused the music to warn that the lyrics would become rough and intense, offering anyone the chance to leave and return in five minutes if needed. Only a couple of clients departed. After the song, I engaged Rocko in discussing how the music made him feel and the memories it evoked. It was revealed that the music had surfaced repressed memories of his friend's traumatic experiences, which he had previously been unable to articulate. This discovery was pivotal, helping him to seek peace and begin the process of healing (The Music4Life® USA, 2024).

Scan this QR code to hear Rocko discuss his entire story.

These stories demonstrate music therapy's effectiveness and highlight the importance of careful music selection and thoughtful guidance during sessions. Madison and Rocko's significant changes show how music therapy can influence mood states and support healing.

Creating a Healthy Music Diet

Music hygiene involves consciously selecting and maintaining a music "diet" that positively influences one's mood states, consciousness, physiology, and behaviors. This proactive approach to music consumption encourages listeners to engage with music that provides immediate pleasure and promotes long-term emotional and mental wellness. The importance of music hygiene lies in its ability to cleanse our emotions and enhance desired moods, much like how eating the right foods can improve physical health and emotional well-being. By forming new insights about our music consumption and its effects, individuals can create tailored playlists that act as prescriptive tools to manage various moods and situations effectively.

Just as food cravings can indicate underlying emotional needs, cravings for certain types of music or repeated thoughts of specific songs—known as "earworms"—can also reflect deeper emotional states. Diane Javelli, a registered dietitian in the Nutrition Clinic at the University of Washington Medical Center - Montlake, notes that food cravings occur to help satisfy emotional needs, such as stress, anxiety, and sadness (Cabotaje, 2020). This concept aligns closely with why people experience earworms: music that continuously plays in one's mind. In my clinical experience, the earworm may persist until the listener resolves their connection to the music or deciphers the message behind it. For instance, a parent might constantly recall a tune they frequently play for their child, which resurfaces in moments of emotional connection or longing. Similarly, an earworm could relate to other life experiences, prompting listeners to ask themselves about the lyrics' relevance to their current life, the memories they evoke, the moods they trigger, and whether the music describes positive or negative experiences. These introspections can lead to greater awareness of how lyrics and music are tied to one's emotional health, akin to how food impacts physical health.

Cravings for a particular music selection or hearing a song repeatedly in your head, known as an "earworm," often happen because the beat controls one's mood and makes you want to move, making the song feel good. People might play a song repeatedly without fully grasping the lyrics, which could reinforce either positive or negative mindsets or behaviors. Similarly, you might use music to address or shift moods, such as a soothing melody to alleviate sadness or an upbeat track to dispel anxiety.

When a song becomes an earworm, it might persistently replay until you resolve its connection to your life or decipher its message. This could be as simple as the music your child repeatedly plays, which lingers in your mind and is connected to your child's thoughts or the emotions the music evokes. On the other hand, they might remind you of your child's absence, triggering memories and feelings tied to their presence. Earworms also link to broader life experiences. The "6 Habits of Music Medicine for Highly Empowered People," specifically in Empowerment Habit #3, "Mood Control," offers insights into understanding earworms better. It encourages asking questions such as: How do the lyrics relate to your current life?

Do they bring up stories you cherish or wish to forget? Do they keep you anchored to unresolved past issues or help celebrate present successes? What moods do they trigger? How do you connect with the instruments or the singer? Does the music reflect positive or negative experiences, and does it inadvertently align with your unresolved emotions?

Addressing these questions can heighten your awareness of how closely connected an earworm is to your current emotions, potentially helping to end its repetitive influence. For more complex earworms that evoke mixed emotions or remind you of unrepeatable past experiences, leading to sadness or confusion, a deeper music-based intervention like a Music Medicine Pill® might be recommended. This approach is part of the broader strategies discussed in Empowerment Habit #4, "Music Hygiene," and #5, "Emotional Fluidity," aimed at refining your music listening habits to manage your emotional health better. By developing three new specialized playlists, individuals can gain new insights into the "music diet" and its influence on states of consciousness, emotions, physiology, and behavior. This proactive management of music consumption allows for a holistic application of music as medicine, bridging the gap between therapeutic practices and daily emotional self-care.

Maintaining a healthy balance in music listening habits is essential for effectively using music for emotional support while ensuring diverse coping mechanisms. This balance involves recognizing signs of over-reliance on music for mood management and implementing strategies to address it effectively. A striking illustration of this is found in the experiences at Sheppard Air Force Base under the leadership of the installation commander, Colonel Kenyon Bell, who has since ascended to the rank of

Major General. During a two-day airmen training event, a Music Medicine Pill® guided meditation was to be introduced to help arm 66 crew chiefs in training with emotion regulation strategies. In the command center, the track "Bodies" by Drowning Pool blared through the speakers before the anticipated soothing music to advise the leadership of this cathartic protocol. This choice of music initially caught the base commander and three other Colonels off-guard in the command center.

Their reaction underscores the critical importance of music selection in therapeutic settings. The unexpected music prompted acute attention from the leadership, leading to an immediate evaluation of the psychological tools employed in training. Recognizing the potential for music to influence mood and mental state significantly, the base leadership, in consultation with Colonel Kevin McCal, the 82nd Medical Group Commander, decided to enhance the training with dedicated mental health support. This decision was informed by prior discussions and preparedness that included insights from the Music4Life® support team, comprising experts such as Donnie Lee, III, LPMT, MT-BC, and Dennis D. Burkhardt, D.C.

This event highlights the immediate impact of music on mood states. It illustrates the broader applications of music as a therapeutic tool in military settings and emphasizes the need for careful consideration and selection of music in therapeutic interventions. Reflecting an understanding of its profound psychological impacts, this case at Sheppard Air Force Base is a compelling example of how music, when applied like medicine, can enhance emotion regulation and potential resilience among military personnel (Pinkerton, 2020).

Practical strategies for a balanced music listening regimen include diversifying coping mechanisms to ensure music does not become the sole method for managing stress or emotional turmoil. Integrating music with other stress-relief strategies such as physical exercise, meditation, and social interaction is crucial, enhancing overall emotional resilience.

Recognizing signs of overreliance on music is also critical. This might manifest as excessively using music to escape from reality, ignoring other important aspects of life, or experiencing increased stress or anxiety when unable to listen to music. Assessing whether music consumption is helping or hindering mood management is essential.

In addition, the Music4Life® program offers structured educational tools that help individuals understand the impact of music on emotional and mental health. eCourses such as "Is Your Music Toxic?" and "Danger Zones of Music Listening Habits" at MusicMedicineAcademy.com educate how particular music patterns might be detrimental or beneficial, aiding in making informed choices about music consumption.

Furthermore, structured music listening practices such as creating specific playlists for different emotional needs—Unsettled, Soothed, and Energized—can significantly aid emotion regulation. This approach mirrors the training methods used at Sheppard Air Force Base, where music therapy-informed strategies and training were tailored to enhance focus and reduce stress, with the potential of boosting overall mental resilience among airmen. These practices were supported with empirical evidence, demonstrating the protocol's capability of improving performance and well-being through clinically guided methods, highlighting music's significant role in emotional and physical health management. ("Music Medicine with Military," 2019).

During the recent training session at Sheppard Air Force Base, experiential learning took center stage, mainly focusing on the effects of different rhythmic patterns on physical well-being. Dr. Dennis Burkhardt, a chiropractor, provided a compelling demonstration using kinesiology to assess the impact of anapestic beats—characterized by their rhythmic pattern of two short beats punctuated by a longer one—on muscle strength (Diamond, 1979; Hawkins, 1995). Seven airmen who were skeptical from the previous day's virtual training on how anapestic beats could weaken muscle strength participated in this live test. Each participant's arm strength was evaluated while listening to Eminem's "Mockingbird," which features an anapestic beat, and then compared to their muscle strength while listening to Pachelbel's "Canon in D," a piece with a classical structure. The results were precise: after a baseline was established, participants showed significantly weakened muscle strength under the influence of the anapestic beat, whereas their strength remained robust while listening to classical music.

These findings highlight the potential disruptions that anapestic beats may cause to synchronizing the central and peripheral nervous systems, potentially leading to weakened muscular structure and compromised physiology. Therefore, choosing music without anapestic beats during physical fitness training sessions is advisable. Selecting music with a steady and consistent rhythm, such as a simple four-four time signature, can promote better alignment of neural signals and enhance muscle activation. Although this approach supports the coordination and efficiency of muscular contractions, leading to improved strength gains and reduced risk of injury, research is just beginning to connect the neural processing of music with physiological responses to music. In a recent study, the neural processing of beats (the regularly recurring pulse in music) and meter (a repetitive pattern of strong and weak beats) was found to predict HRV - Heart Rate Variability, establishing a neural–physiological link. This link presents new research in the realms of music cognition and auditory neuroscience (Zhao et al., 2020).

Additionally, the training incorporated a comprehensive Music Medicine Pill® guided meditation, created from three specialized mood playlists—Unsettled, Soothed, and Energized—each representing specific emotions as found within the Emotional Profile Quiz in the Key2MEE® Music App. Clinical evidence reports the potential influence of Music Medicine Pills on the use of medication with physician-directed reduction, cessation, or prescription of drugs. This innovative approach to music therapy, documented by a case report of a veteran with PTSD, features the transformative power of prescriptive music playlists to address specific emotional and physical needs, thereby enhancing overall well-being and resilience among military personnel (Wellman et al., 2015).

The training also featured breakout groups where airmen segmented according to their preferred music genre—ranging from hip-hop/rap to classical and metal—were tasked to collaborate, enhancing peer support by populating specialized music playlists. This collaborative effort was designed to utilize music strategically to improve emotional intelligence and psychological resilience. Pre- and post-assessment results indicated that 92% of the participants learned new strategies for harnessing the power of music, with 62% improvement in Emotional Intelligence and 67% reduction in emotional disturbances, such as anger, anxiety, depression, and sadness (Pinkerton, 2020).

This comprehensive approach educated the airmen about the scientific underpinnings of music's effects on the body and mind. It provided practical tools and strategies to improve their overall quality of life, echoing the program's goal to enhance military readiness and personal development.

Music Diet's a Therapeutic Tool

The Music Medicine Protocol incorporates various principles that can be effectively applied to promote stress relief, emotion regulation, and overall mental health improvement. By utilizing music to address physical, emotional, cognitive, and social needs, this protocol empowers individuals to manage their stress levels and regulate their emotions more effectively.

Integrating a music diet into daily routines can be both enjoyable and therapeutic. One practical exercise is singing, which oxygenates the body and releases endorphins, elevating mood and alleviating anxiety. Playing easy wind instruments such as the didjeridu, recorder, or Native American flute can strengthen the lungs and provide mental clarity. The controlled breathing required for these instruments enhances lung capacity and has a calming effect on the mind. One executive reports playing the didjeridu for hours, creating the desired transcendental groove experience with his mind quieting and changing his concept of self.

Another valuable music diet is creating a transition playlist. This involves compiling music that starts with slower tempos, lower pitches, and fewer instruments and gradually includes tracks with faster tempos, broader ranges of pitches, and more instrumentation. This playlist can help regulate your energy throughout the day, aiding in emotion regulation. Tony Drexel Smith's journey is another testament to the power of music in regulating energy and aiding emotion regulation to overcome life's challenges. Tony is a Marine Veteran of Desert Shield and Desert Storm who has faced a multitude of challenges, including recovering from gambling addiction, managing bipolar disorder, and now dealing with diabetes. Despite these obstacles, Tony has found success with weight loss and mood management through a carefully managed, medically monitored Keto diet. His resilience and determination have allowed him to continue working in finance, where he provides third-party due diligence with compliant documentation to achieve maximum valuation in minimal time to funding.

Music has been a key stabilizer throughout his varied career as a Marine, football player, business finance consultant, and restaurant owner, helping him navigate life's hurdles. Tony prefers YouTube for its visual effect, enhancing his musical experience. When he needs to assess business plans quickly, he listens to sports themes played by symphony orchestras, such as those from the Polish Varèse Sarabande label, particularly the score from "Rudy" and "Remember the Titans." This music, combined with the movie's messages of self-belief and overcoming adversity, inspires him to deliver excellence in his work.

For reading, Tony focuses on the uplifting sounds of children's choirs, such as "Glorious" by David Archuleta and the One Voice Children's Choir. For financial details, he relies on "Waking Up" by Explosions in the Sky from the movie "Lone Survivor" to maintain complete concentration.

When deadlines loom and intense focus is required, Tony immerses himself in the opening scene of the "Top Gun" movie. This motivates him and evokes memories of his Marine days, particularly his role in the Aviation Ordinance, which demanded precision and quick execution. With its powerful impact, music helps Tony navigate his demanding career and personal challenges, providing a steady anchor in his life.

Similarly, subscribing to "Power Up 365" offers a daily boost of inspiration, leveraging the power of music and positive messages to enhance motivation and positivity. This service sends daily empowerment texts that include an inspiring quote, a matching beautiful image, and a music link from Spotify spanning various genres. This regular infusion of motivational content can help maintain a positive mindset and encourage daily engagement with uplifting music.

Moreover, it's essential to assess and adjust music listening habits. Evaluating whether your music consumption is continuous (24/7) and how it impacts your emotional and mental health is crucial. Tailoring and how you engage with your music diet can ensure that it serves a therapeutic purpose rather than becoming a potential disruptor.

By consciously incorporating these techniques into daily routines, individuals can leverage the therapeutic powers of music to enhance their mental health and emotional well-being significantly. These practices improve personal mood management and enrich the overall quality of life through music's thoughtful and strategic use. Such transformative experiences are vividly illustrated in the inspirational stories shared by individuals and therapists who have witnessed firsthand the profound impact of music as a tool for healing and emotional growth. These narratives share personal transformation journeys and highlight the outcomes and lessons learned from integrating music into therapeutic practices.

One notable story is that of Barry L., who experienced a substantial shift in how he perceives music after engaging with Music4Life®. Barry explains, "I've always loved music, but Music4Life changed my outlook. The way music is prescribed is better than any medicine. I will never hear music the same way again: my eyes and ears were opened to music, healing every wound that impaled my body, mind, and spirit." Barry's experience demonstrates the power of music to transcend traditional therapy and provide deep healing for the body, mind, and spirit. His journey with music therapy began in a residential treatment center. Barry first learned the concepts of Music Medicine. Years later, he successfully decoded an earworm during a virtual session, which led to personalized therapeutic insights and the creation of a tailored Music Medicine Pill® based on his specific emotional and life circumstances.

This story, among others, sheds light on essential outcomes and insights from using a music diet as a therapeutic tool. From my professional experience working with over 11,000 clients in residential addiction treatment facilities, I've learned that recovery is a lifelong process. Emotions in recovery can be complex and layered, often resembling the peeling of an onion. For example, repressed anger might initially present as depression, a pivotal trigger for emotional relapse. Once depression is addressed, significant anger connected to past memories or current life conditions may surface, posing challenges to sobriety. According to the American Addiction Centers, emotional relapse, such as unresolved anger, can lead to a mental struggle in maintaining sobriety, with individuals potentially seeking substances to numb their emotions (Ackermann, 2024).

The Music4Life® psycho-education program emphasizes the importance of increased awareness of emotional triggers. Teaching clients to apply music therapeutically—akin to medicine—can effectively resolve problematic moods. This proactive approach helps clients manage potential stressful triggers like anxiety, depression, and anger, which are common precursors to relapse. As individuals learn to harness the healing power of music, it becomes equally important to cultivate a balanced approach to their listening habits. While music offers profound therapeutic benefits, including stress relief and mood enhancement, maintaining a healthy, balanced music diet ensures that it complements rather than replaces other essential coping mechanisms.

To address potential overreliance on music, it is advisable to integrate it into a broader context of stress management techniques. This integration can include physical activities such as exercise or yoga, meditation, social activities, and nursing therapy. Diversifying coping strategies helps reduce the risk of dependency on music and enhances overall emotional resilience and well-being.

Moreover, developing a comprehensive emotional support system that extends beyond musical engagement, listening or making music, is critical. Engaging in diverse hobbies and interests can significantly improve emotional and mental health. Activities such as sports, reading, crafting, or learning new skills provide opportunities for personal growth and stress reduction that complement the therapeutic benefits derived from music. Building solid interpersonal connections and participating in community activities, such as drum circles, also offer essential emotional support that music alone cannot provide. These relationships foster a sense of belonging and are crucial during emotional distress.

While music is a valuable resource for emotional support, maintaining a balanced approach to its use is vital. By integrating various coping mechanisms and developing a broad-based support system, individuals can ensure that their engagement with music remains healthy and beneficial. This holistic approach prevents over-reliance on music and enriches the individual's emotional landscape, improving overall well-being and resilience.

Throughout this chapter, we've explored the dynamic relationship between music, mood control, and emotional healing, as well as the significant, often subtle, impact of music on our mental states and overall well-being. The National Center for Complementary and Integrative Health has emphasized how music activates brain regions involved in cognition, sensation, movement, and emotions, offering considerable physical and psychological benefits. This capability of music to stimulate neurotransmitters and hormone release evokes emotions. It fosters social bonds, with early musical training potentially leading to structural changes in the brain.

Reflecting on personal experiences and the educational content shared in the chapter, it's clear that music is more than just a background element in our lives—it is a powerful medium for emotional expression and regulation. Whether through my own early musical training on the violin or the strategic use of music in family settings and therapeutic contexts, music has demonstrated its profound capacity to enhance bonding, provide comfort, and serve as a coping mechanism for individuals across various circumstances, particularly those with different abilities.

The techniques for emotion regulation highlight how different music choices—varying in genre, rhythm, and tempo—can significantly affect our emotional and physiological states. By actively engaging with music, individuals can harness music's therapeutic potential to enhance emotion regulation and emotional self-awareness. The case studies presented, including transformative experiences of individuals like Madison and Rocko, demonstrate the real-world impact of music therapy in managing moods and facilitating personal growth and recovery.

The power of music extends beyond mere entertainment; it is a transformative tool that, when integrated thoughtfully into our lives, can significantly enhance our emotional health and well-being. Considering the lessons learned from this chapter, it becomes evident that creating a personalized and healthy music diet is essential. This diet should support the individual's emotional and mental health journey and enrich their daily living, providing a balanced soundtrack to life's complex emotional landscape. By developing a deeper understanding and strategic use of music as a special diet, we can all tap into its healing power and enjoy a more harmonious world with moods controlled in a healthy way.

5

EMOTIONAL FLUIDITY WITH ENVIRONMENT CONSCIOUSNESS

Imagine you're in a morning meeting at work, presenting a project you've dedicated weeks to, only to receive harsh criticism. As the room's atmosphere shifts, you feel your face flush with embarrassment and then stiffen with anger. Instead of letting go, you stew in this frustration, allowing it to darken your mood for the rest of the day. This bitterness shadows your lunch with colleagues, taints your interactions, and even affects your drive home. Every conversation is colored by the frustration of that morning's feedback.

This experience reveals a lack of Emotional Fluidity, where you struggle to move beyond the initial feelings of anger and disappointment. Emotional Fluidity, however, would involve acknowledging these intense emotions, reflecting on their triggers, and consciously transitioning to a more productive mood state. It might include stepping aside to process the feedback, identifying constructive criticism amidst the harsh words, or sharing your feelings with a supportive colleague. Mastering Emotional Fluidity requires regular practice navigating through your emotions with agility to maintain balance, support your ability to adapt, and build resilience as you face daily challenges.

To cultivate the skill of Emotional Fluidity, individuals must train their brains to manage transitions between different mood states effectively. This training helps control physiological responses, such as adrenaline rushes, within 10-15 minutes. By consistently practicing Music4Life® Mood Sequence Formulas™, individuals develop the capability to achieve a flow state on demand. These formulas guide listeners on the frequency of prescriptive music listening and how to sequence music effectively to facilitate smoother mood transitions (The Music4Life® USA, 2013).

As these practices become integrated into daily life, Emotional Fluidity manifests as a sign of good mental health, reflecting an individual's ability to experience and articulate their emotions effectively. Mastering this skill allows a person to transition smoothly between emotional states, such as moving from frustration to calm following challenging feedback at work. This capability enhances mood control and facilitates a deeper emotional connection in various situations. Employing tailored prescriptive playlists with mood sequencing, for example, can help shift from stress-filled anger to peace and then optimism, improving emotional presence and engagement. As individuals become more adept at managing their moods by applying music like medicine, they are better equipped to face daily challenges with mindfulness and adaptability, resulting in richer interactions and a more balanced life.

As discussed in the previous chapter, the "6 Habits of Music Medicine for Highly Empowered People" incorporates five specific activities designed to foster Emotional Fluidity. These include journaling, which helps participants reflect on their emotional experiences and the impact of music on their mood states; emotion regulation for intense feelings; teaching techniques to manage strong emotions through music; learning about 24/7 music listening habits to promote awareness of how constant music listening can hinder emotional fluidity; prescriptive listening techniques that encourage the use of music with specific therapeutic goals in mind; and mood sequence formulation, instructing on how to create and use music playlists that are strategically sequenced to foster a seamless flow of emotions. These activities are integral to developing a deeper connection with one's broad emotional continuum, enhancing the ability to move through emotions quickly and fostering a balanced mental state conducive to overall well-being.

Music can influence and manage our emotions, making it an effective tool for achieving emotional balance. Two techniques that stand out involve using different genres to guide emotional transitions and the practice of Mindful Listening. Embracing the Power of Mindful Listening is critical to harnessing this capability. In my own practice, I dedicate time to immerse myself fully in music during Mindful Listening sessions. I select pieces that resonate with my current emotional state or uplift my spirits. I pay close attention to every aspect of the music—all ten elements, such as melody, rhythm, intensity, plus lyric content—observing how each element affects my mind, body, actions, and feelings. I name the mood it evokes, usually categorizing it under U.S.E. (Unsettled, Soothed, Energized), and then pinpoint the specific emotion the music ignites.

Each music component contributes to its overall emotional resonance, reflecting and amplifying my inner emotional landscape. This attentive engagement deepens my emotional awareness and enhances my ability to navigate through various mood states more smoothly.

I craft personalized playlists to enhance daily activities, extending beyond the specialized U.S.E. playlists. For work-related tasks, I rely on "Neon Outback" by Rick Dusek, an energetic didjeridu album with electronic beats that keep me focused. Rick's music came into my life during a Music4Life® class. I learned about the therapeutic benefits of didjeridu music for conditions like snoring and sleep apnea (Belcher, 2013). "Cellular Awakening" by Kelly Howell helps me tap into my inner creativity for creative tasks.

For driving, I curate a playlist that helps me focus and calm on the road, avoiding songs that might induce road rage or drowsiness. I also apply a similar principle of careful music selection to my study environment. For studying, I curate a playlist featuring tracks primarily within the 55-70 bpm range, mostly classical music. The 55-70 bpm range in music helps synchronize brain waves with the heart's natural rhythm, promoting focus and calm, ideal for concentration and learning. This tempo range enhances concentration and boosts memory recall, a strategy that aligns with the principles of neurologic music therapy.

Starting my day, I opt for a playlist with a slower tempo and gradually introduce more energetic songs to build momentum and set a positive tone for the day. My meditation and relaxation playlists are thoughtfully composed to align with my energy levels, promoting tranquility and mindfulness through carefully selected ambient sounds or classical pieces without solid beats. In exploring the significance of lyrics that resonate deeply with me, I engage in lyric analysis, especially when a song becomes an earworm. This helps me understand the emotional or other implications attached to these songs, as noted by music therapist Dr. Connie Tomaino, who suggests that songs that spontaneously come to mind often have deeper personal connections (Taylor, 2024). Additionally, I actively participate in community music-making, which enriches my emotional experiences by creating a sense of connection and belonging. Whether playing in a small ensemble or joining a drum circle, these activities amplify my joy and creativity. Reflecting and journaling about my emotional responses to music is also integral to my routine. This process helps me articulate and explore the emotions, memories, and associations evoked by different songs or genres, using music as a powerful tool for introspection and self-discovery.

An example of how I use music effectively is my walking/jogging playlist, which lasts 2 hours and 21 minutes and includes 33 songs specifically chosen to match my movement tempo and support my desire for a positive mindset. I begin this playlist with "Promontory," the theme from "The Last of the Mohicans." This song holds special meaning for me, as it brings back memories of when I used it to improvise on the violin at residential addiction treatment centers. This helped clients deepen their commitment to walking through emotionally charged danger zones, supported by this music within a Mood Sequence Formula™. For the full list of tracks and their sequence, please refer to Appendix B.

These strategies can help you navigate mood states through music. Whether reviewing the latest hits for their medicinal content or comparing music to lyrics to deepen personal connections, I continuously learn and adapt my music choices to support my emotional well-being, ensuring that my engagement with music remains a reflective and enriching part of my life.

Creating Positive Environments

Music has the remarkable power to transform both physical and psychological spaces. It enhances physical environments, turning quiet spaces into vibrant areas that improve mood and social interactions, as seen in restaurants and shopping centers. Psychologically, music impacts emotions and cognitive functions, helping to alleviate stress and improve focus, which is leveraged in settings from therapy rooms to classrooms. Thus, music is a dynamic tool that shapes experiences and influences outcomes in diverse aspects of life.

One remarkable example of music's transformative power is observed in the experiences of individuals involved in Music4Life® wellness programs. For instance, one member, Karen, describes how a prescriptive playlist altered her mood, significantly reduced healthcare costs, *To hear direct-* and enhanced overall well-being. This personal testa- *ly from Karen* ment underscores the profound impact that music can *and learn more about her jour-* have on one's life, extending beyond mere entertainment *ney, scan the* to become a pivotal component of health and wellness *QR code here to* (The Music4Life® USA, 2013). *watch.*

Music's role in transforming environments is particularly evident in educational settings. As music influences emotions and cognitive functions to enhance mood and focus, integrating music into the classroom is a potent strategy to benefit student learning and development significantly. The George Lucas Education Foundation champions this approach through Edutopia, supporting innovative educational practices that foster lifelong skills and innovation (American Institutes for Research, 2023). For instance, a creative method involves students writing lyrics incorporating math vocabulary and performing these in front of their classmates. This practice reinforces their understanding of the concepts and leaves a lasting impression, often remembered and recited years later.

Music also plays a crucial role in signaling transitions within the classroom, providing rhythm for movement breaks, and celebrating diversity—practices often chosen collaboratively by students and teachers. On the first days of class, educators can engage students by asking about their favorite songs, which aids in building deeper relationships and understanding their preferences, which can provide insights for lesson planning and set a positive tone for future interactions (Saavedra, 2022; Herrity, 2023).

Research supports music's significant role in enhancing environmental quality in educational settings. According to a study published on PMC-PubMed Central, music plays a crucial role in adolescent emotional expression, social connection, and cognitive development (Chen, 2023). However, the study also notes that the misuse of music can lead to adverse effects such as hearing damage or emotional distress. This underscores the importance of responsible music consumption, guided by educators and parents.

Furthermore, creating a healthy music environment in schools involves more than just exposure to music. It requires comprehensive support from families, schools, and society to foster safe music spaces and provide ample educational resources. Music educators are central to this effort, as there is a growing need for them to help students understand music's emotional and mental health benefits, enhancing their social skills and self-confidence.

Music's transformative impact on physical and psychological spaces is deeply recognized, especially in educational settings. The National Center on Safe Supportive Learning Environments (NCSSLE) advocates integrating music into classrooms to enhance student learning and development significantly. This practice supports project-based learning and social-emotional development. It increases access to technology in schools, a vision also promoted by the George Lucas Education Foundation through Edutopia (Saavedra et al., 2022).

In an illustrative project, students were tasked to write lyrics that included math vocabulary words. The lyrics were then performed in front of their classmates, which helped solidify their understanding of the concepts, with many students still able to recite their songs years later. Such projects demonstrate how music can create memorable learning experiences and ensure a lasting grasp of academic concepts.

Moreover, integrating music into educational settings extends far beyond mere enjoyment, profoundly impacting students' mental health and cognitive development. Consider the approach taken by Judy Poteete in Chapter 1. In her anger management groups, she found that the participants became so conditioned by the prescriptive playlist that the music itself was no longer required; simply entering the group room immediately shifted them into a more calm state. This illustrates the powerful influence music can have on emotion regulation.

A study highlighted by the National Institutes of Health examines the intricate link between music and adolescent mental health, suggesting that while music offers numerous benefits, misuse can lead to adverse effects such as emotional distress. Therefore, educators and parents need guidance in ensuring responsible music consumption, including avoiding hearing damage. (Gonzalez et al., 2022)

The study emphasizes the importance of creating a healthy music environment at home, in schools, and in society. This environment advances music life skills with social skills to boost self-confidence in young individuals. Music educators are pivotal in this, as they impart musical knowledge and an understanding of its benefits for emotional and mental health.

The personal impact of music is also evident in military settings, where cadences play a crucial role. These rhythmic calls, which began with simple chants like 'left, right, left' in Basic Combat Training, help synchronize soldiers' steps during marches and runs. A popular cadence, "My Old Granny," illustrates this point vividly:

1, 2, 3, 4

1, 2, 3, 4

My old granny, she's 91

She does P.T. just for fun

My old granny, she's a 92

Stand in her way, she'll run you right through

My old granny, she's a 93

She does P.T. in a tree

My old granny, she's a 94

Knock down the walls and busted the door

My old granny's she's a 95

She does P.T. and that's no jive

When my old granny was a 96

She done P.T. just for kicks

When my old granny was a 97

She up and died and went straight to heaven

She met St. Peter at the pearly gate

She said "Hey, St. Peter, I hope I ain't late"

Saint Peter looked at her with a grin

He said "Get down Granny and knock out ten"

This cadence, and others like it, are more than just songs; they are integral to the training environment, enhancing unity and lifting spirits among soldiers.

As we examine the varied roles of music in both personal and institutional settings, it becomes clear that its impact reaches far beyond simple auditory enjoyment. Music's ability to shape and redefine both physical and psychological spaces positions it as a significant tool in educational and therapeutic contexts. It enhances learning environments and serves as a conduit for cultural and emotional intelligence. Educators and therapists can greatly enhance their influence by integrating music into daily routines and strategic interventions, creating more inclusive and empathetic communities. This deep integration of music highlights its lasting role in strengthening human connections and enriching our collective experiences.

Respecting Others with Music

Engaging in mindful sharing of music allows individuals to express emotions and experiences that might be difficult to articulate otherwise. This practice can serve as a bridge to understanding, opening up lines of communication, and nurturing empathy among family members or within community groups. By carefully selecting music that resonates with the emotional undertones of a situation, participants can find common ground, alleviate tension, and create a shared experience that might lead to resolving long-standing issues and improving relationships.

When addressing chronic family or community issues, mindful music sharing can take you a step closer to influencing positive changes in relationships, whether with your spouse, kids, friends, or even strangers. Instead of distancing yourself from their music listening habits, start by engaging respectfully and curiously about their choices. Ask about the music they listen to and how it affects their feelings, initiating conversations that can lead to deeper understanding and empathy. Recognizing that their music preferences often mirror internal desires, needs, or experiences can open discussions that help prevent conflicts and deepen connections.

It's important to consider that while some individuals may appreciate sharing music as a way to connect, others might prefer music that shifts their mood rather than matching it. For instance, when reviewing Colby Buzzell's playlist from "My War: Killing Time in Iraq," my evaluation concluded that 80% of the selections were "U" Unsettled music, and only 20% were soothed and happily energized music, which is not a balanced mix. A balanced music diet should have equal time in each mood category. To achieve this balance, I expanded his playlist by adding more soothing and energizing tracks. This adjustment aims to reduce the risk of getting stuck in unsettled emotions, promoting a state of calm to enhance alert concentration. While this playlist serves as a communal touchpoint that resonates with shared experiences among soldiers in more diverse settings, it's important to consider varying musical tastes and the need for music that can change mood states rather than just reinforcing them. For the full list of tracks and their sequence, please refer to Appendix B.

This approach respects individual preferences and adheres to social etiquette when sharing music in shared spaces. By being considerate of others' listening habits and the impact of music on their emotional well-being, we promote a more inclusive and harmonious environment. This mindful sharing of music underscores its role as a powerful medium for social connection and emotional expression, enhancing our interactions and collective experiences. Psychology and music psychology focus on answers to the question: Is it possible to develop music-based interventions that help break habits with a negative environmental impact and help to form and strengthen habits with a more positive environmental impact? (Prior, 2022)

Integrating music into communal spaces can enhance the environment significantly. Still, careful consideration is required to balance individual preferences with collective harmony. Maintaining an appropriate volume level to ensure everyone enjoys the shared space without feeling over-whelmed. Too loud music can be intrusive and disruptive, especially in multifunctional spaces where people might also need to concentrate or communicate with others. Choosing neutral and widely acceptable genres, such as classical, light jazz, or ambient music, can minimize discomfort and enhance the overall atmosphere. Additionally, the timing of music plays a critical role; energetic tracks might be perfect for boosting morale during a communal work session but could be less appropriate during late evening hours in residential areas or quiet times in offices. There are stores (i.e. Safeway) that choose to blast music in their parking lot to repel undesirable people and inadvertently affect the surrounding neighborhood with music they don't want to hear 24/7 (Schultz, 2023). I've created a lesson in the MusicMedicineAcademy.com called "Music May Murder," citing incidents where neighbors have been killed because of music disagreements.

Personal headphones are a respectful solution for those who prefer to listen to music in quieter settings, such as libraries or study areas. This approach allows individuals to enjoy their choice of music without disturbing others. Engaging with the community by seeking feedback about music choices and volume is beneficial to promote a considerate music environment. This can be achieved through informal conversations or structured surveys. For environments like shared offices or communal living areas, establishing specific times for music play can help manage expectations and reduce potential conflicts. For instance, agreeing on music-free periods during high-concentration tasks or designating times for more lively music can cater to diverse needs. Moreover, encouraging the creation of collaborative playlists for shared sessions can cultivate a sense of community and ownership, allowing everyone to contribute their favorite pieces and enhancing the feeling of inclusivity and mutual respect. For example, my hair specialist, Lisa, who owns her own studio called Dare to Dye, invites each hair stylist to contribute their favorite songs to the salon's environmental playlist. The ambiance is special, and it's apparent when I'm there that the stylists and customers regard each other as family, showing sincere interest in each other's lives.

Music and Mindfulness

Mindfulness is a practice that focuses on being intensely aware of what you're sensing and feeling in the moment, without interpretation or judgment. It involves breathing methods, guided imagery, and other practices to relax the body and mind and help reduce stress. Integrating music with mindfulness practices offers a distinctive approach to enhancing meditation and awareness exercises. By weaving music into these exercises, individuals can connect more profoundly with the present, using sounds to help focus their minds and ground themselves.

For instance, actively listening to the natural sounds of a forest or stream while being acutely aware of the environment around you—engaging all senses to see, smell, touch, taste, and hear—can significantly amplify the mindfulness experience. This method encourages participants to anchor their attention in the now, deepening their engagement with the moment rather than automatically drifting through the motions.

Additionally, structured mindfulness exercises incorporating music can enhance the depth of the practice. One such method is Music4Life's Power Up 365 program, which combines empowering quotes with striking imagery and pertinent music, encouraging individuals to form active connections that reinforce their mindfulness practice. Another creative technique involves producing an echo chamber effect by playing a piece like "Be Still" by Beautiful Chorus on two slightly offset devices to foster intense listening and focus. This setup, where one tracks the overlay of vocals and instruments, is a powerful focal point for mindfulness, promoting relaxation and stress release through deep concentration and controlled breathing.

Incorporating music into mindfulness exercises can significantly enhance the practice by helping participants connect deeply with their emotions and achieve a more profound state of relaxation or alertness, depending on the intended outcome. For effective music-based mindfulness, it is crucial to select music that resonates with the participants' current emotional state, not merely their music preference. This selection process ensures that the music genuinely facilitates the mindfulness experience, aligning with the individuals' psychological needs.

A practical approach to integrating music into mindfulness practices involves a step-by-step method where each piece of music matches and gradually alters the listener's mood. According to the Sonatina Center, a Mood

Regulation Playlist can be highly effective if composed correctly. Their blog, "Music for Big Emotions: Emotion Playlists," offers invaluable insights into creating playlists that effectively manage emotional transitions (Hooks, 2022). The blog emphasizes the importance of avoiding common mistakes, such as choosing songs that mismatch the emotional tone needed for the moment, thereby undermining the therapeutic potential of the music.

For example, a well-curated Mood Regulation Playlist should begin with songs that validate the listener's feelings before moving on to tracks that gently guide them toward a more regulated emotional state. The Sonatina Center points out that while some playlists purport to address mood regulation, they often fall short because they are not sufficiently tailored to the individual's unique emotional landscape. Each person's response to music is highly personal, and what works for one individual may not work for another. Therefore, mindfulness practitioners should consider the general mood associated with a piece of music and how each participant might uniquely interact with and respond to it (Hooks, 2022).

In exploring using music as a therapeutic tool to manage moods, specifically anger, I employ the Music Medicine Protocol, which provides a structured approach to selecting songs that resonate with and influence the listener's emotional state. I evaluate a series of songs based on their ability to match and modulate anger, revealing the complexity of music's impact on our feelings.

To validate anger, I critique three popular songs to demonstrate their effectiveness within the Music Medicine framework. "We're Not Gonna Take It" by Twisted Sisters, although seemingly appropriate for its angry lyrical content, is paradoxically coupled with upbeat, dance-like instrumentals, which might undermine the true essence of anger, making it less suitable for expressing or processing this emotion. Olivia Rodrigo's "Brutal" exhibits a fluctuation between soothing tones and aggressive energy, reflecting not just anger but a mix of sadness and depression, failing to capture the target emotion singularly. Billie Eilish's "Happier than Ever" starts with a slow, soft tempo more indicative of depression and anguish rather than pure anger, highlighting the importance of selecting music that precisely matches the intended emotional response.

The soothing category features Taylor Swift's "Out of the Woods," which, according to Swift, deals with the fragility and unpredictable nature of certain relationships (Mali, 2023). However, the song's energetic rhythm and poignant lyrics might provoke rather than soothe, suggesting a deeper analysis of the listener's current emotional state to guide the music's therapeutic application more effectively. Dolly Parton's "Wildflowers" and Van Morrison's "Brown Eyed Girl" exhibit cheerful rhythms that encourage movement and nostalgia, which might not be calming but could be transformative if aligned correctly with the listener's emotional needs.

For uplifting emotions, I find "Here Comes the Sun" by the Beatles and Rachel Platten's "Fight Song" effective in fostering a positive, energized feeling. These selections are ideal for transitioning from a state of anger to one of motivation and resilience. Nicki Minaj and Beyoncé's "Feeling Myself" also fits into the uplifting category, particularly for listeners who find the song's vibe empowering and self-affirming. However, its impact may vary across different generations.

These evaluations reveal the detailed application of the Music Medicine Protocol, stressing the importance of carefully selecting music that reflects the emotion and aids the listener's journey through emotional processing and healing.

6

TURNING LIFE CHALLENGES INTO LEARNING EXPERIENCES

Resilience is the ability to bounce back from challenges, enabling one to navigate unsettled emotions without repressing them and to think clearly and respond appropriately in any situation (American Psychological Association, n.d.). Music, particularly through the Music4Life® Music Medicine Protocol, is a powerful tool to foster resilience. This protocol guides individuals to deeply feel and release emotions by moving through the Mood Sequence Formula™ with mood-specific music.

In my personal experience, resilience has gained profound meaning through music. One of the most significant moments when music helped me recover from a difficult situation was during my pregnancy with twins. At four months, I couldn't feel them moving, and an ultrasound revealed they had died. Despite carrying lifeless fetuses for almost a month, which posed severe health risks, I struggled to accept their loss. During this painful period, I frequently listened to "The Rose" by Bette Midler, which helped me express my grief and find solace through tears.

Three months later, I attended the baby shower for my dear friend Goldie, who was pregnant at the same time. Feeling out of place, I found refuge in a low-light craft room, where I was mesmerized by Enigma's soothing yet powerful music, which resonated deeply within my wounded womb of sacral and root chakras. Immersed in creating quilt squares, I felt a profound healing as Enigma's music became my medicine, helping me shift focus to my one-year-old son and regain a sense of life and purpose.

I encouraged my husband to listen to Enigma. Although he initially disliked it when played in the wrong setting—driving our children on a road trip—he later appreciated its impact when a co-worker left hurriedly upon hearing it because of strong memories of making love. Enigma's music became a part of our love-making playlist, and it played a crucial role in rekindling intimacy for a client who had become disengaged from life and family. By recommending Enigma, she and her husband were able to rejuvenate their connection, demonstrating how music can support emotional and relational resilience.

Personal stories of Barbara Wood and David Haman further illustrate the transformative power of Music Medicine. These accounts reveal how Music Medicine facilitates significant moments of healing and change, offering tangible benefits to those grappling with health crises or emotional distress. The stories exemplify the profound effects of the Music Medicine Protocol, showcasing its role in providing solace and empowering individuals in their most challenging moments. Through these experiences, the undeniable value of music applied like medicine in promoting healing and hope is ever more apparent, reinforcing its importance in the journey toward recovery.

Barbara Wood's experience with the Music Medicine Pill® offers compelling insight into this protocol's profound impact on emotional and physical states. As Chair of a nonprofit creative arts therapy agency, Barbara was no stranger to the concepts of healing through creativity. Yet, the immediate and tangible benefits of music applied like medicine became clear during a personal health crisis. When faced with sudden chest pains—a situation that naturally triggers concern and fear—Barbara opted for a Music Medicine Pill to be followed by conventional medical treatment as needed. Supported by a close friend who was also a music therapist, she embarked on a journey that offered her a unique form of relief and underscored the therapeutic potential of music.

Within less than 30 minutes of engaging with the Music Medicine Pill, Barbara experienced a significant reduction in her symptoms, finding relief from the pain and anxiety that had abruptly encroached upon her day. This rapid alleviation of her distress exemplifies how carefully chosen and therapeutically applied music can transcend its traditional role as entertainment or aesthetic enjoyment to become a potent tool for health and healing. Barbara's choice to rely on music as a healing agent in acute discomfort demonstrates her trust in music's healing powers, and she was rewarded with swift and effective relief without the aid of conventional medical intervention.

Exploring techniques and practices for using music to navigate life's hurdles can reveal powerful tools for emotion regulation and resilience. In my personal experience, specific music practices have been instrumental in overcoming challenges. For instance, I recall an incident where I received an upsetting response to a project just as I was arriving at a parking lot to attend an important meeting. This meeting would initiate programs requested by a new facility. I sat in the car, waiting for a colleague, and immediately turned to my U.S.E. playlists. Although I don't remember the exact song, I vividly recall screaming in rhythm to the music with untethered loudness, which helped me release all my unsettled emotions. I mindfully monitored my satiation level and then shifted to quiet music from the "S" category to soothe myself and transition from the intense experience. By the time my colleague arrived, I was composed and ready to focus on the meeting, free from the feelings of rejection I had experienced just minutes earlier.

Selecting music that aligns with my emotional needs during tough times involves a mindful approach. Music is very effective at initiating conditioned responses, so having a library of preferred music immediately accessible on my mobile device is optimal for addressing any situation anywhere. I practice deciding whether a conditioned response from soothing music will work better than music from the U or E categories. This decision depends on the depth of my feelings, my target mood, and the time available. Sometimes, it's trial and error; I may not know what I'm feeling, so I'll start with several pieces and notice if they resonate with my mood, whether it's anger, anxiety, depression, or sadness. Once I find the right piece, I listen to it until I feel the emotion release and subside, then follow it with soothing music (S) to ensure the emotion is fully released, like applying a calming, moist bandage after antiseptic. I then shift to E music as the calming bandage is removed to expose the wound to air.

David Haman's experience with Music Medicine illustrates the profound impact of prescriptive music on alleviating stress-related physical symptoms. After experiencing what felt like chest pains—a symptom often associated with high stress levels—David was introduced to a unique solution: the "Stress Brake" CD from the standardized Music4Life® series. Opting for this music-based intervention over traditional medical approaches, he embarked on a journey that tested the power of music and showcased his willingness to explore alternative healing methods.

To hear directly from David and learn more about his journey, scan the QR code here to watch.

David's method of integrating prescriptive listening with the CD while matching the beats with running—demonstrates an active engagement with the therapeutic process. This physical activity, combined with the carefully selected music, significantly reduced his stress and symptoms. The aggressive beat of the first song encouraged a physical response that mirrored the intensity of the music, facilitating a form of psychological and physical release (The Music4Life® USA, 2011).

His testimony, "I just pretty much calmed down... it really worked. It just really calmed me down. Without any drugs or ambulances or any other intervention just listening to music," emphasizes the effectiveness of this Mood Exercise Regimen® in providing immediate relief without the need for conventional medical intervention. David's experience is a powerful endorsement of the potential benefits of prescriptive music in managing stress-related symptoms, suggesting that non-traditional approaches may offer valuable alternatives or complements to standard medical treatments.

Music4Life strongly recommends pursuing medical treatment when dealing with life-threatening symptoms.

As the innovator of the Music4Life® Music Medicine Protocol, I have been immersed in Mood Sequence Formulas™ with thousands of cathartic experiences. When tough times confront me, I have developed a natural response to pivot with deep emotion and clarity about the situation. While I can experience raw states of anger, anxiety, depression, and sadness and feel them deeply, often, I don't need music because my emotional health makeup prevails with an auto-cleanse in place. This response has been conditioned for decades by intense Mood Sequence Formulas, developing a profound capability to take care of my emotional needs when confronted with chaos, rejection, business disruption, death, serious illness, life-changing surgery, addiction trials, and more.

Learning from Marital Experiences

After eleven intense years, I was tired of the control my parents exerted over me, particularly my father. My regular music schedule started before second grade with violin lessons twice weekly from my father, and my mother, Carol, a violist, pianist, and vocalist, coached my daily practice sessions. I remember being excited about going up to the big high school where my father started his first orchestra director position (after graduating from Eastman School of Music) in Los Alamos, New Mexico—a government town of 13,000, the birthplace of the atom bomb and me, with secure gates requiring our visitors to be escorted by us. Two years later, we moved to Anchorage, Alaska, where my father founded the string program with my help. Typical of the organ grinder's monkey, he would schedule PTA meeting appearances featuring me playing the violin so he could advocate starting a string program in the Anchorage School District. It worked. He became the district Music Coordinator, and I continued as the "monkey." He was very specific about how I needed to act in order to be acceptable. I readily complied because I loved the violin, learned quickly, we got along well, and I was able to perform frequently. Today, I am the only concertmaster of the Anchorage Youth Symphony he founded in 1965 to sit in the first chair from age 11 until I graduated high school. I led a traveling string quartet and learned the fine art of leading chamber ensembles. I played in the Anchorage Symphony, Opera, church solos, large events, and summers at Kings Lake Fine Arts Camp, which my father founded. My calendar was filled daily with practice, rehearsals, performances, and schoolwork, mostly under the watchful eye of my father ("Our History," n.d.).

When it came time for college, I knew that Europe was the family's destination for six months, so I planned accordingly. I was accepted into the American College in Paris and invited to audition at the Lucerne Music Conservatory. The year's first half was spent traveling with all seven family members. I graduated early from high school as the eldest of five kids (myself, Gary, Nancy, Jim, and Dan), with the youngest in first grade. My father had arranged for his six-month sabbatical to be located in Europe, where we traveled in a Commer Highwayman campervan my parents purchased when we arrived in England from Alaska (1972). We drove and camped in towns from England through Germany, Switzerland, Austria, and Yugoslavia to Greece, Italy, France to Spain, and then back to France and England. Jesus Christ Superstar was released in 1971, and my brother Gary and I listened continually to it, teaching our younger siblings the lyrics while traveling, creating a special, shared space in close quarters with seven people.

After being accepted to the Lucerne Music Conservatory in Switzerland, with plenty of desired opportunities and it looked like a tiny Alaska, I declined to attend the American College in Paris as I was not in sync with the large city nor the French lifestyle. I studied violin performance with Valdimir Skerlak, Wolfgang Schneiderhan, and Rudolph Baumgartner in Lucerne. I learned to breathe and play even more musically. My facility with French and German from junior and senior high school courses, as well as an intensive submersion that summer in a Zurich German language school served me well as my German fluency improved to participate in all-German music classes: theory, history, private violin and sight-reading lessons, master classes, chamber groups, and orchestra. I played in the Lucerne Symphony and opera and provided support for the Lucerne Music Festival, where I was assigned to support the Canadian Brass. As an astronomy buff, having led planetarium programs at Mears/Dimond Junior/Senior High School, I assisted the Zurich Planetarium as a volunteer and helped translate one program into English.

I spent eleven months in Europe. It was my first time away from family. And, as I was used to a much more progressive culture in Alaska (Swiss women gained voting rights in 1971), after I returned home for Christmas, my homesickness prevented me from wanting to return, crying uncontrollably so that my father canceled my return air ticket. It also meant giving up my assignment to join the Lucerne Strings in the Spring and figuring out how to get Maestro Skerlak's violin returned and my new Cremona Italy violin back home.

All these experiences took a toll on me, and freshly back in Alaska, with my parents wanting to control my life again, living in their house didn't work for me. I decided to separate myself and found an old friend who became my love, and we got married six months later. It was my exit from parental control and heavy schedules demanding constant vigilance of behavior and performance.

Music played a significant role in shaping our relationship during my first marriage to Bob at age 19. We shared a love for soothing music, which was intertwined with his strong interest in metaphysics and meditation, matching my interests. Metaphysical discussions and ethereal music were like a balm for my soul. However, the practicalities of life soon intruded. Bob quit his job one week before we married, and I had to start working immediately to support us. My first job was as a "floater" in the record department of the Anchorage JC Penney store, where I became aware of all kinds of music and even became a shopper's guide for music purchases. Management soon elevated me to the hardware department, where I was responsible for inventory management. Despite my efforts to motivate Bob to work, he wouldn't stay with a job for very long, often complaining of illness and relying on his parents for help. I eventually tired of having a husband who lacked the desire to thrive and have fun. We divorced after three years.

In my second marriage to Thom at age 27, I continued with the JC Penney management training program, evolving through the ranks and traveling frequently. My last position was as Senior Merchandise Manager, in charge of $4 million of inventory, and I won the store's Manager of the Year award. I met Thom as my neighbor when I purchased my condo at the intersection of Prosperity and Success. Even though he was Catholic, I respected his family's faith, and we avoided talking about religion. He was fun-loving, loved to travel, and listened to all kinds of music. After two years of being together, I quit JCPenney because I was close to a nervous breakdown, departing just before Christmas so that I could be with family in Denver, Colorado. Music performance had not been a major force in my life, so I traveled from coast to coast in the lower 48 states for a month to experience life differently as I figured out what was next. My brothers "kidnapped" me to Boston, and I returned to the West Coast on a Greyhound bus, formulating my next career. Then, Thom wanted to support my decision to start a talent agency called Pinkerton Performances. I quickly learned that I needed to engage musicians playing all styles of music, not just classical music, or the agency would not survive. I totally immersed myself—this time my choice—into the music scene, initially focused on booking my Friends Trio (variations of vocal, violin, flute, cello, piano). The agency quickly grew into managing a couple hundred different musician groups and entertainers, concert series, and clientele numbering around 500. Simultaneously, I co-founded the Alaska Conservatory of Music with my father and located it at a private university for grades 7-12.

Running Pinkerton Performances and the Alaska Conservatory of Music required a delicate balance between professional obligations and personal life. Thom's support was crucial during this period, and his love for diverse music genres added a new dimension to our relationship. His encouragement helped me expand my musical horizons and professional network, bringing a variety of talents under the agency's umbrella. This venture allowed me to leverage my musical background and helped me build a community of musicians and music enthusiasts who shared a passion for performance and education. However, a significant problem arose: Thom didn't want to work as much as I did. He was having too much fun enjoying the traveling lifestyle, making quick money, renting his condo to others, staying with me, and having me alongside when mutually convenient. After two years of living together, he knew he needed to propose, or we were done. I'll never forget his proposal: "Well, I guess let's do it." I had no clue if it meant we were getting married or splitting up. The music in our shared life was mainly my business. Although he was the life of the party, loved music, and did well-earning commissions in car sales to be able to travel, we were not grounded in a shared faith, and he was not interested in deepening our relationship. Instead of traveling together to Australia as originally planned, we separated our travels and later divorced. Reflecting on this period, I recognize music's critical role in both the highs and lows of my marital experiences. Music was a source of connection, growth, and fulfillment, but it also highlighted the complexities of balancing personal and professional ambitions. Each marriage brought unique lessons and insights, shaping my understanding of relationships and music's profound impact on my life journey.

In my third marriage to Peter at age 32, we met at a private ARCO Alaska event that booked me as a strolling violinist. He was captivated by my violin playing and asked me out. He was charismatic, had a great job as Vice Chancellor of Human Resources at UAA, and I soon discovered I was pregnant. Surprising both of us, I had to cancel plans that were in place to move to Australia and start a talent agency in Sydney with a dear friend who was well-respected in the industry and whom I met during my travels in the Land of OZ. Peter loved my business and fully supported it. I gradually discovered he was severely challenged with alcoholism. He would not be kind when drinking and sometimes disappear for a couple of days without communication. Not knowing anything about recovery, I was determined to fix him. When I played the violin in the evening, we would notice that he slept better and sometimes did not need his high blood pressure medication. When he was admitted to the hospital for emergency back surgery, out of my love for him, I recorded my solo violin music into a mono microphone connected to a tape recorder. I brought the Walkman cassette tape player and headphones to the hospital for him after surgery. It was noon in his hospital room at Providence Hospital in Anchorage, Alaska (1986). The nurse read his vital signs at 12:15 and returned at 12:30 to administer the high blood pressure medication. After reading his vital signs, she whipped around to me and asked, "What's he listening to?" I replied sheepishly, "Me?" as I was embarrassed about the bad quality of the recording. She emphasized, "What do you mean 'me'?" I responded meekly, "I play the violin." She immediately apprised me of the situation: "I'm supposed to give him medication right now and he doesn't need it!" Mystified, I queried, "Isn't that good?" And she requested, "Can I have a copy of that tape?" I shuddered weakly, claiming I needed to go into a recording studio first. She walked to his hospital documents and scratched out medication, writing instead that music had been used to bring his high blood pressure into a normal range.

I was stunned. How did that happen? My entrepreneurial spirit was motivated to tell the world about this! My passion was ignited to learn more. I created what I coined "SeminarConcerts" and started playing the violin connected to chakras. I researched what healing music was all about, not knowing anything about music therapy. Then we discovered Peter lost his university job as part of the statewide university system restructuring from the economic effects of the 1986 severe recession. Subsequently, his accepted job in Santa Clara, CA, fell through. Immediately, the Las Vegas position at UNLV opened up, and he moved to Las Vegas with our baby and me following by the end of the year (1988). I thought that moving to Las Vegas, Nevada, would be a better change of scenery for Peter's alcoholism. I was hoping to keep our family together for our two-year-old daughter, Meghan.

Las Vegas' party environment appealed to Peter much more than Anchorage had offered. I soon realized that three years of living with an alcoholic was taking a toll on my emotional health. His verbal and emotional abuse was more than I could handle, and I didn't want Meghan growing up thinking this was normal and attracting that kind of relationship. I could no longer hide what was happening from friends and family. When I left the first time and communicated we were leaving him, I didn't take anything with us, and he changed the locks on the house. I had no recourse but to return. It got worse. I went to Al-Anon for help, seeking to understand. I privately hired an attorney who directed me step by step to plan our exit.

I hid what had been happening over the years so well that even my mother called me in the morning. We were planning to secretly move out with half the detailed household inventory, wondering if I was making the right decision. We went into hiding for months, staying with friends. I found an apartment for my daughter and me and continued steady work as a violinist, took temp jobs, and made it work. I'm grateful to Peter, now deceased, for being the catalyst for relocating to Las Vegas. Otherwise, I would never have left Alaska.

As I began to rebuild my life in Las Vegas, an "intuitive" informed me how I would meet my soulmate (1990, August). It happened to the letter that she stated: We would see each other in September but not recognize each other until January. I was playing the violin in September at church. Dennis saw me there but thought I was a "stuck-up violinist" and did not approach me. Three months later, I decided to lighten my hair color and exclusively use my birth name, Judith, not Judy. The next month in January, Dennis and I were at the same church, in a new location, participating in a "Jump-a-thon" fundraiser, counting how many jumps our kiddos made on our individual mini-trampolines to convert into dollars pledged. At the potluck luncheon thereafter, he was discussing music publishing with the church board president, and I interrupted them, wanting to know more, and sat down uninvited. Our children began playing together, ages 3, 4 and 7. Dennis came to my office the next day to continue talking. We had both signed up for a church retreat the next holiday weekend, and people started noticing sparks flying. As a result of the retreat's call-to-action, I committed to Sunday evening Peace Concerts to support the cease-fire of Operation Desert Storm. And Dennis brought a large TV with VHS tape capability to show a calming video, and I played the violin. Every morning at 7 am, I was out in the desert on a hill I hiked up to with my 4-year-old daughter carrying earth in her hands—an inflatable ball. I discovered army tanks at the foot of my hill overlooking Las Vegas, requesting people across the USA to join me in meditation for the cease-fire. On Feb 25th, I announced it was our last Peace Concert, and on Feb 28th, President Bush declared a cease-fire. Dennis had proposed marriage on Valentine's Day, and we were married at Mt. Charleston Mahogany Grove on July 20, 1991, with two dear friends singing and playing guitar "I Will Always Love You."

Creative Life-Line

THE NEWSLETTER BY & FOR CREATIVE LIFE COMMUNITY CHURCH

FEBRUARY 1991   VOLUME VII, NUMBER 2

Concert in the Key of Peace™

Sundays at 7:00pm beginning Jan. 27th

Each concert features Judith Pinkerton and friends embracing inner peace and personal wellness through MEE™ performances. Judith creates these special performances of Music Exercising Emotions™ based upon research which shows how music can effect positive physical, emotional and behavioral changes. Performance of these live music sequences demonstrates how music may be used to move through undesirable emotional states.

Judith says, "I believe in the power of music!" The effectiveness of Judith's solo violin music is documented from an unexpected hospital experience years ago. An audio-cassette of her violin performance provided music, post-surgery, which was able to replace her husband's high blood pressure medication.

Every morning at sunrise, 7 am PST, Judith is playing her violin on a hill surrounded by mountains with the Nevada National Guard Armory, its tanks and artillery, beneath her feet. Hundreds of people nationwide join her in prayer and meditation to send peace and love globally. Donations will be accepted to benefit the Center for Creative Therapeutic Arts.

Each phase of my marital journey is marked by distinct musical genres and pieces that reflect the emotional landscape of that period. With Bob, metaphysical and soothing music provided a spiritual connection central to our relationship. This music's calming and introspective nature helped us navigate the challenges we faced together. During my time with Thom, the diverse range of music we enjoyed brought joy and variety to our lives, reflecting our relationship's dynamic and adventurous nature, even as it became clear that our paths were diverging. With Peter, classical violin music played a significant role in managing certain health issues and providing comfort during difficult times. The therapeutic use of my violin music during his hospital stay and our evening rituals highlighted the power of classical music to soothe and heal. Finally, my relationship with Dennis is characterized by the music we shared during our weekly peace concerts and morning violin meditations in the desert. The combination of peaceful, meditative music and the active pursuit of calm during turbulent times created a strong foundation for our relationship.

One of the key lessons I learned is the importance of communication. Music often facilitated conversations that were difficult to start otherwise. Music created a space to connect deeper, fostering conversations and mutual understanding. Resilience was another critical lesson. The therapeutic power of music became evident when playing the violin helped Peter sleep better and manage his high blood pressure. This experience taught me the healing potential of music and motivated me to explore its therapeutic applications further. Music became a tool for resilience, helping me cope with the emotional turmoil and ultimately guiding me toward personal healing and growth.

The significance of personal autonomy and self-discovery also emerged as a central theme. My journey through these marriages highlighted the need for personal space and the pursuit of individual passions. Establishing Pinkerton Performances and co-founding the Alaska Conservatory of Music allowed me to immerse myself in the music scene and build a fulfilling career. This pursuit of personal ambitions, even in the face of marital challenges, reinforced the importance of maintaining one's identity and passions. Another essential lesson is the power of adaptability. Moving to Las Vegas and rebuilding my life after Peter's alcoholism and our subsequent separation required adaptability and openness to change. Music was crucial in this transition, helping me find strength and solace in a new environment. Meeting Dennis and sharing our love for music and peace concerts during Operation Desert Storm's cease-fire efforts further emphasized the importance of adaptability and finding common ground in new relationships.

Overall, these experiences have contributed to my personal growth and resilience. Music has been a source of connection, healing, and understanding through the highs and lows of my marital journeys. It has taught me the importance of communication, resilience, personal autonomy, and adaptability. These lessons have shaped my understanding of love and life, reinforcing the value of emotional connection and the transformative power of music.

Compassion and Addiction

I often visited my adult daughter Meghan in the detention center during her 30+ day stay. The visits were conducted remotely, with me watching her on a monitor connected to a telephone. In those moments, I secretly held one earbud to the sending part of the telephone receiver for her to hear and the other earbud to the receiving part so I could listen as I played portions of various songs. Applying music like medicine in a mood sequence, I knew it would resonate deeply with both of us. We both cried and shared profound messages of unconditional love. This was the mood sequence of songs: "Lose Yourself" by Eminem, "Human" by Christina Perri, "Hidden Song" by Staind, "Love's Lullaby" by Kathy Zavada, "I am Remembering" by Melissa Phillippe, "Kingdom in the Clouds" by Chris Spheeris, "Headed in the Right Direction" by India Arie, "Reach" by Gloria Estefan, and "Eye of the Tiger" by Survivor. This playlist became our emotional lifeline, offering solace and understanding.

Having two children struggle with addiction has profoundly impacted my perspective. One of my children successfully overcame it without the need for rehabilitation, while the other continues to grapple with the challenge, now desiring recovery support but still trapped in fear. For years, I kept our family struggles hidden, embarrassed that, as a successful clinician, I couldn't help my struggling daughter in the ways she needed. Understanding the conditions and situations that led to her disappearance and realizing many years later that it was worse than I was told deepened my compassion and concern for her and others facing similar battles. My personal family experiences have driven me to be more compassionately engaged with every client who walks through my music therapy door. Without these experiences, I wouldn't have developed the same depth of empathy and commitment to helping others through the healing power of music.

I challenged my capacity to handle the stress of working with 150 clients weekly. Over the course of seven intense years, I documented more than 35,000 experiences with over 11,000 clients in residential addiction treatment centers. Teaching and constant experiential sessions with the Music Medicine Protocol supported their well-being. It bolstered my resilience and capability to deal with an unprecedented caseload of music therapy clients. The constant use of Mood Sequence Formulas™ played a significant role in this process. Every face became instantly familiar as I sought to see the Divine within each person, drawing it out so they could feel, touch, recognize, desire, and embody it. I broke down emotional barriers to help them build a more sustainable, positive mindset. I heard thousands of stories, each one deepening my understanding of my daughter's struggle. Every person counted. I remembered, honored, and respected each one, unrelenting in their discovery of who they really were. Clients often called me a mind reader. They waited in line for my arrival, craving certain sessions and requesting them specifically. I was always honest, transparent, and real with every person, respecting ethical boundaries. I didn't hesitate to change up a session when situations, clients, or interactions demanded it, and I had a treasure trove of options beyond Plan A, B, or C. I began to trust that God would deliver the words I needed to say that would be best heard, often finding the courage to open my mouth without deliberating on the best delivery of words. Each time I connected deeply with a client, my confidence grew. There were only a few instances I recall missing the mark. Still, I learned from these moments by commiserating with other therapists and understanding what I could have done differently, especially when unraveling the severity of mental illness became more apparent.

One success story from my music therapy practice stands out, particularly in the context of addiction recovery. A client who had experienced a personalized prescriptive playlist reconnected with me recently to share the importance of this playlist in her recovery nine years ago. She explained how it neutralized emotional triggers of trauma, helped her cease medication and alcohol dependency, and taught her life skills she continues to use today. She shared, "I lost my son to suicide and years later lost my husband to lung cancer. My grief was so overwhelming I finally turned to alcohol to numb my feelings because I couldn't eat a lot after surgery. Thirteen years after my son's death, I admitted myself into rehab and found Judith and music therapy through my therapist. I agreed to try the personalized approach with her support, creating a prescriptive playlist to address anxiety, grief, depression, loneliness, stress, and difficulty relaxing. After ten days of listening, I was elated at my turnaround. Sadness and depression were no longer trapped inside. I felt lighter, unburdened, and open to new opportunities. I even started vocal lessons. Three songs of the eleven on my music therapy CD continue to remind me of feeling deeply: 'It's So Hard to Say Goodbye to Yesterday' by Boyz II Men, 'Say Amen' by Howard Hewett, and 'I Believe' by Sounds of Blackness. I've been sober for more than nine years and stopped antidepressant, anti-anxiety, and alcohol-craving medications nine years ago. I continued my career in school administration, attained my Ed.D., and really enjoy my grandsons. My faith is strong, and I intuitively listen to music a certain way to stay in a certain posture."

Many times, the phrase "music is my therapist" will be chanted among people with a substance use disorder (SUD) who identify with artists and songs that resemble their own journeys. They embrace and share this music with peers, finding validation in the moods and messages conveyed. This validation is crucial, as people struggling with an alcohol/drug problem often do not feel validated and may isolate themselves from loved ones, seeking understanding from peers instead. Music helps foster a compassionate approach towards oneself and others struggling with addiction by helping individuals identify life themes that support greater self-understanding and improved self-compassion.

Determining whether the music and artists represent past, present, or future life themes is important. Understanding the how, what, why, when, and where of one's connection to music can begin to decode the way it resonates with life experiences. For instance, understanding how you found the music, what was happening when you heard it, why it is attractive (whether due to the lyrics, the beat, or something else), when it first mattered, and where it was heard can inform potential entrapment in a negative experience and guide the next steps for recovery. Identifying whether a theme is important to the past, present, or future involves decoding the lyrics and responses to music elements, as these describe life aspects in mental, emotional, behavioral, and physiological expressions.

A music therapist is trained with optimal skill in this analysis, applying the best evidence-based practice of receptive and active music-making interventions, culling from all music genres to achieve identified therapeutic goals. Music therapists understand how to break down emotional barriers and build sustainable positive mindsets, often drawing from a treasure trove of techniques and personal experiences to connect deeply with each client. By fostering these connections, music therapy validates the individual's journey and provides a structured path toward healing and recovery.

Overcoming Loss and Finding Purpose

My daughter Meghan did not want to be born, and hindsight reveals what a difficult life she may have known was in store for her. Thirty-three hours after labor was induced and my water broke, two weeks past her due date, she began her journey into the world after a C-section, putting me through the paces immediately. I remember the exhaustion and grief right from the start, especially when she cried for the promised sugar water during her repeated attempts at breastfeeding. Despite being deeply immersed in music as my profession, I don't remember it helping us much in those early days. I now realize I had unrealistic expectations of her resilience, ego strength, and interests.

Three years later, I decided we needed to separate from an abusive home environment. She held this against me, not understanding why, even plugging her ears with tiny balls that had to be removed by my friend Bob, a physician assistant. We moved to St. George, Utah, hoping for a better environment for our blended family. After building a house there, we realized it wasn't a good location, as I frequently traveled to Las Vegas for shows. During this time, Meghan struggled with recurring UTIs, which exacerbated her issues with peers, making her more withdrawn. She was also without a mother up to fifty percent of the time, causing constant grief for me as I was separated from my husband, infant son, daughter, and two stepsons.

When Meghan started fifth grade, we relocated back to Las Vegas because my show work was unrelenting. However, upon re-entering Las Vegas, my show work was suddenly canceled based upon rumors I discovered were circulated by peer violinists who wanted my jobs. So, I immediately networked, advocated, and landed a job providing music therapy at a girls' group home run by Catholic Charities of Southern Nevada. I was consumed with making a difference for these teenage girls who were abandoned, neglected, or abused. I remember bringing Meghan to the home a few times, and in retrospect, I wonder if she thought she needed to be like them for me to love her more—a sad thought indeed.

In mid-eighth grade, Meghan returned from church camp very angry and unable to share why. She withdrew more from me. Though she had been playing the violin for a couple of years, she changed her last name to her bio-dad to avoid being compared to me, a known professional show violinist. She auditioned and was accepted into the performing arts high school, where my girlfriend Carol, a violinist, was her orchestra director.

I started noticing a jar of pain pills was less full and faulted myself, refusing to think one of my kids was taking them. Then, just before Christmas in ninth grade, I received an urgent call from her school. She had ingested Soma for a reported headache given by another student. As I rushed to her school, I discovered her pulse was so faint it was unreadable. I authorized immediate ambulance transport. She survived the hospital experience, and we enrolled her in an outpatient program while she was assigned to an alternative school for a semester. Concurrently, her older brother was involved with men dealing in counterfeit checks and drugs, which we later found out were shared with her. She saw a therapist who warned me she had been caught stealing and advised me to quit everything to spend more time with her. I tried to allocate more time, realizing it took hours for her to open up and start talking about what mattered. No matter how much time I spent, it never seemed enough. Nothing I said made a difference; everything I said made her angrier. I was at a loss. I sought family therapy. Meghan turned more to her boyfriend's mother and less to me. I was devastated. She became pregnant at 17 and quickly married her boyfriend, who enlisted in the army.

Music therapy for others also supported me, as I'm not immune to music activating my central nervous system. This professional involvement with music helped me navigate my grief, though it was a constant struggle. Being faced with the constant fear since 2014 that I might hear my daughter died from an overdose is a heavy burden to carry. There was one dramatic music therapy event that left me hysterical that night. This incident occurred during a session I referred to in Chapter 4 with Rocko's story. The intensity of the session brought all my fears and grief to the surface, leaving me emotionally overwhelmed. That night, I turned to my own prescriptive playlist, created spontaneously from specialized mood playlists, to find solace and regain my composure.

Music therapy has been an essential part of my healing process from such a significant loss. Engaging with music allowed me to process my grief, find understanding, and begin healing. Each session was a step towards confronting and releasing the accumulated emotional pain over the years. One particular session stands out in my memory. I was working with a group of teenage girls who had experienced significant trauma. I felt a deep connection to their pain and resilience as we created music and listened to music together. The shared experience of music created a space where I could privately channel my own grief and begin to understand it in a new light (Peterson, 2000).

This transformative moment reminded me of the power of music to reach the deepest parts of our souls, to express what words cannot, and to foster a sense of connection and understanding. By helping these girls navigate their emotions through music, I was also navigating my own. The process of creating and engaging with music became a therapeutic practice that not only supported my clients but also facilitated my own healing journey. The prescriptive playlist I used that night and many nights thereafter became a lifeline, guiding me through waves of grief and helping me find moments of peace and clarity amidst the turmoil.

These experiences ultimately led me to find a renewed sense of purpose and direction in life. Music was central to this transformation, providing strength and guidance as I navigated life after loss. I am constantly looking for new music to add to my specialized mood playlists to satisfy my desire for strength and resilience. My life now revolves around my four-year-old daughter Kaylan, my adopted (grand)daughter, who brings immense joy and a sense of a do-over opportunity. I fully embrace her life with us, and my travel is minimized in this virtual world of connection, allowing me to maintain a productive home office that connects me with the world instantly. Our rec room, filled with music instruments, an art studio, a library, and all her babies and educational resources, has become a sanctuary of creativity and learning. I need help organizing her constant production of art daily! Life is very full now, and my grief is actually minimized, knowing Meghan continues in a lifestyle of her own choosing, having birthed two sons after Kaylan, who have been adopted by another family member. Music continues to be a source of strength and guidance, helping me navigate life's complexities with resilience and hope.

7

ACHIEVING GOALS AGAINST ALL ODDS

When facing challenging circumstances, perseverance, resilience, and adaptability are your most powerful allies. By setting clear, achievable goals and being resourceful, you can overcome obstacles, maintain focus, and continue moving forward. Dedication, thorough preparation, and staying calm under pressure are key to success.

I vividly recall navigating the vast Alaskan wilderness in a small aircraft, where every decision could mean the difference between safety and disaster. One particular memory stands out: learning to land a plane on a narrow riverbed. The meticulous preparation and unwavering calm required for such a task were crucial. Another time, I was a passenger flying treacherous mountain passes, where staying focused and unruffled was the only way to ensure my safe journey. These experiences taught me that remaining composed and flexible can lead to success even in the most high-pressure situations.

These personal stories serve as a reminder that no matter what your aspirations may be, applying these principles can guide you through any adversity. You can achieve your goals with determination, careful planning, and the ability to adjust to unexpected challenges.

My dad's passion for flying was inspired by his father, who flew and taught flying during WWII. After our family moved to Alaska, my dad quickly earned his private pilot license. Over the years, he flew various bush planes, including a Champ, Super Cub, Kitfox (which he built), and his favorite, a Cessna 172 he called the "Bluebird of Happiness." He even flew in the Iditarod Air Force and piloted a Cessna 206 and Beaver for Ketchum Air Service.

As the eldest child, I often accompanied my dad on flights around Alaska, including bear and moose hunting trips, as our family exclusively ate the game we hunted. We had several memorable experiences, such as when we ran out of fuel while flying and had to land in the duck flats across the inlet from Anchorage. We patiently waited there until a kind person brought us more fuel.

I'm told I inherited my dad's charisma and ability to work under pressure, multitask, and constantly challenge myself. By age 25, I grew tired of always being the passenger and decided to get my pilot's license. I reconnected with my family after my divorce at age 23. Prior to that, I had been on a break from my family and intense music commitments, working instead as a retail manager for JC Penney.

In my typical out-of-the-box thinking, I set a firm goal of acquiring my pilot's license, no matter what. I broke down the steps needed to achieve this and figured out when, where, and how to start. First, I sought a partner for motivation, stability, and camaraderie. The pieces quickly fell into place. I convinced my fellow JC Penney manager, Randy, to join me in enrolling in the Anchorage Community College's ground school semester to pass the required written exam.

During that semester, I also persuaded Randy to buy a Cessna 150 airplane with me from my friend James, who flew it into Anchorage from Central Alaska. My dad inspected the plane for flight worthiness and provided recommendations for necessary fixes, which James completed. We then purchased the plane and tied it down at Merrill Field, the world's largest and busiest small airplane airport. This airport shares complicated airspace with the most extensive seaplane base at Lake Hood/Lake Spenard, a nearby dirt airstrip, the International Airport, Elmendorf Air Force Base, and Ft Richardson Army Base, all operating within identified air corridors.

After completing ground school, passing the required medical examination and FAA written exam to receive my student pilot certificate, Randy and I hired an independent flight instructor and insured our plane. Little did we know we would be his first students to get a license. I quickly soloed to accumulate the necessary flight hours, balancing solo flights with instructional sessions to study navigation, cross-country flying, night flying, emergency procedures, and maneuvers. Due to the lack of legal night flying during the summer months, I had to delay completing the required hours until late summer, finishing all requirements in September 1980. Although the average time required was 60 to 80 hours, I completed everything in 47 hours, surpassing the required 40 hours with an individual instructor.

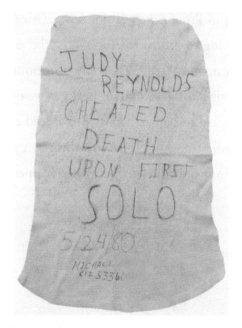

I completed the final check ride with my scheduled FAA-approved examiner on my last day as a student pilot. This included an oral examination of aircraft systems, rules, and regulations and a final flight demonstration. During the flight, my eyes widened in disbelief when the examiner demanded I fly at the ceiling of my air corridor to cross Cook Inlet. We observed a fast-approaching Air Force jet near the bottom of the AF air corridor, with only a few hundred feet separating us. I was sure he was testing my ability to handle wake turbulence, which, fortunately, did not severely compromise my C-150's air stability.

Flying in Alaska is different, presenting numerous challenges that require both skill and courage to overcome. One particularly challenging moment stands out vividly in my memory. On a beautiful clear day, my dad, mom, and I flew to Lake Clark Pass in my dad's Cessna 172, meeting a friend midair who joined us from Wasilla. Both planes stopped at Port Alsworth before continuing to Proenneke's cabin, now part of the National Park Service. Not wanting to return to Anchorage the same way, we decided to continue through Merrill Pass, a site notorious for many crashed bush planes. Clouds hid the mountain peaks as we flew down the entry canyon, which seemed to be narrowing into a dead end, with many left and right-side canyons revealing glaciers. As this was my first flight into this area, I soon became anxious about what would happen.

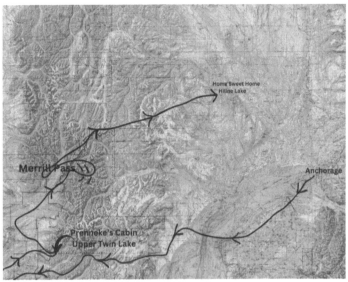

Merrill Pass Trip

Prenneke's Cabin on Upper Twin Lake

My parents (Frank & Carol Pinkerton) and I at Hiline Lake

I noticed my mom sitting calmly in the back. I asked my dad, "When do we decide to turn around?" He responded, equally calm, "About now," as we approached what looked like a dead end. Unbeknownst to me, he was silently calculating the cloud ceiling to ensure it was high enough to make an abrupt left turn at the end. He entered the pass at the right altitude, 500 feet higher than the current ground level, staying just under the clouds and successfully clearing the ground.

As we quickly flew through Merrill Pass, I saw wrecked bush planes scattered everywhere, with little space between the slopes and our plane's wings due to the low cloud cover. I repeatedly exclaimed, "Oh my God, oh my God, oh my God," with wide eyes as I saw one plane carcass after another. I noticed the hole in the cloud we were aiming for slowly closing. We shot through the hole into pure, cloudless sunlight, with a mountain directly in front of us and two canyon passes below forming a "V." Hugging that mountain, Dad quickly turned left, preparing for immediate up and down drafts from the 500-foot drop-off.

We then did a U-turn high over the clouds, with beautifully rugged, snow-capped mountain peaks sticking through. We returned to the spot far below the clouds at Two Lake, where we had left our friend with his bush plane. We informed him to turn around and go through Lake Clark Pass, where we originally came in. Then we flew straight to my parent's home on Highline Lake, where they lived for 20 years, 70 miles from Anchorage and 40 miles from the nearest road. My dad had fulfilled my request: to go on a trip to forget the recent stress of working in Las Vegas.

My pilot training experience taught me that there's always a next time and that using different perspectives is essential for success. We practiced multiple touch-and-go landings and takeoffs, experimenting with various approaches: high/long, low/long, high/short, and low/short, on dirt, grass, water, and pavement.

I remember flying my dad's Super Cub—a two-seater with a front/back arrangement, unlike my side-by-side Cessna-150. I was the pilot, and he sat in the back seat as we practiced touch-and-go landings on riverbed sandbars in the Matanuska Valley. He instructed me to land with a low/short approach at "that bush," but I landed at a different bush. We had each picked different bushes, which we realized only afterward, and shared a quick laugh instead of me getting into trouble.

Reprinted with permission photo 238942849 | Matanuska Valley River by Andreas Edelmann | Dreamstime.com

One memorable lesson in resourcefulness occurred on one of my teenage birthdays when I received a cut-off broomstick as a gift. My dad installed it in the back seat of the Super Cub so I could fly from there. Flying from the back seat requires instinctive flying because you can't see the instruments. Dad taught me to rely on my gut instincts (which I interpret as guidance from God) to make critical life-or-death decisions while flying.

This pilot training experience culminated in countless personal flights in the Alaskan bush, with or without my dad, for over 45 years. He mentored me on how to react and bounce back quickly, no matter the situation. I learned to become more focused when times were tough, always look for "what's next," and remain flexible and open to all possible solutions when committed to a goal. Being well-prepared by researching precisely what is required to accomplish the goal is crucial. Finding a safe outlet to release stress and quickly get back on track is vital when stress overwhelms. Decades of violin performance with regular disciplined practice also helped me release anxiety and regain focus.

Overcoming Near-Death Experience

During one particular flight to Birchwood, where we would practice touch-and-go's away from the busyness of Merrill Field, we were returning to Anchorage when my instructor decided to put me through an emergency landing practice. As we approached a road under construction, he directed me to target it, aligning for a typical flight pattern. Suddenly, he changed the plan abruptly with, "land here, not over there," ordering me to land at the beginning of the road rather than the opposite end. He then turned off the mags, not just throttling back, and directed me to apply flaps and slip in.

His mistake was turning off the mags instead of just pulling the throttle back, forgetting we had to hand-prop the airplane to get it started. The prop died midair, and multiple attempts to restart with the key failed. We quickly descended from 900 feet towards the construction road, littered with big rocks and large vehicles. My instructor immediately took over, raised the flaps, and dove the plane straight down. Rather than hit the ground, he pulled back quickly on the yoke to raise the airplane nose, then sped down the road just above the rocks. Ahead was a forest, and I saw my life replay in my head, certain this was the end. Just before careening into the trees, my instructor made a quick right turn under power lines and landed on an unforeseen uphill grade.

Relief washed over me, and I was thankful I had used the bathroom before the flight. My instructor ordered me out of the plane to switch places so he could become the pilot. Cars suddenly appeared, expecting a crash site, with people asking if they could help. My instructor assured them we were okay. We quickly turned the airplane around. He hand-propped the plane with me at the controls, then got in as the pilot. He narrowly missed the power lines as he accomplished a short downhill takeoff, another miracle in an airplane not known for high-performance feats. Upon our late return to the airport and hopping into partner Randy's truck, I stated we needed to fix the prop before flying again. Instead of taking his turn at flight instruction, we met at my condo for an after-party to de-stress.

Instantly angered by my instructor's carefree attitude, as if nothing extraordinary had occurred, I left them to break down crying at my girlfriend Bonnie's nearby condo, a fellow JC Penney manager. The following day, I recounted the entire episode to my dad over breakfast at a restaurant. He was ready to confront the instructor, but I intervened, saying, "I want to give him another chance. I'm almost done with him and just want to get licensed. If I report him, he could have his instructor license revoked." The instructor had experienced an emergency landing as a student pilot that resulted in a crash, motivating him to ensure his students had different experiences with plenty of opportunities to learn emergency landing practices. I returned to him with compassion and increased awareness of potential problems. I also hired another flight instructor from a Merrill

Field flight school to support my first nighttime cross-country flight from Anchorage to Homer.

Another harrowing experience occurred with my dad on a moose hunting trip in the remote Alaskan wilderness when I was a teenager. It was a crisp, clear morning, and we had flown deep into the wilderness, far from any signs of civilization. We spotted a moose and landed the Super Cub on nearby rough ground, preparing for what we thought would be a routine hunt. As my dad began to gut the moose, his knife slipped, creating a deep, bleeding wound on his knee. Panic surged as I realized we were miles from help, with only our wits to rely on.

With my heart pounding, I listened to my dad's calm but urgent instructions. I had to gut the moose myself, the stench of gut and blood mixing with the cold air and the ever-present fear of attracting predators. Every snap of a twig or rustle in the brush heightened my anxiety, knowing that fresh kills always invite other animals to the scene. The adrenaline coursed through me, pushing me to work quickly and efficiently, balancing the need to be fast with the need to be thorough.

These experiences, filled with suspense and danger, taught me the importance of quick thinking, resourcefulness, and staying calm under pressure. They also underscored the value of preparation and the necessity of having a safe outlet for stress, which, for me, came through music acting as a healing agent. Music's discipline and emotional release helped me manage—afterward—the intense pressure and anxiety of these high-risk situations. These lessons taught me to navigate life's challenges with resilience and determination.

Adapting to Unusual Circumstances

Life as a show violinist in Las Vegas demands adaptability and resilience, which have defined my career. From my nerve-wracking debut with Frank Sinatra Sr. to my years of performing with Wayne Newton, my journey has exemplified the necessity of flexibility in the face of ever-changing challenges.

My first show performance was with Frank Sinatra Sr., where I had to prove myself by making no mistakes, sight-reading music with conflicting markings, and playing with a microphone on my violin, all without rehearsal. This experience set the tone for my career, emphasizing the importance of adaptability.

In 1989, I began performing with Wayne Newton, embarking on a journey that would blend my musical and therapeutic talents. A memorable tour in Wayne's private jet took place in 2003, shortly after I had earned my music therapy certification. To manage documents for grants, staff, partnerships, and marketing for the nonprofit music therapy agency I founded in 1990, the Center for Creative Therapeutic Arts, I needed my best communication tool at the time: a fax machine. I remember my bandmates grunting as they lifted my suitcase from the jet's cargo, incredulous at its weight. They teased me about its contents until they discovered it was a fax machine for my music therapy projects. Although they continued to tease, they were more accepting of the weight once they understood its purpose.

Wayne and the band traveled by private jet, which felt like a special privilege. He traveled with his family and his core group of musician section leaders, picking up additional musicians during a two-week tour around the country, including Canada. As the lead violinist, I had the opportunity to work with other violinists from across the country. This experience gave me a new perspective on what my musician colleagues go through when they come to Las Vegas to perform a series of shows with their significant entertainers and collaborate with local talent like me.

During a nighttime flight on this tour, I looked down sadly on a town where my ex-husband was incarcerated for multiple DUIs, recalling three years of emotional abuse before I left the marriage to protect my sanity. This personal reflection was a stark reminder of the resilience required not just in my professional life but also in my personal life.

Traveling with the band forged deep friendships through friendly camaraderie. Mike "Bear" Forch, Wayne's bodyguard, who had a black belt in karate, even mentored my son, who struggled with teenage life in Las Vegas. We often faced the challenge of ensuring "the show must go on no matter what." Once, I was so sick before a show in New York that I had to leave the stage to throw up. Bear escorted me to the bathroom and immediately back on stage to continue performing. This instance reinforced the idea that professionalism and dedication are paramount, regardless of personal cost.

Working continuously in Las Vegas as a show violinist and gigging with various ensembles, from symphony orchestras and chamber symphonies to string quartets and solo violin performances for events or weddings, requires immense flexibility to ensure a perfect performance that satisfies those in control. I would often sight-read music and perform with friends or strangers, adapting spontaneously to match bow techniques, leading with strength or following with support depending on my position as lead or section violinist. Being polite, respectful, friendly, and dressed to please was essential, often in white and black formals, as Wayne Newton required white. Regular workouts at the gym were necessary since wearing clothes that showed skin was usually desired. My female colleagues and I constantly shared makeup tricks and tips on where to find formal dress sales.

However, the life of a musician isn't just about performances and appearances; it's also about resilience in the face of unexpected challenges. On October 2, 2017, the day after the mass shooting in Las Vegas, where a gunman opened fire on a crowd of concert goers at the Route 91 Harvest country music festival, killing 58 people and injuring hundreds more, I sensed something was wrong when I received an early morning text from my sister asking if I was okay. Later, I was called to play in the Catholic ensemble that evening at the Guardian Angel Cathedral on the Las Vegas

Strip after a long day of music therapy groups in addiction treatment facilities. A memorial mass was held with dignitaries, a dozen interfaith leaders, and a large gong center stage, which each religious leader struck to memorialize every person who died (excluding the shooter). I agreed at the last minute to play a solo violin rendition of "Amazing Grace" to open the memorial event.

These experiences have underscored the importance of adaptability and resilience in my personal and professional life. From the pressure-filled debut with Frank Sinatra Sr. to performing with dozens of major entertainers, including the enriching tour with Wayne Newton, and from handling personal trauma to providing comfort through music therapy, my journey has been one of constant learning and growth. Each challenge has reinforced the necessity of being prepared, flexible, and resourceful. The moments of camaraderie and professional dedication, coupled with the ability to adapt in the face of adversity, have shaped my career and approach to life. Embracing flexibility and resourcefulness has allowed me to create meaningful and personalized music-based interventions, ensuring that moments of spontaneity bring comfort and healing to those in need. Through these experiences, I have understood that true resilience is about staying committed and adapting to whatever life throws your way, reminding myself to move forward (sometimes after screaming internally) with grace and determination.

Achievement in the Face of Adversity

Achieving significant milestones requires overcoming substantial obstacles, and my journey in music therapy has been no exception. Through innovative fundraising events, strategic networking, and relentless advocacy, I navigated the complex landscape of legislative processes to secure recognition and funding for music therapy in Nevada. Along the way, I forged alliances, faced political challenges, and demonstrated the transformative power of music. This section delves into the pivotal moments and strategies that defined my path, illustrating how persistence and vision can turn ambitious goals into reality.

Circa 2005-06, I created the Attorneys vs. Doctors basketball game at UNLV's Thomas & Mack Arena as a fundraising event for music therapy services at my nonprofit, the Center for Creative Therapeutic Arts (which I founded in 1990 after relocating from Alaska in 1989). The event was attended by the sister of the Nevada Governor, who connected me to Governor Guinn. As a result of constant networking, Governor Guinn added a line item for music therapy in the state budget 2007 before leaving office.

At the time, I had no idea what state recognition meant when our music therapy profession's leadership decided to launch a national campaign for music therapist involvement. In January 2007, I decided to target receiving legislative appropriation for funding and began amassing significant support quickly. Having connected with the past Governor Guinn through his sister, who loved my nonprofit, I hoped the budget he created, which included music therapy, would be accepted by the incoming Governor Gibbons. I thought it would be easy to influence the new governor, but I needed to be corrected. I soon discovered that most people objected to everything Governor Gibbons did. He was challenging to work with, unavailable, and singularly focused on not supporting anything related to taxes. I quickly found an ally in Senator Dina Titus through my good friend Ted DeCorte. I received a video testimonial of support from Nevada Senator Harry Reid, who was responsible for appropriating $1M for music therapy research in the amendment to the Older Americans Act in 1991. With my CCTA Board of Trustees assisting in duplicating DVDs, we mailed this video invite to all legislators to attend the Nevada Governor's Mansion Music Therapy event in Carson City, NV, on February 21, 2007—one month and 433 miles away from my home—and scheduled an "ER - Experiential Room" on February 22, 2007, in the Nevada State Legislature building to build relationships with legislators (Dornan, 2007).

I employed several strategies to achieve my goal. I created a binder for legislators to write notes about their staff, best contact methods, requests for information, party affiliation, occupation, and interests. I solicited and coordinated support, confirmed attendance, and advised when, where, how, and with whom to network at the event and the ER room. National leaders from the American Music Therapy Association (AMTA) in Washington, DC, including Judy Simpson, Director of Government Relations, and Jane Creagan, Director of Professional Programs, attended. The music department chair, Jonathan Good, from UNLV, President of the Western Region Chapter of AMTA, Lillieth Grand, and REMO Health Rhythms Manager Alyssa Janney, who shipped drumming equipment to Carson City, were also present.

To further bolster our efforts and ensure comprehensive representation, I badgered Reno music therapist Manal Toppozada (who was MIA as she was due to give birth) to detail what music therapy equipment she needed for her nonprofit Note-Able Music Therapy Services and to schedule some of her clients to attend the ER Room. Music therapist Diane Bell attended with her Marvin Picollo students performing at the Governor's Mansion and submitted a desired equipment budget. My family (husband Dennis Burkhardt and son Michael) drove up from Las Vegas with equipment and materials; everyone advocated with flyers and pocket folders containing relevant materials. We scheduled spontaneous meetings over three days in Carson City with my team presenting to legislators, the Department of Education, and Nevada DHHS Director Mike Willden, who had previously labeled me "a pitbull" in my Las Vegas office in Building L on the West Charleston Campus of the College of Southern Nevada, where we had our second meeting.

With our collective efforts in full swing, I presented before the Senate Committee on Finance, requesting statewide music therapists to receive equipment funding. Senate Bill 558 was created, with the committee selecting Senator Barbara Cegavske to sponsor it. I continued to trust the process from February through May, staying in touch with legislators. I'll never forget the voicemail received at home from Senator Dina Titus' office on the final day of the legislative session, informing me that funding was approved in Nevada Senate Bill 579 - Chapter 354 Cultural (2007): "$109,590 to various recipients for the purchase of instruments, equipment, music, supplies, and software for music therapy services." Another large nonprofit, which had spent months preparing and submitting a large binder for funding programs for medically challenged children and testifying before the same committee, received no funding. I had a thin packet of mighty materials, networked strategically (I'll never forget one bathroom discussion with a senator), conversed spontaneously, and boldly demonstrated the power of music to support people from womb to tomb with only seven music therapists in Nevada (Dornan, 2007).

After receiving legislative funding for equipment in 2007, my next step was to enact state music therapy licensure. This had never been done before, and I love a challenge. I hold tightly to my vision and find ways to achieve it. I treat every "no" as an eventual "yes." It may be first-child-of-five syndrome, but I enjoy being first.

I thoroughly investigate all aspects to understand what is required and inquire about deciding the best sequencing and delegation, always prompting "tell me more" answers. I don't trust chance unless I know I've done everything possible and now must focus on God's will.

Reflecting on this monumental achievement, I realized the importance of understanding what brings joy and fulfillment. Identifying what makes you smile and what you enjoy most is essential. Even though I shifted from retail management to creating the first talent agency and music conservatory in Anchorage, Alaska, it still did not keep a big smile on my face (Piper, 1982). So, I decided to list what puts a smile on my face. After reviewing about 100 items, I categorized them into four major areas and meditated on them daily in the sauna adjacent to my bedroom. These four areas are performing, being with people, helping others, and traveling.

To fully embrace these areas and stay focused, I followed a simple approach, which I like to call the SMILE Process:

1. **Set a Goal:** Define clear, achievable objectives that provide direction and purpose.

2. **Map the Steps:** Break down the goal into manageable tasks and milestones.

3. **Invite Support:** Seek help and collaboration from others to build a strong support network.

4. **Leap into Action:** Take proactive steps and maintain momentum towards the goal.

5. **Evaluate and Adapt:** Regularly assess progress and be willing to adjust strategies as needed.

By using the SMILE Process, I have been able to focus on these four areas for decades, allowing my life to evolve and embrace more people, conditions, opportunities, and locations (McPherson, 1988). This approach has kept me motivated and resilient, helping me overcome challenges and continue moving forward with a smile on my face.

When pursuing your dreams, identify and focus on what truly brings you joy. By doing so, you can stay motivated and resilient, even in the face of challenges. Keep smiling, but not in a "grin and bear it" response, which could repress unsettledness and trap you in a Chronic Comfort Zone^{TM}. Use your prescriptive playlist to manage moods and stay committed to your passions, as they will guide you through any obstacles.

Reflecting on my journey, I want to share the importance of perseverance and vision in achieving your goals, regardless of odds. My family's mantra, "What's next?" constantly rings in my ears. Always plan several goals ahead of the current one and adjust your course of action based on the responses and feedback you receive. Never accept "no" as a final answer; view it as a temporary setback or a sign that another path needs to be explored and revisited later. Have the courage and fortitude to speak up and lead and support others in becoming leaders, embracing them to replace you eventually.

Having this big vision for Music4Life® is like trying to boil the ocean, so I need solid and influential voices to "change the culture of music creation and consumption." While I have often been too severe and focused on multitasking and considering all paths, leading with a great sense of humor is essential. Take the time to celebrate accomplishments with those who support you, honoring their part in the achievement. I regret that I rarely did this, focused instead on generating the next achievement - "What's next?"

Reflecting on this, I have learned that achieving ambitious goals requires more than a clear vision and hard work. In addition to these qualities, it also involves perseverance, resilience, and adaptability. By incorporating these traits, setting clear, achievable goals, and being resourceful, you can overcome obstacles, maintain focus, celebrate WINS, and continue moving forward. Furthermore, dedication, thorough preparation, and staying calm under pressure are key to success.

8

TURNING LEMONS INTO LEMONADE

Navigating the complexities of an emotionally abusive relationship while striving to maintain a thriving career in the music industry is a daunting challenge. My story begins with an unexpected pregnancy, a tumultuous partnership, and a series of personal and professional trials that tested my resilience at every turn. Through the lens of my experiences, I share how music has provided solace and strength, illustrating how passion and creativity can be powerful tools for overcoming adversity. My story demonstrates the power of finding light in the darkest times and the importance of surrounding oneself with a supportive community.

Recognizing and confronting emotional abuse within the family was a harrowing journey that began when I found myself in a dire predicament. I became pregnant with someone I barely knew, Peter, who was initially attracted to my solo violin playing at a private event for ARCO Alaska. Seduced by his charisma, we went on a date to a wilderness cabin in the middle of winter, and while staying warm and cuddled in front of the fireplace, I conceived my daughter. As my pregnancy became apparent, I realized my immediate plans to relocate to Australia were no longer realistic, so I stayed with Peter because I really wanted this baby, hoping for a daughter, and believed strongly in the sanctity of marriage. After a difficult birth in August 1986, Peter found fault with everything I did, mainly when he was under the influence of alcohol.

I quickly began noticing he preferred hanging out in bars, had a host of friends he met there regularly, and then had a bad accident when he stumbled from too much alcohol, falling on his face with his glasses embedded into his forehead. He would disappear for days at a time with no contact. Then, he would show up and make amends by taking me out to exquisite dinners, cleaning the house, supporting my business, and taking me on vacation to Hawaii. The cycle started all over again. I started dreading life with him, questioning my worth and why this was happening to me. I was very secretive with family, colleagues, and the public—I could not let anyone know what was happening. I could fix this. I had a positive public image to maintain.

I realized he had one unsavory friend who sought him out for shady business dealings written on a paper napkin in a bar setting only. He would not heed my caution as the business deal eventually trapped him in a significant tax fraud. Fortunately, I insisted on filing taxes separately, which protected me when an IRS agent appeared unannounced at our house.

Amidst these challenges, music became my sanctuary and source of strength. My business was music, and I immersed myself completely in it. I booked talent, including myself, around Alaska, growing the business from waiting for the first call in 1981 to a burgeoning roster of

500 clients and 200 entertainers and musicians. Promoting concerts with Spyro Gyra, Pure Prairie League, Al Hirt, Lola Falana, David Grisman Quartet, Nicolette Larson, Scott Cossu, the Montreux Band, Michael Tomlinson, and Australian entertainers Banish Misfortune, along with producing a Renaissance Festival at Prudhoe Bay, Alaska, kept me deeply engaged. I booked my "Friends" trio with treasured friends Betsy on flute and Bob on cello from the Alyeska Ski Resort to Valdez (Vegas Star opens Civic Center, 1982). I produced a summer outdoor weekly concert series for seven years, featuring dozens of genres and talent, from a community chorus to Tommy Rocker of Las Vegas fame (Piper, 1982). My custom shows for corporate events with my 5-piece band "Creation," and my involvement in recording, speaking, concert promoting, and consulting kept me focused and resilient (Kleeschulte, 1984). The musicians I worked with and my office staff became my extended family.

Despite facing challenges, like a concert promoter embezzling funds, cash missing from concert ticket sales connected to receiving a mysterious package of drugs, a staff member leaving to start her own talent agency, and the police wanting me to go undercover to expose a pornographic ring, I managed to navigate these crises with the help of trusted colleagues. Additionally, dealing with a local dancer wanting extra cash jobs to escape entrapment added another layer of complexity to our environment. Through it all, bonds strengthened, and I emerged more resilient.

Two things occurred as a result of the economic downturn in 1986. Peter lost his job, and I had a decline in bookings. He started scouting for a job anywhere, and I pivoted to offer more: consulting, healing recordings, concert promotions, seminars, and speaking. The next two years were a whirlwind of activity for me, suddenly needing to stop with Peter accepting a job out of Alaska.

Ultimately, I sold the business in 1988 and moved to Las Vegas, closing one chapter and opening another.

Star Services

On Entertainment

ALASKAN WELL-BEING / Summer 1987

There exists an entertainment company whose philosophy is publicly stated as promoting entertainment and related services that stimulate in the performer and audience a positive introspection mentally, emotionally and spiritually. Star Services, based in Alaska, is that company.

Star Services promotes events that concentrate on a person's well-being: physically, mentally, emotionally and spiritually. This is always the goal, and the following take us closer to the ideal.

Concerts are provided for non-smokers, in a setting that is more relaxed.

Seminars are sponsored to provide specific topical information necessary for mental stimulation and awareness.

Concerts are promoted to stimulate emotional well-being, creating a positive response for the performer and audience.

Entertainment presentations are coordinated to incorporate one or more of the fine arts together as one with the audience. Audience reaction and interaction is very important to personal growth of each participant (performer and audience). Color, music, dance, and drama presented with the awareness of metaphysical concepts weaves an experience conducive to personal growth.

It is not always so easy to achieve all of the above. This day and age in entertainment, many performers and audience participants are still using old concepts of what "show-biz" is: ego-centric for the performer and idol-worshipper for the audience.

The audience puts the performer on a pedestal which is very demanding on the performer's physical, mental, emotional and spiritual states. It's hard to live up to millions of peoples' expectations, yet it's a wonderful feeling to have millions of people admire your talent. However, the performer and audience must be aware that that talent comes from God to share: the performer is merely the tool. This perspective then becomes a new relationship between performer and audience.

This transition in perspective is everyone's responsibility as our society begins to realize the God within rather than the God without (which is believed to exist outside of one's body).

Star Services strives to present entertainment and services that produce this quality. Projects are chosen very carefully so that these goals are always in sight.

What type of entertainment do you seek?

What kind of entertainment setting do you most enjoy?

How does entertainment effect you?

Cultivate your relationship with entertainment in a new way.

Be aware of what entertainment cultivates energies in you that are happy, joyous, courageous, relaxed, loving, gentle, gracious, peaceful or confident. Conversely, what entertainment stimulates sadness, distress, fears, scattered energies, apathy, anger, acrimony, dis-ease and doubt?

Be attentive to your relationship with entertainment. Know yourself first to better understand what energy patterns you can effect through what, where, when and why you entertain yourself.

Star Services Inc.'s special summer event presented with the above ideal includes: "Scott Cossu" (Windham Hill Recording Artist) concerts, June 24, the Anchorage Hilton Ballroom, "The StoryTeller" June 10-September 19, Wednesday-Saturday, at Sydney's, Anchorage Hilton Hotel, and Art Exploration: Hands-On Experience, Egan Center, August 10-15. For additional ticket information, call 277-2277 or 277-3135.

Music was my lifeline during the most challenging times, helping me manage emotions and find solace amidst the chaos. From 1981 through 2004, I performed constantly as a professional violinist, pouring my heart and soul into the music. This immersion in music was not just a profession but a therapeutic refuge that fed my spirit and provided an emotional outlet. I performed in various settings: solo recitals at the Alaska Conservatory of Music I managed, ensemble performances booked through my talent agency, the Anchorage Symphony, and Anchorage Opera. Playing music allowed me to channel my emotions constructively, transforming pain and confusion into melody and harmony.

Certain songs and types of music were particularly influential during these times. I resonated deeply with the show music required for my job, finding exhilaration in sight-reading music "perfectly," whether on stage or in a recording studio. Playing Frank Sinatra's music charts was a unique pleasure due to their exciting and demanding arrangements. Similarly, the music of Johnny Mathis, John Williams, Barry Manilow, and Paul Anka captivated me with its complexity and beauty. I enjoyed the intimate connections formed through classical music in smaller ensembles for weddings, events, and conferences. These performances, whether part of a magic show like "Classical Magic" or other events, provided a sense of stability and joy. The intimate connections with other musicians in these settings fostered a sense of community and support, further helping me navigate the turbulent waters of my personal life. Music was not just a job but a sanctuary that sustained me through the darkest times.

Rebuilding Life in New Environments

Leaving behind the familiar embrace of Alaska for the bustling energy of Las Vegas was nothing short of a monumental leap. This move demanded not only a physical relocation but also a complete emotional and psychological overhaul. I left the business I had nurtured and the serene

landscapes I had cherished, stepping into the unknown with a mix of trep-
idation and excitement. The journey was fraught with intense logistical
challenges and emotional upheaval, yet it was also a path of resilience and
self-discovery. Shutting down the business and preparing for the move was
an exhausting process. I boxed up my entire life, mailing belongings to Las
Vegas, sold my car, and took care of my condo rental. On the night of my
final performance in Alaska, I felt relief and sadness as I bid farewell to the
life I had built there. Navigating the vibrant, fast-paced environment of
Las Vegas, I had to rebuild my life from the ground up, all while maintaining my professional identity and striving for personal stability. It was
a transformative period that tested my adaptability and determination at
every turn.

While these achievements provided a sense of accomplishment, rebuilding my life was not without its challenges. The logistics of packing up
my entire life, mailing my belongings to Las Vegas, selling my car, and
managing my condo rental were overwhelming. Additionally, I missed my
infant daughter terribly, as she had moved down earlier with Peter and his
mother to be cared for until I could arrive. Without the usual research
and preparation about living in Las Vegas, I relied on the hope that this
new beginning would offer us a chance to repair our marriage and start
fresh. The drastic change in climate and lifestyle required adjustments;
the bustling environment of Las Vegas was a stark contrast to the serene,
remote landscapes of Alaska. Despite the challenges, I was determined to
rebuild my life, utilizing the resilience I had developed through previous
adversities.

Transitioning to this new life was not just about environmental adaptation; it required a profound, personal transformation. Rebuilding my life in Las Vegas required strategy, adaptability, and sheer determination. The exhaustion of shutting down my business and the emotional strain of moving away from Alaska were significant. Still, I focused on practical steps to establish myself in the new city. I immediately immersed myself in the local music scene, auditioning for the Nevada Symphony Orchestra within weeks of my arrival. Being accepted into the orchestra provided an instant connection to a community of musicians, which was crucial for my sense of belonging and professional continuity.

Music played a huge role in assisting my transition. I constantly immersed myself in playing violin, whether practicing, rehearsing, or performing. I even invited musicians to my home to play quartets, fostering new friendships through shared music experiences. My first significant engagement was presenting a Seminar Concert to the Nevada Dental Hygienists Association in April 1989. This event began my integration into the Las Vegas music community and helped establish my reputation in a new market.

Opportunities continued to arise as I connected with local musicians. I joined the Nevada Chamber Symphony, became the first paid Concertmaster for the Las Vegas Civic Symphony, and played a Mozart Violin Concerto with LVCS in October 1989. Forming a local trio called "SoundSynergy" with two talented musicians, Erika (violin) and Aggie (cello), further solidified my place in the city's musical landscape. Within months of arriving, I had the chance to play with Frank Sinatra Sr., which marked the start of my show career. Additionally, I wrote music-related articles for Darlene's magazine, "New Dimensions of Las Vegas." I also started "The Music Therapy Project" to advocate for a music therapy degree program (Starr, 1990). These professional milestones were more than just jobs; they were lifelines that provided stability and joy amidst the upheaval of relocating. The vibrant Las Vegas music scene and the support of new friends and colleagues helped me adapt and thrive in my new environment.

At the same time, I hoped that Peter's move to Las Vegas five months earlier, living with his mother, would mark a fresh start, distancing him from his old habits and social circles. When I moved later to join him, I focused on learning about the city's culture, neighborhoods, cost of living, transportation options, and local laws while searching for a new house. I was thrilled to discover that groceries cost almost half as much as they did in Alaska. Establishing a routine and identifying local services, such as healthcare providers and gyms, helped create a sense of normalcy and stability.

Networking also played a significant role in my adaptation. Joining local groups and attending self-development and industry events proved to be the best way to build social connections and establish networks for professional and personal support. Today, social media greatly enhances networking. Connecting with local colleagues and joining professional associations provided valuable opportunities for growth and integration into the Las Vegas community.

Exploring my new surroundings with an open mind helped me embrace the new culture and adapt to different ways of doing things. Staying active by joining a local gym, church (or faith center), and participating in activities like hiking and cycling contributed to my physical and mental well-being. Practicing self-care and joining a study group were also important aspects of maintaining my health.

Setting short-term and long-term goals motivated me and provided direction during this transition period. Creating a budget to manage expenses and maintain an emergency fund helped ensure financial stability. Embracing the adventure of moving to a new city with a positive attitude allowed me to view the experience as an opportunity for growth and new experiences.

Finding Strength in Community

Establishing a new network of friends and supporters in Las Vegas was essential for my emotional and professional well-being. I was optimistic about our new life in Las Vegas, hoping that Peter and I could have a fresh start away from his drinking buddies. Music played an instrumental role in forming these new relationships. Within weeks of arriving, I auditioned for and joined several local orchestras and symphonies, immediately providing a sense of community and belonging. These connections were not just professional; they also became personal, forming the backbone of my support system.

Through music, I met many like-minded individuals who shared my passion and dedication. For instance, joining the Nevada Symphony Orchestra introduced me to a network of musicians who welcomed me into their fold. This camaraderie extended beyond rehearsals and performances, with fellow musicians often gathering for social events, further strengthening our bonds. Additionally, participating in local events and musical productions allowed me to integrate more deeply into the community, establishing lasting friendships and professional relationships.

During this professional integration and personal adjustment period, I discovered a resource that profoundly influenced my journey. Reading "The Artist's Way" by Julia Cameron was a transformative experience that profoundly influenced my creative and personal growth. The book arrived at a critical time, offering a lifeline as I navigated the emotional turmoil of living with someone who had a severe drinking problem. Cameron's emphasis on rekindling one's creative spirit resonated with me, helping me climb out of the negative spiral I found myself in. The exercises and insights in the book encouraged me to let go of negativity and focus on what truly mattered, reigniting my faith and confidence.

One of the most impactful exercises from the book was the morning pages—a daily practice of writing three pages of longhand, stream-of-consciousness thoughts. This exercise became a therapeutic outlet, allowing me to process my emotions and clear my mind. It helped me confront and release the fears and doubts that had accumulated over years of emotional abuse. Additionally, the concept of the artist date, a weekly solo expedition to explore something that interests you, provided a much-needed escape and a chance to nurture my inner artist. These activities boosted my creativity and restored a sense of autonomy and self-worth.

The book's emphasis on recovering a sense of safety, identity, and possibility was particularly relevant as I rebuilt my life in Las Vegas. Creating an organized altar of creative success, painting rocks, and engaging in various artistic endeavors helped me reconnect with my creative self. These practices reinforced my belief in my artistic abilities and reminded me of the joy and fulfillment that creativity brings. "The Artist's Way" guided me to transform my mindset from fear and low self-worth to empowerment and possibility. It was instrumental in helping me navigate the challenges of my new environment, fostering resilience and personal growth through creativity and self-expression.

Turning Challenges into Opportunities

Finding hope and positivity in adversity has always been central to my resilience. When I quickly discovered that moving to Las Vegas did not alleviate Peter's drinking problems but instead worsened them, I had to find new ways to cope and thrive. His heavy drinking and emotional abuse intensified in a city that seemed to cater to every possible vice. Despite this, my faith guides me through these tumultuous times. I believe that God is an omnipresent force accessible at all times and that aligning my thoughts with love, peace, and joy transforms my reality.

Embracing my faith allows me to find strength and a new perspective on life's challenges. This philosophy not only helped me navigate my tumultuous relationship with Peter but also shaped my approach to overcoming other adversities, including my battle with cancer. I don't just survive; I thrive. I identify not as a cancer survivor but as a thriver, demonstrating a life anchored in deep faith and embracing universal truths. Love, peace, and joy are at the core, spontaneously creating and supporting life. Alaska's nature taught me to connect deeply with God in a very personal way, a relationship I hold sacred and private, honoring everyone as "the face of God, the light of God, the heart of God." My faith shapes my truth in prayer, meditation, and connecting with others through deep compassion.

My first transformative spiritual experience happened at ten, during a United Methodist Sunday School session. While others drew traditional depictions of God, I drew a wavy circle with alternating ears and eyes, symbolizing an all-encompassing presence. This early sense of a personal relationship with the Divine continued to grow, especially during moments of deep emotional distress. Later, my encounters with religious leaders deepened my faith journey. I learned to see the face of God in everyone and everything, believing that God is always available, no matter the circumstances.

This foundation in God helped me navigate the challenges of living with Peter's worsening behavior. I could counteract the negativity and abuse by centering my thoughts on gratitude, love, and peace. Affirmative prayer and meditation became essential for maintaining my inner peace and resilience. Nature also played a significant role in my connection with God, reinforcing my belief in the power of the Divine when I walked barefoot on hot coals without harm. This act symbolized my trust in the omnipresence of God and my ability to overcome any obstacle with Divine support. My relationship with God, immersed in religious principles and practice, allowed me to embrace challenges with hope and transform adversity into opportunities for growth and awakening.

Just as God provided a foundation for my resilience, music emerged as a powerful ally in my healing journey. Music has been an indispensable therapeutic tool throughout my overcoming obstacles, providing a means to express and process deep-seated emotions. Playing and engaging with music offered a sanctuary where I could heal and grow, transforming pain into creative energy. For instance, music was my refuge during the darkest times with Peter. Performing as a professional violinist allowed me to channel my emotions into something beautiful and constructive. The discipline and focus required in music provided a necessary distraction and a way to regain control over my chaotic life.

One poignant example of music's therapeutic power was my participation in the Nevada Symphony Orchestra and other local ensembles. These opportunities allowed me to perform and connect with fellow musicians who shared my passion and provided emotional support. The camaraderie and mutual understanding within these groups created a safe space to explore my feelings and find solace. Playing complex and demanding pieces, such as those by John Williams, composers of show arrangements and classical music required intense concentration and technical skill, which helped me temporarily escape from the emotional turmoil at home.

"People often tell me that you are one of the few violinists that is so completely successful in communicating a warm, joyous, and magnetic personality as you are performing."

- David P. Peterson, Chaplain (LTC), Ft Richardson Army Base, Alaska.

This feedback highlights how my connection with music allowed me to communicate a positive and uplifting presence, even amidst personal struggles. My collaborative therapeutic music projects created a sense of community and belonging. These collaborations were more than just professional engagements; they were therapeutic interactions that reinforced my sense of identity and purpose. Music's ability to evoke and manage emotions was essential in my healing process, enabling me to transform negative experiences into sources of strength and resilience.

Furthermore, teaching and mentoring others in music amplified its healing effects. By sharing my knowledge and passion, I helped others discover the therapeutic benefits of music and reinforced my healing journey. The sense of fulfillment and joy derived from these interactions underscored music's profound impact on my emotional well-being and personal growth. Through music, I found a way to heal, grow, and ultimately thrive, using its transformative power to navigate and overcome life's challenges. As my experience has shown, to thrive in the face of adversity, it is important to increase our capacity to deal with more stress, or as I like to say, "Take this (Music Medicine) pill so you won't be one."

Resilience Through Music and Positivity

Reflecting on my experiences, I've learned that resilience, adaptability, and creative expression are key. My mother's motto, "Turn lemons into lemonade," perfectly captures my journey. Facing adversity, whether it was emotional abuse, relocating to a new city, or professional challenges, I found strength in turning obstacles into growth opportunities. My definition of success now focuses on helping others, channeling my experiences into actions that support and uplift those around me. Maintaining a positive public image while dealing with personal turmoil required immense strength and taught me to compartmentalize and focus on my goals despite the chaos. God and music became fundamental in navigating these challenges, with religious standards and "The Artist's Way" helping me maintain a mindset of hope and possibility.

Community and connection were also essential. Building supportive networks through music provided emotional support and practical opportunities for growth. Shared experiences and collective creativity reinforced the idea that we are stronger together. Turning challenges into opportunities became a guiding principle. Each setback invited innovation, adaptation, and new pathways, demonstrating the practice of pivoting with ease. This mindset allowed me to thrive in adversity, continuously evolving and finding joy. I've seen adversity as a catalyst for growth, creativity, and deeper connections with others. When one window closes, another window opens; look for it with expectancy and anticipation, and follow the signs from God to it.

When advising others facing similar challenges, I emphasize the importance of service, positivity, and resilience. Focusing on helping others provides purpose and direction. Maintaining a supportive network of individuals who uplift and encourage you is essential. Periodic vision meetings with my staff build synergy and ensure alignment with our goals, creating a positive and proactive environment. Learning from mistakes is crucial for building resilience. Each setback provides valuable lessons that help avoid future pitfalls. Visualization and religious practices play significant roles. Visualizing myself surrounded by Divine light helps me maintain a positive mindset and avoid problems. God is a deeply personal experience for me, and I honor every person's right to express God in a way that is meaningful for them as together we focus our attention on positive outcomes.

For those seeking to develop resilience, embrace a mindset of continuous growth and adaptation. Set short-term and long-term goals, celebrating small victories along the way. Stay open-minded and embrace new experiences, as they offer unexpected opportunities for growth. Ultimately, resilience is about thriving, not just surviving. By focusing on service, maintaining a supportive network, learning from mistakes, and embracing a positive mindset, anyone can overcome challenges and turn them into growth opportunities. This approach has allowed me to navigate life's adversities and find fulfillment and success.

The positive feedback I've received has guided my journey. Testimonials and words of encouragement underline the impact of my work. For example, the words of David P. Peterson, Chaplain at Ft. Richardson Army Base, deeply moved me in my final year of retail management when he described my ability to communicate a "warm, joyous, and magnetic personality" while performing. Bob Marley's words, "One good thing about music, when it hits you, you feel no pain," encapsulate how music served as my refuge during challenging times. These principles embody my approach to life, performance, and overcoming challenges:

Golden Rule: "Do unto others as you would have them do unto you."

Platinum Rule: "Treat others the way they would like to be treated" (Hall, 2017).

They remind me that our thoughts shape our reality, and by aligning with positivity and love, we can transcend adversity. Reflecting on these experiences, I recognize that the resilience, adaptability, and creative expression I've cultivated are deeply rooted in the principles discussed in Chapter 1. Our brains constantly reshape and rewire in response to experiences, showing the difference between positive and negative patterns. Embracing music and spirituality has led to emotional strength and resilience, while dwelling on negativity or succumbing to despair can reinforce harmful neural pathways. By consciously choosing to focus on positivity, service, and connection, I have used the power of positive change to overcome adversity and thrive. This ongoing journey shows the profound impact of our choices on our brain's wiring, reinforcing the idea that we can shape our reality through intentional thought and action. As Beethoven eloquently put it:

"Music is the Mediator between the Life of the Spirit and the Life of the Senses."

Beethoven's insight subtly captures the transformative essence of music, serving as a bridge between our spiritual and sensory experiences. The significance of these principles becomes even clearer through the feedback and insights from those who have observed and benefited from my work. For instance, one director of a university military and veteran services center remarked on the practical benefits of my approach: "Increase your capacity to deal with more stress using Music4Life®." His words demonstrate how integrating music into our lives can effectively manage stress and enhance well-being, reaffirming the powerful connection between our mental state and the choices we make.

These testimonials and quotes affirm the power of resilience, the healing potential of music, and the importance of a positive mindset. They inspire me to continue encouraging resilience and creativity in others. My journey has shown that success is about navigating the journey and embracing each challenge as a stepping stone toward greater resilience and fulfillment. By focusing on service, maintaining a supportive network, learning from mistakes, and embracing a positive mindset supported by life-affirming, God-embracing signs that signal the path of a fulfilling life, anyone can overcome challenges and turn them into growth opportunities. Through the power of music, we can find light in the darkest times and create a supportive community around us.

9

CHANGING LIFE PATHS AND STANDING UP TO HARASSMENT

F rom a career in retail to one in music performance and education, this transition marked a defining chapter in my life. This transition was driven by a need to forge a new identity and escape the overwhelming stress that had begun to take a toll on my well-being. From leaving a stable job at JCPenney to embarking on adventures across the country, each step was a bold move toward rediscovering my passion for music. The experiences gained during this period helped me reconnect with my roots and laid the foundation for a fulfilling career in music, bringing with it profound lessons in self-care, resilience, and the importance of following one's true calling.

The decision to leave a career in retail for one in music performance and education was a major moment in my life. I needed to excel in something non-musical to establish my own identity. With my last name changed to Reynolds during my first marriage, no one at JCPenney readily knew of my strong connection to music in Anchorage, allowing me to forge a new identity. Although I loved Iron Butterfly's "In-A-Gadda-Da-Vida" and the music of Super Tramp and the Alan Parsons Project, my spirit was imploding after seven years of limiting my focus on performing music. The stress of dealing with my final management supervisor was overwhelming, and despite peers advising me to tough it out, my spirit was dying, and I almost had a nervous breakdown. So I did the unthinkable: I quit one week before Christmas and flew to Denver, CO, for a family reunion. I remember the District Manager flying to Anchorage and trying to persuade me to take a six-month sabbatical and return to the same management position. But I couldn't do it. I wanted out. It felt like leaving family, choosing to flee the nest of tolerance, success, and acceptance.

Deciding to have some fun, I traveled with my brothers Gary and Jim in the Lower '48 to the East Coast after Christmas, staying with Jim in his M.I.T. fraternity house—a memorable experience! I then stayed at Gary's house before creating some art during the 3,000-mile journey via bus, traveling the "milk run" from the East Coast to the West Coast. I also stayed with a dear friend, Bonni, before venturing back to Anchorage.

*My embroidery art (1981) - see
my JP signature?*

Upon returning to Anchorage in February, I decided to work on the North Slope. At a recent party, I was told that the only way to get up on the slope was to sleep your way there, and one guy in particular was willing to show me the way. I refused. Instead, I joined a temp agency that advertised jobs on the North Slope. I'll never forget the look on this guy's face when I walked into a social area at MCC "Main Construction Camp" as the receptionist. He was incredulous that I was there without his "help!" The job was fun—scheduling movies and social events (thematic dance contests—never forgetting one professional dancer choosing me as his partner and flinging me all over the place!), answering the telephone, and getting tours of the area at BP and ARCO camps and oil rigs. I couldn't believe the attire of people flying to the North Slope to work. Women wore high heels, nylons, and suits—not pants. I wore bunny boots, warm pants, and a heavy coat, and they smiled and laughed, knowing I was "new." However, my boyfriend Thom was tired of me being gone 50% of the time, so I quit my slope job, found local part-time work, and started my talent agency, Pinkerton Performances, with his support and several other partners.

By 1983, I was no longer satisfied with the Morassi violin I had purchased in Cremona, Italy, so I bought my current violin, a Gilkes 1867, from a shop in Seattle, WA, favoring its chamber music timbre. Desiring to reconnect with my family's focus on music, I partnered with my dad to found the Alaska Conservatory of Music when another music school went out of business. It provided income through tutoring junior high and senior high students with violin sight-reading lessons (my dad provided private violin lessons), and I had performance opportunities with recitals. With the new violin and the establishment of the conservatory, performing became very natural for me, and I knew how to practice, learn quickly, and avoid wasting time. Emphasizing small chamber ensembles over symphonies allowed me to play as a soloist with much more flexibility than being one of many violins focused on merging into a single sound in unison. I enjoyed duos with excellent guitarist Vance, string quartets, and various other ensemble sizes.

Transitioning careers came with its challenges and successes. After leaving my stress-filled retail work family, I needed time off to soak up love from my immediate family. Choosing different landscapes, traveling, and doing something completely unrelated to my past work history was a healthy transition. It allowed me to reconsider what was important without work agendas, connect with non-judgmental people, and have the space and time to think, meditate, and reconnect with myself.

Music played a key role in supporting this career change. Even though I didn't travel with my violin, my brothers loved music, so we listened to our favorites in the car, often using the car's tape deck, filling our ears with Journey, Phil Collins, and the Grateful Dead during this transformative period. For private listening, I used my Walkman to enjoy meditation music, which provided a personal retreat amidst changes in life.

Dealing with Workplace Harassment

Entering the professional world often brings a mix of excitement and challenges, but sometimes, it also introduces unexpected and difficult experiences. Harassment in the workplace is one such experience that can severely impact an individual's well-being and career trajectory. These encounters can be harrowing and test one's strength and resolve. In my journey, I faced multiple instances of harassment that deeply challenged me. These experiences affected my professional path and reinforced my commitment to self-care and advocacy.

When I accepted the offer to be a management trainee at JCPenney in 1976, I was assigned to "Larry" (a pseudonym), one of the store's general managers. He was likable and attentive until I realized he wanted more at a managers' after-hours party. In 2005, I documented a required experience of being "socially disadvantaged" to the U.S. Small Business Administration's 8a/SDB application when this manager almost cost me my job because I would not accept his sexual advances. In retaliation, Larry set me up for failure in management situations, withholding necessary training. I risked reporting the problem to the store manager, who was close to firing me because "Larry" had rated my performance evaluation with a low score. Instead, the store manager transferred me to another general manager, giving me one last chance. This new manager further interviewed me about the sexual harassment because other management trainees were quitting under Larry's supervision, and management couldn't understand why. The District Manager learned of my situation and traveled from California to Alaska to interview me after the store closed off-location. This occurred the same year as Williams v. Saxbe, causing the first quid pro quo sexual harassment judgment ("A History of Sexual Harassment," 2023). Larry was subsequently transferred and demoted.

After completing the training, my second assignment involved managing many departments under a new general manager who made work conditions very stressful with unreasonable demands. The previous female manager had almost quit due to the extreme stress provoked by this supervisor and was transferred to another city in the Lower '48, where she continued to be promoted to senior positions before retiring. I reported to the SBA that the stress produced such anxiety for me that I was forced to quit in 1980 or suffer a nervous breakdown, declining a six-month sabbatical offered by the District Manager to return to my life with music and my violin.

As a consultant, I accepted the position of Statewide Director for Alaska Expo '88 in Australia, independently contracting with the State Chamber of Commerce. I created marketing programs to generate revenue to support Alaska's booth featuring a large iceberg. I was introduced to a unique fundraising idea: a Murder Mystery aboard the Air France Concorde. Intrigued, I agreed to fly to Vancouver to meet the team and board the jet back to Anchorage. Unfortunately, I failed to confirm in writing that I would be on the Concorde. In Vancouver, the team lead from the Middle East insisted on meeting me at the pool and followed me to my hotel room to have a private discussion. He insinuated that I could guarantee my return if we had sex right then or if I joined the Mile-High Club. I declined. The next morning, this team lead had scheduled my breakfast interview with the lead actor for the Murder Mystery, who wore a big red clown nose. He described my role and what I needed to do, but I still had no ticket to board. I played the part of a fun-loving participant in the boarding line and finally received the boarding pass just in time. I acted out my role of being poisoned on the flight convincingly, even though I missed the dramatic landing, wrapped "dead" under the Air France red plaid blanket, which I still treasure as saving my life from coercion.

"Sacre bleu, mes amis. Was that Judith Pinkerton, president of Star Services, lying dead, dead, DEAD on the Concorde last weekend? Alas, yes. Judith was struck down most foully five minutes before the plane landed in Anchortown, en route from Vancouver. Of course, d'Ears, it was just a high flying and tres expensive murder mystery weekend" (Toomey, 1988).

These experiences of sexual harassment were similar: I refused to participate in their schemes. Working with major Las Vegas entertainer "Joe" (a pseudonym), I faced psychological harassment. Injured before a show I played but was sent to Urgent Care afterward due to a large hematoma, Joe refused to pay me for that night, claiming I did not play, and immediately issued an unrelated reprimand. With the support of the musician's union, I protested. Joe's administration continued issuing unreasonable reprimands over several months, ending with termination, which I refuted with the union's support. Eventually, the grievance of wrongful termination resulted in the receipt of a large settlement, the first in Las Vegas entertainment history. Despite Joe's attempts to reconnect, I refused to tour with him and instead focused on building a successful nonprofit music therapy practice on the College of Southern Nevada's West Charleston Campus.

Reflecting on these many disturbing experiences with Joe, I employed several strategies to confront and overcome harassment. I detailed incidents in writing for potential legal action and to process my emotions. I confided in trusted individuals for emotional support, researched my rights, and sought advice from organizations or attorneys. I set boundaries where I felt safe and filed formal complaints when advisable. Legal advice guided my understanding of options, and in one instance, I proactively became well-liked with passengers before boarding the Concorde, creating a safety measure in case I needed to expose his coercion. The Musicians Union proudly proclaimed their success with my grievance against a major entertainer, strengthening their position with other members. When I experienced sexual harassment in 1976, it was still the "menace with no name" (Blakemore, 2023). Engaging in well-being activities like exercise, hobbies, and relaxation techniques helped manage the stress and anxiety related to harassment.

These strategies were not just about facing harassment but building resilience and empowerment in my personal life. My journey was filled with stories of power-filled tenacity, shaped by my adventures and the inspiration of my father, an adventurous mentor who traveled the world, even hiking the Inca Trail into Machu Picchu (1983). His confidence and fortitude motivated me to travel and live independently in various places.

Flying solo in the Alaska wilderness, backpacking along the Chilkoot Trail, and exploring the wilderness near our family cabin taught me to stay hyper-focused while enjoying the beauty around me. Whether it was facing moose encounters, driving on narrow, snow-covered roads, or exploring new countries, I found strength and joy in these challenges. I quickly made friends in Australia, visiting places that intrigued me, including the Green Room and connecting with musicians in the Sydney Opera House. In

Switzerland, my open and mindful approach led to unexpected rewards, such as traveling by rail to Solothurn and staying in the mansion of the owner after finding her expensive watch. Embracing discoveries brought pleasant surprises and strengthened my resilience.

These personal adventures paralleled my professional experiences, where navigating the professional world often means confronting unexpected and challenging experiences, such as workplace harassment, which can deeply impact one's well-being and career. My journey through various instances of harassment was marked by a series of trials that tested my strength and resilience. From facing unwanted advances and unfair treatment during my career in retail management to dealing with coercion and psychological harassment in later roles, each encounter taught me valuable lessons about self-care, advocacy, and the importance of standing up for oneself.

Throughout these experiences, I found solace and support in documenting incidents, seeking legal advice, and relying on trusted friends and colleagues. My commitment to self-care, through activities like music, exercise, and travel, helped me manage the stress and anxiety that accompanied these challenges. The support of organizations like the Musicians Union and the guidance of mentors, such as my father, were instrumental in reinforcing my resilience.

Advocacy and Empowerment

The concept of self-advocacy has evolved significantly over time. Initially developed to support individuals with disabilities, it has since gained recognition as an important skill for anyone seeking to stand up for their rights and interests. Self-advocacy involves effectively communicating your needs and rights, enabling informed decision-making, and promoting personal responsibility. Mastering this skill can lead to healthier work relationships, a successful career, and greater job satisfaction. Yet, knowing about self-advocacy is different from applying it in the workplace. To guide you in becoming an effective self-advocate, here are three key elements to consider (Fisic, 2023):

1. **Understand Your Needs:** Learn to listen to yourself and identify what you need at any moment.

2. **Be Aware of Your Support System:** Know who you can turn to for help.

3. **Communicate Your Needs Clearly:** Articulate your wants openly and understandably.

Before diving into the practical aspects, it's important to approach the topic of workplace bullying with sensitivity. Because many individuals have experienced the negative impacts of harassment, it's essential to understand how pervasive and damaging it can be. Workplace bullying encompasses verbal, physical, social, or psychological abuse, and in today's increasingly common virtual work environment, harassment can also occur remotely, often through private and group meetings ("Workplace Bullying," 2024).

Psychological harassment, in particular, can severely affect a person's well-being, making them feel belittled both personally and professionally. This can lead to a domino effect, harming their physical health, social life, and work performance. Examples of psychological harassment in the workplace include:

- Excluding or isolating the victim

- Undermining the victim's thoughts or ideas

- Spreading rumors about the victim

- Consistently opposing the victim

- Gaslighting the victim

- Establishing a hostile or excessively competitive work atmosphere

Music can be a powerful tool to build confidence and self-esteem during such challenges. A prescriptive playlist can help recover from incidents of harassment and bolster confidence. Consider starting your playlist with Demi Lovato's "Warrior" to match "U-Unsettled" energy and validate unsettled feelings. Then, immediately follow with a "S-Soothing" song like "Hope Deep Inside" by Samuel Fresh to neutralize those feelings. Finally, shift nonstop into an empowering mindset with an "E-Energizing" song like "Excuse Me" by Irene Boggs.

In summary, the journey toward effective self-advocacy is both challenging and rewarding. By actively listening to your needs, seeking support, and communicating clearly, you can confidently navigate the complexities of the workplace. Recognizing the prevalence of workplace bullying, espe-cially in our increasingly virtual world, highlights the importance of being prepared and resilient. Utilizing tools like music for emotional support can help you face and overcome these challenges.

Inspiring Others To Take A Stand

When facing challenges like harassment, you must network with your support group. They will provide valuable perspectives and bolster your resolve. Even though one dear friend trembled at what I was disputing with Joe, the major entertainer, she knew I was resolved to make him accountable for absurd reprimands. Be firm with the harasser: set healthy boundaries, document everything in writing, journal the date and time of all interactions, and take legal action if necessary by connecting with HR, a union, or an attorney.

To effectively advocate for yourself and others, assertiveness, knowledge of rights, and support systems are crucial. Know the law, understand the details accurately, avoid sidebar chats that aren't in alignment with your goal, and find and enlist allies. Grow your network for good, respect requested confidentiality, and stay focused on your mission.

I know a woman who advanced her career by engaging in relationships with influential people, ultimately becoming a formidable, likable force for good. Despite her unconventional path, her determination and strategic approach were crucial to her success. She was private, calculating, positive, and strategic to ensure her position. Only you know your path and what you are comfortable with. Ensure you align with your values, conscience, goals, and God. It's essential to stay true to yourself and choose a path that you can confidently follow without regret.

While navigating your career, it is equally important to be aware of the challenges that can arise, such as sexual harassment in the workplace. A comprehensive survey involving over 86,000 respondents revealed that 58 percent of women have encountered sexually harassing behaviors at work (National Academies of Sciences, 2018). Sexual harassment can manifest in various forms, focusing on gender-based discrimination, unwanted sexual attention, and coercion. This behavior can be direct, such as inappropriate comments, physical advances, or demands for sexual favors. It can also be indirect, creating an uncomfortable or hostile work environment by spreading rumors, making suggestive jokes, or displaying offensive materials. Understanding these different forms of harassment is essential in recognizing and addressing them effectively ("11 Types of Workplace Harassment," n.d.).

In addition to sexual harassment, gender and ethnic discrimination are prevalent issues that can stem from implicit bias within company decision-making processes. Involving diverse ethnic and gender groups on interview committees helps produce fair and relevant questions, promoting inclusivity. Furthermore, workplace bullies who excel in their roles can negatively impact professional environments, as management often fears revenue loss if they are removed. However, taking decisive action can lead to positive outcomes. For instance, Shanice convinced management to fire Jon, a bully, and sales increased (Janove, 2018).

Understanding these examples of harassment and discrimination emphasizes the importance of assertiveness, self-awareness, and strategic networking. By committing to these principles, you can effectively advocate for yourself and others, transforming challenging situations into opportunities for growth and empowerment.

DIVING DEEP INTO YOUR PASSION AND COMMITTING TO FAMILY

F rom a young age, my life was deeply intertwined with music, shaped by intense training and a relentless pursuit of excellence. Yet, as I transitioned into retail management, my musical aspirations took a backseat. It wasn't until a transformative experience reignited my passion that I found my true calling in music therapy, blending my business acumen with a profound desire to heal through music.

Amidst this professional evolution, my family and I faced significant life changes, relocating multiple times in search of better opportunities and a nurturing environment. These moves tested our resilience and unity as we balanced personal challenges with the demands of my burgeoning career in music therapy. Through it all, the support of my husband and the shared experiences of our blended family have been crucial, teaching us the importance of adaptability, communication, and unwavering commitment to each other.

KEY2MEE

I began my musical journey with intense training throughout elementary, junior, and senior high school. I eventually attended a music conservatory in Switzerland. However, music took a back seat as I pursued independence and excelled in retail management. When retail management no longer fulfilled me, I launched music businesses, amazed at the intersections God placed in my path to ensure I stayed true to my life's purpose. While managing these music businesses, a transformative experience at a hospital with Peter ignited my passion to explore further. Like many musicians who hear that their music has healed others or alleviated their physical or emotional pain, I naturally became a "therapeutic musician," a term that has gained prominence today. My background in retail management, where I gained speaking experience through public presentations for the Growth Company, led me to talk about healing music.

However, I sought a more scientific basis for the therapeutic effects of music. During a short-term stay with a friend before leaving Alaska, I was introduced to the profession of music therapy. I connected with a music therapist in Las Vegas, began co-presenting with her, and eventually, after 15 years of perseverance following that initial hospital experience, I became certified. Life's challenges never distracted me from this goal.

*1988*₂

Judith Pinkerton **Solo Violin**			**Music to Heal** **In Concert**	

1	Ovaries/Gonads	Transmute Frustration/Passion Into Pro-Creative Energy	CM CM Am	Schubert "Ave Maria" Bach-Gounod "Ave Maria" Haydn "Serenade"
2	Spleen/Liver/ Pancreas	Reject Anxiety/Infection Allowing Well-Being	DM DM DM Bm	Old Irish Air "Danny Boy" Massenet "Thais Meditation" Strauss "Blue Danube" English Folk Song "Greensleeves"
3	Adrenal	Recognize Desires/Fears Fueling Emotional Power	EM EM Cm	Bach "Gavotte en Rondeau" Brahms "Lullaby" Russian Gypsy Folk Song "Dark Eyes"
4	Thymus	Transform Grief/Hatred Into Love	Dm	H.F. Von Biber "Passacaglia"
5	Thyroid	Free Repression With Creative Self- Expression Through Divine Communication	GM GM Em	Dvorak "Humoresque" Mozart Cadenza Mendelssohn "Andante"
6	Pituitary	Understand Obsession Realize Soul's Vision Through Intuitive Balance	AM Fm Fm	Schumann "Traumerei" Schubert "Serenade" Bizet "Carmen Habanera"
7	Pineal	Recognize Reality beyond Duality In Unity	Gm Gm BM BM BM	Tchaikovsky "Canzonetta" Bach "Adagio" Bach "Jesu, Joy of Man's Desiring" "O Holy Night" "The Lord's Prayer"

1988 concert program

This journey came full circle when I arrived in Las Vegas on January 1, 1989, with a renewed sense of purpose and a mission to get certified in music therapy. The Anchorage Times had featured my departure from Alaska, declaring my commitment to fulfilling my fantasy: performing, connecting with people, helping others, and traveling, as noted in "Sound Therapy, Sound Body" (McPherson, 1988). "Pinkerton is a woman with a mission. She wants to tune you up," the newspaper proclaimed. Although I had heard of music therapy, I had never met a music therapist. This changed in 1990 when I attended the National Music Therapy Conference in San Diego, California. Surrounded by hundreds of music therapists, I felt an overwhelming sense of unity and inspiration from the music-making and conference sessions. I cried throughout the event, realizing I had found my true calling. I knew I needed to become certified in music therapy, and my passion became unstoppable. The emotional reward of supporting another person's healing through music is incomparable. Despite the recognition my violin playing received, I sought a deeper understanding of the scientific basis for music therapy. Although I advocated for a local music therapy degree program in 1990, I faced resistance from music therapists because I was not yet certified: U.N.L.V. still lacks such a program. I found an out-of-state equivalency program where music therapy Professor Barbara Crowe at Arizona State University believed in me and my mission and was willing to accommodate my challenging needs. I am forever indebted to her.

Balancing Career and Family

Life has a way of surprising us, often leading us down paths we never anticipated. I found my perfect partner in Dennis, a man whose love for our family was as deep as his commitment to health and service. Dennis, now a retired sports official, teacher, and chiropractor, brought a unique blend of skills and passions into our lives, from playing the didjeridu to ensuring we stayed active with outdoor adventures. Our shared values created a harmonious balance, emphasizing quality family time despite our busy schedules. Yet, the most unexpected journey began with a phone call from C.P.S. in 2019, altering our lives in ways we could never have imagined.

When we were awarded custody of our (grand)daughter Kaylan, a tiny miracle waiting for us in the NICU, our world shifted profoundly. The initial days were a whirlwind of legal and medical challenges. Still, when Dennis laid eyes on Kaylan, any doubts vanished. Her presence demanded all our attention and love, drawing us into a new chapter filled with joy and immense responsibility. Co-locating between Nevada and Idaho amid the pandemic added another layer of complexity. Yet, it also brought us closer to extended family and provided the support needed for this new venture.

Our adventures with Kaylan began early, spanning multiple states for family events, conferences, and work commitments. As an infant, she charmed everyone she met, and her easygoing nature made even the most hectic travels enjoyable. Through it all, the heartbreak of my daughter's struggles was a constant shadow. However, as we grew closer to Kaylan, it became clear that she was a miracle for us. Her arrival transformed our lives, filling them with unexpected love and purpose. In adopting Kaylan, Dennis and I embraced a new role later in life, proving that the heart has a boundless capacity for love and that sometimes, the most incredible gifts come when least expected.

As we transitioned through different locations, the importance of a supportive network became clear. Leaving Las Vegas was pivotal in providing our family with a safer, more nurturing environment. Our initial stay in St. George offered professional growth and a healthier lifestyle. The co-location between Nevada and Idaho brought us closer to extended family, ensuring both personal and professional stability.

Creating a supportive environment was instrumental in our journey, involving forging new professional connections and integrating diverse family dynamics. Focusing on fostering a balanced, thriving home, we navigated the complexities of our lives through strategies like vision boards and the Virtues Project, reinforcing our family's resilience and adaptability. Now, let's explore how these elements fortify our ability to thrive amid life's changes.

Creating a Supportive Environment

Our family's journey took us from Las Vegas to St. George and eventually to Idaho, each move driven by the pursuit of better opportunities and well-being. Leaving Las Vegas was a significant decision, influenced by the need for a safer, more nurturing environment for our family. We found a community in St. George that supported our professional endeavors and provided a healthier lifestyle. However, as our needs evolved, we relocated to Idaho decades later to be closer to extended family and help my aging parents. Each move significantly affected our personal and professional lives, requiring us to adapt to new communities, build new professional networks, and constantly reassess our priorities to ensure our family's stability.

Amid these personal transitions, in 2004, while my daughter was giving birth to our first grandchild at Nellis A.F.B., I met a military nurse intrigued by my music therapy-assisted childbirth manual. This encounter led to a referral to Major Kevin McCal, then Deputy Commander at the N.A.F.B. Mental Health Flight. Our collaboration began that year, expanding to include Colonel Gerald Curry, Commander of the 99th Security Forces Group. Our discussions focused on supporting military personnel, leading to Colonel Curry advocating for our programs and setting up key meetings, including Dr. Hendrick W. "Henk" Ruck from the Air Force Research Laboratory. Before deployment, I presented to security troops, gaining positive feedback and referrals to present at a national military conference. Despite the consistent denial of grant applications for a Community Resilience program, music therapy was not recognized until much later. This changed with the 2009 Army program, which finally acknowledged the existence of "invisible wounds." This recognition opened the door for various therapies to be utilized. More recently, the U.S.O. showed interest in a music therapy program at Creech A.F.B. However, it has yet to be fully implemented. Training at Sheppard A. F.B. further demonstrated the effectiveness of our Music4Life® Team's approach in supporting airmen's performance goals and resilience through personalized music therapy-informed strategies (Pinkerton, 2020). However, the program lacked scalable technology until the development of the Key2MEE® Music App. On a personal note, my daughter's challenges with her Army veteran husband's P.T.S.D., acquired from a 2005 deployment, highlighted the emotional strain on military families. Despite efforts to support them, we faced significant barriers, including my daughter's eventual estrangement in 2014.

Simultaneously, managing a blended family requires a thoughtful approach to integrating different parenting styles and emotional dynamics. Our wedding, held under a majestic Mahogany tree, symbolized strength and resilience and included a special ceremony for our children. Open communication, patience, and flexibility were critical in building solid and harmonious relationships. We emphasized fairness, coaching each other to avoid favoritism. The 7 F's—Family, Friends, Finance, Firm (business/career), Fitness, Fun, Faith—were reminders to maintain balance. Vision boards were a practical tool for setting and achieving goals, with updated boards prominently displayed to inspire daily reflection and progress. The Virtues Project reinforced positive character values, focusing on positive language, teachable moments, clear boundaries, respect, and genuine listening. These principles helped us adapt to new conditions and thrive in changing environments. Embracing change, staying curious, being resilient, problem-solving creatively, managing emotions, and effective communication were essential skills in navigating life's challenges.

Fulfillment in Music and Family

While creating a supportive environment for our family, I found another avenue of fulfillment through music. Discovering music therapy sparked the desire to attend my first national music therapy conference in San Diego (1990) which reinforced my commitment to creating The Music Therapy Project and founding SeminarConcerts International Inc. (Pinkerton, 1990).

My journey into music therapy was filled with challenges as I initially advocated for a music therapy degree program at U.N.L.V. (1990). Rick

Soule, the music department chair, agreed and supported the feasibili-
ty of attaining a music therapy degree while staying local with my large
family. However, ten years later, the new music department chair revealed
that a departed faculty member was adamantly against the music therapy
program, preventing it from being included in the department's strategic
plan, deeming it impossible to match Kansas City's standards. Also, during
that time, I was dealing with troubling communications from out-of-state
music therapists about my intentions with the lack of music therapy cre-
dentials.

Simultaneously, in 1990, amidst dealing with an alcoholic husband and
raising my 4-year-old daughter, I consulted an attorney. I meticulously
followed her advice: record abusive episodes, inventory household items,
and secretly move out. My mother doubted my decisions, but with the help
of friends Tony Wells and Darlene Mea, I quickly moved in temporarily
with music therapist Linda and her husband. Working temp jobs and gigs,
I met Joe K., an architect and guitarist who offered a back office for my new
business, SeminarConcerts International Inc., and I accepted the support
of another mother from our new apartment complex to provide daycare
for my daughter.

Despite these challenges, I presented SeminarConcerts with Linda (Starr,
1990) to expand Las Vegas programs. I founded the nonprofit Center for
Creative Therapeutic Arts and received C.E. provider approval for course
accreditation from the Nevada State Board of Nursing. In 1991, I met and
married Dennis and birthed baby Michael in 1992. We moved into our first
house, transitioning from apartment living, and navigated the complexities
of raising each other's children, supported by our faith-centered life. Our

children's positive response to our union reinforced our commitment to providing healthy family experiences.

In 1992, we moved to St. George, Utah, where Dennis accepted a new job, and I became the first Development Director for Tuacahn Arts & Humanities Complex. My business calls were forwarded to St. George, allowing me to continue working shows in Las Vegas. Despite my second-trimester miscarriage of twins, I continued working and coordinating with builders on the construction of our new home. During this period, I pursued alternative music therapy education through AAMT - the American Association for Music Therapy, supported long-distance by music therapist Jacqueline Birnbaum. Concurrently, I wrote "The Sound of Healing" with a ghostwriter, published by Alliance Publishing in New York.

By 1996, the strain of commuting led us to move back to Las Vegas, where Dennis found a new job, and we purchased a home. I provided music therapy at a girls' group home for nearly seven years, and it became my official internship site. When NAMT - the National Association for Music Therapy and AAMT, merged in 1998, my education program became obsolete, prompting me to finish my bachelor's degree at Thomas Edison State University. With support from Barbara Crowe at A.S.U., I completed my music therapy equivalency and passed the national exam in 2002. Throughout this journey, my family faced challenges. Our eldest son, Thomas, struggling with drug abuse, was supported with special education, alternative schooling, and therapy and now thrives in managing his own construction business. Our middle son Tim thrived in bowling and now enjoys a casino management career, and our youngest son Michael shifted from violin performances to the Army Reserve and now has a corporate career in risk finance management.

Reflecting on these experiences, I've learned the importance of balancing passions with family responsibilities. In the past, I often prioritized work over family. Now, I give my 4-year-old (grand)daughter the attention she desires. Working virtually from home makes it easier to balance work and family. Here are some tips I practice daily:

1. **Set Priorities and Plan:** Identify what's most important and create a schedule that effectively balances your time and energy.

2. **Communicate with Family:** Discuss your goals with your family and listen to their feedback to maintain harmony.

3. **Set Realistic Goals:** Break your goals into smaller, manageable tasks and stay flexible to adapt to family needs.

4. **Involve Your Family:** Find ways to include your family in your interests and use their support to stay motivated.

5. **Practice Self-Care:** Take care of your physical and mental health, ensuring enough rest and personal time.

6. **Celebrate Small Wins:** Acknowledge your progress and share successes with your family to stay motivated.

7. **Seek Inspiration and Support:** Find role models and join supportive communities to stay inspired.

These strategies have helped me navigate the complexities of my dual roles. They have allowed me to balance my career aspirations and responsibilities better as a mother, wife, and caregiver. By incorporating these practices into my daily routine, I can stay grounded and focused on what truly matters.

Looking back on my journey, blending the demands of a career with family responsibilities has been both challenging and rewarding. From my early immersion in music to the transformative path of music therapy, every step has been marked by perseverance, growth, and an unwavering commitment to my passions. Creating a nurturing and supportive family environment has been paramount alongside these professional endeavors. Each relocation and every new venture taught us the importance of adaptability, communication, and unity.

Our experiences have underscored the significance of a strong support network, from the life-changing impact of adopting Kaylan later in life to the numerous moves driven by the pursuit of better opportunities. Establishing professional connections, integrating diverse family dynamics, and employing practical strategies like vision boards and the Virtues Project have all contributed to our resilience and success.

Throughout my journey, blending the demands of a career with family responsibilities has been both challenging and rewarding. From my early immersion in music to the transformative path of music therapy, every step has been marked by perseverance, growth, and an unwavering commitment to my passions. Creating a nurturing and supportive family environment has been paramount alongside these professional endeavors. Each relocation and every new venture taught us the importance of adaptability, communication, and unity.

My passionate commitment to fostering a family-like atmosphere extended to my professional life as well. As the Internship Director at Music4Life®, I had the privilege of mentoring my last two interns, Donnie Lee, III, and Ford Ferrara, during 2018-2019. Their internships were crafted to be supportive family units, nurturing their development as professional music therapists. This approach, anchored in the Affiliate Site agreement with the Directors of Music Therapy at West Virginia University and Florida Gulf Coast University, Drs. Dena Register and Michael Rohrbacher allowed them to grow both personally and professionally. They successfully completed their internships (amidst major stress, such as suddenly relocating the business), graduated with a Bachelor's degree in music therapy, and passed the certification exam through cbmt.org. Additionally, they graduated from the nine-month Music4Life Music Medicine Practitioner program and now hold full-time positions in recovery and hospice care. Working with Donnie and Ford was a true honor, witnessing Ford's transformation into manhood and Donnie's rise to Karaoke Champion of Nevada. Their achievements are a testament to the power of a supportive, family-like internship experience.

Reflecting on these experiences, I realized that balancing passions with family life taught me invaluable lessons about setting priorities, maintaining open communication, and embracing flexibility. The balance is fluid, requiring constant adjustments and a deep understanding of personal and family needs. Celebrating small victories, practicing self-care, and involving loved ones in your pursuits are crucial steps in this journey.

As you navigate your path, remember that balancing your passions with family is dynamic. Celebrate your wins, be patient with yourself and your loved ones, and set a positive example by pursuing your dreams while caring for those who matter most. This approach enriches your life and creates a fulfilling and harmonious environment for everyone involved.

11

TURNING "NO" INTO "YES" SERVING OTHERS

W riting my first book was like setting out on an uncharted adventure, filled with encouragement and wisdom from my Marketing Consultant, Donna. Her deceptively simple advice to "just write one word on a page" dissolved my mental block. Slowly but surely, one word led to another. Before I knew it, I had crafted "Music: The Stress-Release System in 3 Steps" (Pinkerton, 1993), marking the beginning of my literary journey nine years before becoming a certified music therapist.

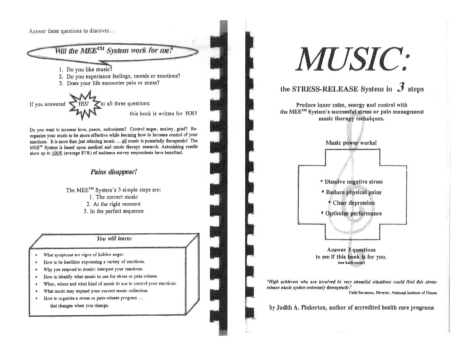

However, the path to publishing my next book brought its challenges. After the initial triumph, I faced a barrage of rejections. Manuscript after manuscript was sent out to dozens of publishers. Each met with a polite but firm "no." It was disheartening, to say the least. Determined, I looked into self-help books and attended self-publishing forums, absorbing all the knowledge I could about capturing a publisher's interest.

Then, in 1995, a breakthrough occurred. Two years after my first book was self-published, Dorothy Harris of Alliance Publishing in New York saw potential in my work and agreed to publish "The Sound of Healing: Create Your Own Music Program for Better Health" (January 1996). The contract was a sign of hope, offering validation and practical support. It included the assistance of a ghostwriter, Kate Fischer, and a $2,000 signing bonus, which, in today's terms, would be equivalent to $4,000.

With this new collaboration, I began another challenging yet exhilarating chapter of my writing journey. The task at hand was monumental, but with the support of Kate and Dorothy's encouragement, I felt ready to tackle it. Little did I know that this experience would further solidify my commitment to integrating music and healing. Billboard Magazine noted, "...to dispel a temporary bad mood, this book can be an invaluable resource" (Rosenblum, 1996). This book set the stage for my future endeavors as a music therapist and author.

Those were the days of fax machines when deadlines felt like insurmountable mountains. The agreement demanded that I deliver a 195-page manu-

245

script in six months—an impossible feat. To meet this daunting deadline, I immersed myself in the world of music, forcing myself to become an expert in all genres. Finding a buddy at Tower Records Las Vegas was like a lifeline, guiding me through the vast ocean of music knowledge, supplemented by an intensive educational course I consumed in one weekend.

Kate Fischer, my ghostwriter, was relentless in her support, flooding me with news articles and books to devour. I also conducted countless interviews with people who harnessed music's power for healing. Halfway through this whirlwind process, Dorothy Harris threw a curveball: she decided the book should be structured so that readers could start with any chapter that caught their interest. This meant splitting up all stories into multiple parts, requiring multiple authorizations, and reorganizing the content.

At the same time, I was commuting for shows in Las Vegas, managing my businesses, and supporting my husband with our blended family of four children, ages 3 to 11. It was a high-wire act, balancing professional and personal responsibilities. Yet, making each chapter self-standing was a stroke of genius. Alyssa Janney, Music4Life's product development consultant, later saw the potential in this format and suggested creating a new series of 12 books. Each book would update a chapter from "The Sound of Healing" with the latest research, clinical evidence, and music insights. We began with Chapter 1, "One New Way to Listen, Many Ways to Heal." It culminated in the publication of my first Amazon book in this series, "Music's Power to Heal: Your Emotional Mind" (Pinkerton, 2021).

Another instance of turning a "no" into a resounding "yes" happened when the publisher of "The Sound of Healing" went out of business. Just as I achieved my board certification as a music therapist in 2002, the rights to my book reverted to me. This unexpected turn of events opened up a golden opportunity. I seized the moment to update and re-publish the book in 2003, this time with the unwavering support of my husband, Dennis Burkhardt. We poured our hearts into the second edition, which featured a striking new cover adorned with purple accents, symbolizing healing and creativity. Alongside this visual transformation, my freshly earned MT-BC (Music Therapist-Board Certified) credential proudly graced the cover. We also introduced a revised byline: "Customize Your Music for Enhanced Well-being," reflecting the book's evolved content and my deepened expertise.

This experience was more than just a re-publication; it was a testament to resilience and the power of turning setbacks into stepping stones. With Dennis by my side, we breathed new life into "The Sound of Healing,"

ensuring it could continue touching lives and promoting music's transformative power.

Rejection to Recognition

In 1991, while I was an active member of the Musician's Union of Las
Vegas Local 369, I discovered the SONG grant program through the
Music Performance Trust Fund (MPTF). This program offered funding
for union members to perform free public concerts, a golden opportunity for musicians. Excited, I submitted a request for funding support
for my 5-piece band, SoundSynergy, to perform healing music seminars.
However, my proposal was rejected because it focused on healing music,
which wasn't a priority for the Fund during that decade. Undeterred, I
refused to let this setback halt my mission. I sought alternative funding
sources and continued to champion the cause of healing through music.
My persistence paid off, and we could perform our seminars, planting seeds
of musical healing that would grow over time.

Fast forward to 2020, and the landscape has changed dramatically. The
NYC Mayor's Office of Media and Entertainment, in collaboration with
NYC hospitals and the local musician's union, initiated a program to
provide healing performances in response to the COVID-19 pandemic.
This was a significant validation of efforts like mine, which had begun
with humble performances in places like the lobby of St. Martin Hospital
in 2008. Over the decades, these efforts have become integral to music
therapy practices across the USA. Seeing the evolution of MPTF's stance
was incredibly gratifying. It was a testament to the growing recognition of
music's therapeutic power and a validation of the work many of us had

tirelessly advocated for. My journey from that initial rejection to witnessing healing music being embraced on such a large scale was a profound reminder that perseverance and belief in music's transformative power can change the world.

Music for the Soul

St. Rose Dominican Hospitals is pleased to present
healing music for our patients in partnership with
music therapist, Judith Pinkerton, MT-BC, and Music 4 Life.

HEALING MUSIC CONCERT PREMIER
Monday, December 1, 2008
4:00 – 7:00 p.m.
St. Rose Dominican Hospitals - San Martin Campus
8280 West Warm Springs Road

Featuring Performances By:
Josh Capp (former pediatric patient), piano
Chaplain Richard Smith, harp
Judith Pinkerton, violin
Michael Burkhardt, violin
Christina Hanschke, flute
Gary Queen, guitar
Jeffrey Neiman, piano

Enjoy refreshments and the unveiling of the 1,000-piece
Holiday Village, donated by Gail and George Tomaio.

Join us each month as we feature different
healing music concerts at San Martin.

For information, call 702-616-4910.

Tuning Into Legislation

Senator Moises Denis became our champion after he participated in our Governor's Mansion event in 2007, attending with his father. He was willing to sponsor the music therapy license bill, but I had to find the health board willing to house the license. Finding the right health board to house the license proved a formidable challenge. Given my long-standing role as a Continuing Education provider for the State Board of Nursing since 1990, this board would be the perfect fit. However, the cost to update their computer system to accommodate only seven music therapists in the entire state was prohibitively high—around $20,000. This was a significant setback, but it did not deter us.

The path forward required creative thinking and relentless advocacy. In 2008, after exhaustive exploration, I finally found the Nevada State Board of Massage Therapy willing to house the music therapy license. Unfortunately, we were on a very tight time frame with the 2009 legislative session starting and only four months to process through both Senate and Assembly. As the Legislative Counsel rewrote the board's regulatory verbiage to include music therapists, they accidentally omitted language prohibiting prostitutes from getting a massage therapy license. Because of the urgency, there was no time to make changes. When that occurred, I just prayed that the bill would die quickly.

Despite this setback, Senator Denis's determination shone through. Reflecting on this period, he shared, "In 2009 Judith Pinkerton asked me to pass a bill to license Music Therapists. At the time Nevada had seven Music Therapists. Many thought it was a 'feel good bill' and a waste of time, but

I knew how music could help to heal people. The bill didn't pass. Judith didn't give up and neither did I because we knew it was the right thing to do." His persistence was instrumental. In 2011, he proposed the bill again with modifications, including the State Department of Health and Human Services managing the license. This time, the bill passed, making Nevada the first state in the country to license a music therapist.

Senator Denis's proactive approach led him to contact Mike Willden, the NV Department of Health & Human Services Director, who agreed to house the music therapy license within his department, ensuring no fiscal impact. This pivotal conversation led to the creation of Senate Bill 190, which began its journey through both legislative houses. The process was anything but smooth. We faced numerous challenges, including staunch opposition from the mental health lobbyist. Each concern raised required a well-prepared, assertive response. Senator Denis had already secured a pre-confirmation from Governor Sandoval that he would sign the bill if passed. An interesting twist came when dietitians, whose own failed bill, rewrote their legislation to mirror SB-190. As a result, the Department of Health & Human Services now offers licenses for music therapists and dietitians.

Manal Toppozada, MA, LPMT, MT-BC, Founder and Executive Director of Note-Able Music Therapy Services in Reno, Nevada, has worked with Judith in various capacities for nearly two decades, recalls, "Between 2007 and 2011, Judith created and chaired the Nevada State Music Therapy Task Force. Her tireless advocacy during those years resulted in increased funding for music therapy throughout the state. Her commitment and networking also resulted in the passage of Senate Bill 190, which made

Nevada the second* state in the country to create a state license for music therapy." This legislation has had a lasting impact on countless individuals in our state who have benefited from the increased recognition and legitimization of the field.

Governor Sandoval signs Senate Bill 190 (2011) for Music Therapy State Licensure. Left to right: Manal Toppozada, Senator Denis, Governor Sandoval, Judith Pinkerton, Diane Bell

Senator Denis's gratitude encapsulates the journey: "We were the first in the country to license a music therapist. Since then music therapists are now recognized in 18 states. Music Therapists are doing amazing things using rhythm and melody to heal. Thanks, Judith for believing in me. Together we did something incredible."

State of Nevada
Department of Health and Human Services
Division of Health
Bureau of Health Care Quality and Compliance

Date Issued: 11/02/2011
Date of Expiration: 11/02/2014

License Number: 11-001

This is to Certify that **Judith A. Pinkerton**

Has been found to possess the qualifications for licensure of:

Music Therapist

And accordingly under the provisions of Nevada Revised Statutes Title 54, this license is issued.

Richard Whitley M.S. / Administrator

* **Note**: North Dakota was the first to create a state license for music therapy, with Governor Dalrymple signing SB 2271 into law on April 26, 2011, but it did not start issuing licenses until January 2012. Nevada Governor Sandoval signed SB 190 into law on June 3, 2011, and Nevada issued the first music therapy license to Judith Pinkerton on November 2, 2011.

 Read our legislative story featured in the American Music Therapy Association's podcast with this QR code.

Transforming Negativity

In the course of my life and career, I've encountered numerous negative experiences that tested my resolve and passion. Each experience could have been a stopping point, but instead, they served as profound learning opportunities, whereby each negative ordeal evolved into positive considerations utilizing a vital life skill: reflecting in nature to mindfully allow the next steps. This life skill was encouraged by a Dimond High School teacher, requiring my class to enter the nearby forest to create a poem about life deciphered from nature. I encourage you to transform negative experiences into positive outcomes by involving various psychological, practical, nature-enhanced, problem-solving strategies to help reframe your perspective and build resilience to thrive through adversity.

Here are twelve techniques, including references to nature, to achieve thought transformation.

1. **Cognitive Reframing.** Consider changing how you think about the negative event to alter its emotional impact.

- Example: Instead of seeing a contract loss as a failure, view it as an opportunity to explore new contracts.

- Related to Nature: Imagine a forest fire that seems destructive, realizing it initiates new growth and rejuvenation.

2. **Mindfulness and Acceptance.** Embrace the present moment by accepting unsettling emotions without judgment.

- Example: Listen to your prescriptive playlist to shift emotions, observing thoughts and feelings about the setback similar to watching your experience as a movie.

- Related to Nature: Watch clouds pass in the sky, viewing your thoughts and emotions as transient and not permanent.

3. **Gratitude Practice.** Focus on what is working positively in your life to counterbalance the negative experience.

- Example: Write in your gratitude journal daily, listing things you're thankful for.

- Related to Nature: Reflect on the beauty of a sunset or a blooming flower to remind yourself of the wonderful things in life that blossom daily.

4. **Positive Visualization.** Imagine positive outcomes and scenarios to generate determination, hope, and optimism.

- Example: Visualize yourself succeeding in future endeavors, including printing pictures to place on a vision board in your contemplation area of your home. This will motivate you to overcome current challenges.

- Related to Nature: Picture yourself walking through a serene forest or along a calm beach to evoke peace and fulfillment. Then, notice the nearby water becoming a mighty river that carves its path through the toughest rocks, growing stronger and more defined with each obstacle it overcomes.

5. **Adopt "This Too Shall Pass" Mindset.** Recognize that all experiences, whether good or bad, are temporary.

- Example: Remind yourself during difficult times that this current situation is not permanent and will change.

- Related to Nature: Notice the season you are experiencing. When winter is harsh, it is followed by the rebirth and growth of spring. When spring has unpredictable weather, it is followed by summer's strength and clarity. When summer's heat is intense, it is followed by fall's embrace of diverse colors. When fall releases vibrant leaves, it is followed by winter's period of rest and reflection.

6. **Find Meaning in Adversity.** Seek to understand, evolve personal growth, and renew purpose from negative experiences.

- Example: Reflect on a previous difficult experience that made you stronger, more transparent, honest (no hidden agenda), or compassionate.

- Related to Nature: Imagine a butterfly emerging from its chrysalis when its wings grow stronger as it struggles to break free.

7. **Practice Self-Compassion.** Be kind to yourself during times of difficulty, recognizing that you are not unique with suffering.

- Example: Talk to yourself in the same tone and with the same understanding you would share with a friend.

- Related to Nature: Observe the tree that continues to stand tall and grow despite the storms it endures.

8. **Engage in Nature-Based Therapy.** Consider a nature-related activity to reduce stress and improve well-being.

- Example: Consider hiking, gardening, flying, swimming, fishing, or camping to cultivate harmony and rejuvenation.

- Related to Nature: Observing nature's resilience, such as a plant growing through concrete, can inspire personal resilience.

9. **Practice Radical Acceptance.** Fully accept the reality of your situation, including aspects you cannot change, to validate adversity.

- Example: Accept that loss occurred and focus on how to move forward rather than dwelling on what could have been or should have happened.

- Related to Nature: Just as a river flows around obstacles, learn to adapt to and flow with life's challenges.

10. **Journal with Reflective Writing.** Write about your experience with emotion to gain clarity and insight.

- Example: Journal about a setback, writing with a stream of consciousness that begins with expressing your feelings, incorporating lessons learned, then shifts into identifying the silver lining (positive prospects).

- Related to Nature: Think of your thoughts and feelings as part of the natural cycle, akin to the moon's influence on the ebb and flow of the tides (Kim, 2019).

11. **Build a Supportive Network.** Surround yourself with positive people who provide immediate validation, perspective, comfort, and encouragement.

- Example: Share your experience with a friend or join a support group to connect with others who understand. If you find a friendship is eroding due to repetitive regrets, engage with the other eleven techniques to develop healthy expressions and save a meaningful friendship.

- Related to Nature: Like a forest where trees support each other through interconnected roots, seek out and build supportive connections.

12. **Engage in Creative Activities.** Use creative outlets to validate, express, and transform unsettled emotions.

- Example: Painting, coloring, woodwork, knitting, writing, or playing music can channel emotions with positive expressions.

- Related to Nature: Just as nature creates beauty through patterns and cycles, use creativity to find beauty and meaning in your experiences.

Apply these techniques to reframe negative experiences in a way that nurtures growth and resilience with a positive vision for life.

A Life Dedicated to Serving Others

My personal motto of "seeking to serve" embodies a philosophy of living where my actions and intentions are guided by my commitment to helping and contributing positively to others. This mindset has profoundly impacted my life through several lenses: psychological well-being, social connections, professional success, and spiritual growth. Adopt a "seeking to serve" motto to enrich your life by enhancing well-being, relationships, professional success, and spiritual growth.

In the spring of 1980, after leaving JCPenney, I found myself in Alaska, seeking new ways to contribute to the community. I joined the United Methodist Women and soon became the statewide Secretary on the Board of Directors. This role required me to travel from coast to coast, attending meetings and progressive rallies. Each journey deepened my commitment to service and taught me the value of connecting with people from diverse backgrounds.

Years later, I took another step in my service journey by mentoring high school students and teaching the first music therapy 3-credit introductory course at UNLV–University of Nevada, Las Vegas (2009). Three of those students were so inspired that they completed their degrees out of state and became certified music therapists. This experience reaffirmed my belief in the transformative power of education and mentorship.

Service through the media became another avenue for me to reach out and help others. In 1997, I produced weekly Music4Life Radio Shows as the host of "The Sound of Healing" on KLAV AM radio. This later transitioned to internet radio on AllTalkRadio, BlogTalkRadio, and iTunes Podcasts as Music4LifeUSA. All radio shows and podcasts featuring dozens of interviews and music therapy-related topics are accessible through TheMusic4Life.com, where they are live-streamed and archived. Sharing the healing power of music with a broader audience was immensely rewarding.

As a third-generation Rotarian, I embraced numerous volunteer opportunities and the guiding principles of the Four-Way Test. This nonpartisan and nonsectarian ethical guide, translated into more than 100 languages, asks: "Of the things we think, say or do: Is it the TRUTH? Is it FAIR to all concerned? Will it build GOODWILL and BETTER FRIENDSHIPS? Will it be BENEFICIAL to all concerned?" These questions have continually guided my actions, ensuring my contributions are ethical and impactful.

My involvement with the Western Region Chapter of the American Music Therapy Association (WRAMTA) from 2007 to 2017, including serving as President-Elect/President/Past President, demonstrated my dedication to professional growth and community service. I chaired the Las Vegas Music Therapy Conference (2010), relying on essential staff from my nonprofit, mentored nine interns from eight states as Internship Director, and helped organize numerous conferences and continuing education sessions.

Initiating the International Foundation for the Healing Arts in California with music therapy colleagues and dear friends Barbara Reuer/

MusicWorxInc.com and Helen Dolas/AbleArtsWork.org and founding the nonprofit CCTA–Center for Creative Therapeutic Arts in Nevada further expanded my service reach. From 1990 to 2010, CCTA provided thousands of grant/state-funded music therapy programs throughout Southern Nevada. I contributed to the field by educating students and allied health professionals about music therapy, and advocating for music therapy in many different settings through brief powerful, inclusive demonstrations, and delivering numerous conference presentations.

In addition to my professional service, I developed DIY programs and products to support mental health, including the "6 Habits of Music Medicine" curriculum taught through mental health organizations. As a lifetime member of CEO Space International, I interact with CEOs in high-level think tanks focused on mutual support and service.

Through these varied experiences, I have seen firsthand how serving others can lead to profound personal fulfillment. Whether through teaching, media, professional organizations, or community initiatives, each act of service has enriched my life and strengthened my commitment to making a positive impact on the world. Serving others not only benefits them but also leads to a more meaningful and fulfilling life for yourself.

Empowering Others Through Music

The journey of empowering others through music therapy began with a transformative milestone on November 2, 2011, when I earned my first music therapy license in the USA. This achievement opened doors I had never imagined. The CEO of a recovery center, influenced by a nurse educator who had witnessed the benefits of my music therapy presentations, reached out to me. Her persistent advocacy led to an invitation to join the new Solutions Wellness Campus. Taking a significant risk, I signed an escalating lease agreement and began building Music4Life's business. I established a Health Club, sold memberships for wellness classes, recruited and trained a variety of facilitators, and delivered more than 1,000 drum circles in partnership with REMO Inc. This bold step laid the foundation for a thriving community benefiting from wellness programs and music therapy.

Initially, I started with a single private group at a residential addiction treatment facility. However, the demand quickly grew with strategic advocacy, leading to several private sessions a day, seven days a week, across multiple facilities. One of these facilities housed 148 beds, with group sizes ranging from 12 to 36 clients. Typically, music therapy groups are most effective with no more than 15 people, with an ideal size of six. Despite this, the CEO and Clinical Director wanted music therapy sessions integrated with the staff therapists during the day. As a result, I facilitated larger groups and tested various music-based clinical interventions. Throughout this process, including significant client feedback, I discovered a way to maximize results utilizing the Music Medicine Protocol, which included psycho-education, music-making, meditations, prescriptive playlist group and individual sessions, emotional processing, and recovery therapy themes.

The impact of music therapy extended beyond addiction treatment facilities to various communities. One memorable encounter involved a state leader whom I met in a small employee lunchroom at a Las Vegas contracted facility. I discovered the music he loved and played it to guide our advocacy meeting in his Carson City conference room. A state grant reviewer later shared that he told his staff his wife had sent him a present in the form of a violinist. This is one example of many types of meaningful, personalized encounters that music therapists create, leading to legislative recognition and funding for music therapy.

Judy Simpson, MT-BC, Managed Healthcare Professional, and Director of Government Relations for the American Music Therapy Association, shared her experience, stating, "Supporting the Nevada Music Therapy Task Force, I arrived in Carson City to fully assist Judith Pinkerton's 3-day schedule of meetings and events, and returned to Washington D.C. with methods firmly imprinted in my mind to support other states replicating what occurred. Now we have 18 states recognizing music therapy."

My work also extended to the City of Las Vegas Young Offenders (YO) Recovery Court, where I created a twelve-week music therapy program after presenting at a Las Vegas Domestic Violence Conference (2005). An attending therapist was so impressed that she recommended my services to Judge Cedric Kerns, who started the YO Court for young adults in 2010. Over several years, I worked with these young adults, helping them navigate their recovery journey. Judge Cedric Kerns (Ret.) reflected on the impact of Music4Life's methods, stating, "Music4Life's music therapy methods supported YO (Youth Offender) Recovery Court members who were ages 18-24, processing emotions connected to trauma which made it easier for them to talk about the trauma with their counselor. Over several years, the music therapy methods Judith utilized with prescriptive listening and music-making involving drum circles supported YO members getting another chance at life." This endorsement highlights the profound effect that structured music therapy can have on individuals, particularly those dealing with trauma, by facilitating emotional processing and communication.

Additionally, I have had the privilege of working with a client, "Annalisa" (pseudonym), for almost eight years. Annalisa is an intelligent, well-liked, and very privacy-conscious 80-year-old who has faced significant challenges throughout her life. Growing up in an extremely dysfunctional and abusive large family led to constant anxiety and genetically predisposed depression. Raised Catholic, she was sent to a convent at age 14. Her memories of nine years in two different convents are filled with rejection and punishment, with leadership dealing with her depression by forcing her to undergo multiple terrifying electroconvulsive therapy (ECT) sessions.

During Annalisa's 46-year marriage to her kind and faithful husband, who was a Marine veteran, she worked full-time and cared continually for him as his physical condition deteriorated. He died within three weeks of diagnosis almost six years ago. Since then, she survived the isolation of the COVID pandemic and the death of her beloved kitty. Enduring a 30-year period of attempted suicide three times, Annalisa was admitted against her will to five psychiatric hospitals over a 50-year period, including one stay when she was raped. Living with post-traumatic stress (PTS) and daily suicidal ideation, Annalisa was referred to music therapy by another client.

Nearly two years ago, Annalisa declined to continue anti-depression and anti-anxiety medications, against the advice of her physician, due to significant physical problems caused by those meds. Recognizing the power of music therapy, her physician regularly prescribes it due to Annalisa's continual struggle with saying "No" to life, but immediately responds with "Yes" to life because her prescriptive playlists support emotion regulation. Through tailored music-based interventions, from drumming and singing to songwriting, her prescriptive playlists provide a core support system for life. She has progressed from being a shut-in to driving, maintaining eye contact, and overcoming her fear of flying by traveling to another state to participate in a remote self-development retreat. Annalisa now utilizes her 18th updated Music Medicine Pill®, plus several other types of prescriptive playlists, to address prevailing therapeutic goals. Annalisa continues to survive by mitigating alarming emotions—anxiety, anger, depression, and sadness, with nurturing love, peace, and joy; she desires to thrive in life.

In addiction recovery, my role as a music therapist in Las Vegas spanned several residential addiction treatment programs from 2012 to 2024. I managed a large caseload at several sites, surviving through the tenures of five CEOs and five Clinical Directors. Jim Goins, LPC, Clinical Director at Desert Hope Treatment Center, praised the program, stating, "I'm really very grateful and very proud of the music therapy that Judith Pinkerton provides on a very large scale. We are a 148-bed facility here in Las Vegas, Nevada, and her music therapy program allows us to divide up our groups into 15 to 30 people. Her approach helps unlock certain areas for clients that they haven't been able to navigate in the past. They find common ground with others, learn how to process events and traumas emotionally, and healthily regulate feelings and emotions to prevent relapse."

Treating more than 11,000 patients in residential addiction treatment centers, Music4Life's Music Medicine Protocol has proven to be a favored music therapy approach. It supports practical life skills utilizing music-based interventions that target therapeutic recovery goals such as reducing anxiety, anger, depression, and grief while enhancing peace and happiness. It also improves Emotional Intelligence, helping individuals reconnect with family and friends, build new healthy relationships, and address mental health issues that may have contributed to substance dependence. This approach creates a safe atmosphere for self-reflection and sharing, introduces and reinforces strategies for preventing relapse, and teaches healthy coping strategies for stress and emotions.

Patients have reported that music therapy sessions infused with the Music Medicine Protocol significantly support their recovery goals. They have shared insights such as using music to control mood, lift spirits, and neutralize emotions. One survey of 603 patients at an addiction detox treatment facility who experienced a one-time 30-minute Music Medicine Pill® guided meditation showed that 94% improved their Emotional Intelligence and 91% improved their mood state. Numerous individual case reports reveal typical therapeutic goals achieved, including reduced stress, frustration, tiredness, insomnia, anxiety, anger, grief, depression, confusion, nightmares, irritability, and worry. Patients also reported enhanced engagement with life, improved ability to focus, communicate, and relax, and increased happiness and job performance.

The Journey of Self-Improvement

The journey of self-improvement has been an ongoing process of learning and growth, both personally and professionally. Since our marriage, my husband, Dennis Burkhardt, has been a constant source of support. He alternated between the Board Chair and Executive Director roles for my nonprofit as I pursued music therapy certification for over two years. Our nonprofit eventually moved to the West Charleston Campus of the Community College of Southern Nevada. Dennis and I completed the NxLevel Business Training to further our growth, graduating in early 2005. During this training, we were asked a core question: "Why be in business?" My answers included helping others, the thrill, fulfilling a dream, personal growth, the challenge, maximizing talent, independence, money, and pleasure.

My primary focus is serving others which translates into financial ebb and flow of business. As an example, after leaving the Las Vegas show business (2004), I hired another music therapist to take over my caseload and income, allowing me to seek more contracts and re-establish my earnings. This cycle of growth continued as my staff expanded to twelve by 2010. Supporting the nonprofit's funded programs while growing the Music4Life® brand and Music Medicine Protocol was challenging. Although we received significant funding and met our goals, the 2008 recession negatively impacted grants in Nevada. In late 2010, I attended CEO Space International, where there was tremendous interest from fellow CEOs, compelling me to aim high: scale the Music4Life Music Medicine Protocol for mass consumption. Due to the economic grant crisis, I had previously recommended to my nonprofit board that my position be deleted and allow the clinical director to continue managing CCTA. Although the shift of terminating my employment was less than ideal, I remained steadfast to the massive project at hand: scale Music4Life.

With support from family and friends and an expanded partnership with REMO Inc., Music4Life became the seventh Recreation Music Center they funded globally. I attended HealthRHYTHMS training and grew as a drum circle facilitator, attracting interest from professionals like Arthur Hull. Expanding wellness programs led to an opportunity to deliver a TEDx Talk at UNLV (2014). This was a monumental task as every word had to be written and memorized. I included a violin performance with a PowerPoint slideshow. A lesson learned: wait to share the video on social media, as thousands of early viewings don't count towards the official TEDx count.

Throughout my career, I sought continuous improvement through a dozen business locations from Anchorage to Las Vegas, moving when the location required change. In Anchorage, my Pinkerton Performances Agency operated from Old City Hall and the Alaska Conservatory of Music from an office within the Burger King franchise corporate offices, then a suite of business offices before expanding Star Services Inc. into a house converted into an office on K Street. Over three decades in Las Vegas, I worked from a home office, then shared a therapist's office, a cardiologist's library/conference room, a college campus, and during my transition from nonprofit to for-profit, an office in a Jewish-owned building. Finally, seven years on the Solutions Wellness Campus preceded the eventual transition to virtual home offices.

In 2014, I spent nine months with Amy Lynn Frost and Sandi Herrera of EducatorDynamics.com, creating a vision for Music4Life® to identify our culture and create a ripple effect of positivity. I recommend others undertake similar efforts for their families and companies. Music4Life's five Core Values encompass embracing change, showing up, taking action when healing is needed, expanding work and connections, being authentic, and building a supportive community. However, it's essential to go beyond merely identifying these core values; teams need to know how to act on them to truly embody and live by these principles.

Embracing change involves being open to new ideas, continuously seeking improvement, and fostering innovation. Showing up means committing fully to responsibilities, being present, and engaging actively with work and team members. Taking action when healing is needed requires recognizing and addressing emotional or physical healing through appropriate support. Expanding work and connections is about seeking growth opportunities, building relationships, and collaborating to broaden impact.

Being authentic means staying true to values, communicating honestly, and maintaining integrity. Building a supportive community involves fostering mutual respect, supporting colleagues, and contributing to a positive team culture. As Joanna McFarland, Co-founder of HopSkipDrive, aptly put it, "It's important to realize that a brand is much more than a logo and slogan. A brand is who your company is: how you function and make decisions." This philosophy has been integral to shaping the identity and mission of Music4Life®. By not only defining but also actively practicing our core values, we create a strong, cohesive culture that drives our mission forward, ensuring our impact is felt both within our organization and beyond.

Music4Life® Core Values: HEALS
- ♥ Embracing the flow of harmonious **HEALING** space
- ♥ Tangible **EXPANSION** vibrating continuously
- ♥ Learning through the tempo of **AUTHENTICITY**
- ♥ **LIKE-HEARTED** synergistic connections
- ♥ Orchestrating a **SUPPORTIVE**, healthy, happy global community

Encouraging PSYCH-K to release personal barriers is also valuable. In a session with Traci Beeson, a Certified PSYCH-K Facilitator, I released an attachment to death, which profoundly impacted my ability to support my family during life-threatening situations, such as my father's ICU experience two weeks later.

Advocating for my father and using music as a prescription for life made a significant difference. My cousin Wayne Moore, a Physician Assistant and Registered Nurse, was an invaluable advocate during my father's health crisis. His extensive medical background ensured my father received the immediate and appropriate care needed to save his life. As my father lay in the ICU, no longer struggling with his last breath, I was able to remain God-centered in the realm of death from the recent PYSCH-K focus and quickly adapted my violin performance to align with his physiological needs. This revitalized his spirit and played a significant role in his miraculous recovery, which was observed and documented by his medical team as scientifically unexplainable. My father continues to be better today than one year ago with my mother, both 93 and celebrating 72 years of marriage.

 Listen to JourneysDream.org podcast with psychologist Dr. Timothy Hayes, describing Judith's experience with her father in ICU, at 36:26.

Reflecting on my journey through the challenges and triumphs of writing, publishing, and expanding the reach of music therapy, it's clear that persistence and a commitment to serving others have been my guiding lights. From the early days of struggling to overcome mental blocks with the simple advice to "just write one word" and facing countless rejections from publishers to working with thousands of people wanting to recover their lives, each step has reinforced the power of resilience and innovation.

Earning the first music therapy license issued in the USA, this achievement opened new avenues for empowering others through music. Establishing Music4Life and integrating it into various communities, from addiction treatment facilities to broader public health initiatives, demonstrates the transformative power of music. Collaborations with REMO Inc., delivering the TEDxUNLV Talk, and producing a music therapy TV spot with Aflac, the Academy of Country Music, country superstar Chris Young, and two children in cancer remission have significantly underscored the impact of my work.

Throughout this journey, the support from my family, especially my husband Dennis, and the inspiration drawn from various mentors and colleagues have been invaluable. Whether advocating for legislative changes, mentoring students, or pioneering new therapeutic approaches, each experience has underscored the importance of a service-oriented mindset. As I continue to navigate the ever-evolving landscape of music therapy and self-improvement, I am reminded that the essence of my work lies in turning "no" into "yes," embracing challenges as opportunities, and continuously seeking to serve others.

12

THE POWER OF NETWORKING AND EMBRACING ENTREPRENEURSHIP

N etworking, especially within the legislative and mental health sec-
tors, has shaped my career path. It has offered invaluable lessons
in resilience, adaptability, and the importance of strategic relationships.
These fields demand a nuanced understanding of policy-making processes
and mental health advocacy's intricate dynamics. Engaging with professionals from diverse backgrounds has broadened my perspective, allowing
me to develop a multifaceted approach to networking that values collaboration and mutual support.

As I continued to hone these skills, I faced a significant turning point in my
career. At the end of 2010, I left my "baby," the nonprofit I had founded in
1990, the CCTA-Center for Creative Therapeutic Arts, to focus on scaling
Music4Life. This departure was fraught with emotional challenges but
ultimately led to a silver lining. I aligned with prominent CEOs through

CEO Space International, who saw the potential in the Music4Life brand and business.

Following my departure from CCTA, I registered as a lobbyist, albeit unpaid, to build a robust advocacy network aimed at passing a transformative bill in 2011. This bill, SB 190, sought to establish licensure for music therapists in Nevada, ensuring that the profession was recognized and regulated. This legislation marked a significant step forward for the music therapy field, providing the framework needed to legitimize and standardize the practice.

In establishing new offices, I focused on strengthening connections with music therapists across Nevada, Oregon, California, and beyond. This network was instrumental in supporting the passage of SB 190, sponsored by Senator Moises Denis. Key figures like Rachel Firchau Gonzalez from the Western Region Chapter of AMTA, Judy Simpson from AMTA (m usictherapy.org), and Drs. Dena Register and Kimberlee Sena Moore from CBMT.org supported members of the Nevada Music Therapy Task Force, immediately responding to legislative issues, ensuring we could address concerns swiftly and effectively.

The in-person meetings in Carson City were transformative, as was the multi-tasking required to communicate effectively with legislators. I learned the importance of presenting a united front, ensuring all music therapists spoke with one voice to avoid conflicting messages. This unity was essential when facing opposition from within our ranks. Expanding my network beyond Nevada proved invaluable. After I chaired the Western Region Music Therapy Conference in Las Vegas (2010), I continued to build connections nationally, serving as President-Elect, President, and Past President for WRAMTA.org (2011-2017). This broadened focus helped me move past the conflicts of 2010-2011 and aim for higher goals.

Effective networking is more than just making connections; it's about creating a synergy that transforms thought processes into collaborative opportunities. This concept, termed "Network Synergy," is about leveraging multiple networks into an interactive system of mutual support, advice, and opportunities.

One must first define their objectives and goals to achieve a synergized network. The starting point is to clarify the main objectives for business growth or personal development and establish clear, measurable goals to guide your efforts. Next, developing a collaborative mindset is essential. This can be achieved through workshops or panels focused on collaboration and mutual support, team-building activities promoting empathy, and sharing success stories to inspire your network with effective collaborations.

Offering mutual support is also integral to successful networking. Centralizing resources and information for easy access, establishing mentorship programs or expert Q&A sessions, and maintaining an opportunity board for job openings and collaborative projects can significantly enhance your network.

The emphasis on establishing the Music Medicine Protocol as an evidence-based practice was crucial in training music therapists. Because this protocol began with teaching nurses first (1990), then the general community and other professions (because I was a "therapeutic musician" - not a certified music therapist until 2002), I realized that developing the Music Medicine training further could benefit mental health providers to utilize music optimally. I also have a deep desire to work with non-music therapists because I worked in the healing music/therapy field for 15 years before finally getting certified. Even though the use of music is extremely popular, I respect the extensive training required for certification as music therapists observe, innovate, adapt, treat, assess, and document music-based interventions working with populations from womb to tomb. With a shortage of music therapists, it's important to train and harness the capability of more therapists to mitigate the growing unsettledness in our country through the effective application of music working like medicine.

The final aspect of Network Synergy is measuring and iterating your efforts to make a significant difference. Gather feedback from network members to understand their needs and experiences, use metrics to measure engagement and collaboration effectiveness, and regularly review and refine your networking approach based on this feedback.

An example of this approach developing in action is Music4Life's Key 2MEE.com Music App. Created with Network Synergy in mind, Music4Life is designed to unite people through music, transforming individual thought processes into a collaborative mindset. Utilizing multiple networks of music preferences and lifestyles creates an interactive system for mutual support. The objective is to encourage innovation and collaboration to improve mental health. This is developed through hosting mental health innovation and peer-mentoring sessions, integrating existing and new meetups, LinkedIn groups, and alums networks, enhancing Music4Life® programs, including Key2MEE®, with channels for different music genres, prescriptive playlists, mental health projects, and wellness interests. Additionally, a knowledge base and scheduled "office hours" with industry experts provide ongoing support. Surveys and engagement analytics measure network effectiveness and iterate based on feedback, ensuring the network remains vibrant and supportive.

Entrepreneurial Ventures in Music Therapy

The journey of founding and evolving multiple ventures in music therapy has shown me firsthand the importance of adaptability in entrepreneurship. Every step has taught me how necessary it is to pivot and adjust strategies in response to changing circumstances and new opportunities (Kirtley et al., 2020). Over the years, I have established a talent agency and a music conservatory, each with challenges and opportunities. The Center for Creative Therapeutic Arts has been a significant part of my life for 20 years, and Music4Life has been a passion project for 24 years. Both ventures required constant adaptation and strategic changes to stay relevant and successful.

Pivoting in entrepreneurship involves recognizing when current products or services no longer align with market needs and making substantial shifts in strategy. This allows quick, effective changes to increase revenue or enhance market position. Pivoting becomes necessary when significant investments yield minimal progress. Business growth stagnates, customer response could be better, intense competition stifles growth or only one aspect of the business gains traction.

Successful pivoting requires avoiding complacency, always striving for improvement, and acting on feedback from clients and stakeholders. Staying informed about industry trends and learning from competitors is crucial. Pursuing bold, disruptive changes rather than incremental improvements encourages innovative thinking and embracing radical ideas. Acting swiftly to match the pace of a rapidly changing market and proactively adapting to industry shifts are also vital.

My entrepreneurial journey is a series of such pivots. When my mental health prevented me from continuing in retail management, I pivoted into self-care, music, and self-employment. When my talent agency struggled by promoting only classical music, I expanded to include requested genres. As my talents grew beyond being a violinist and musician's union booking agent, I founded the Alaska Conservatory of Music and Star Services Inc. to fulfill a growing need in Anchorage, offering services as a booking agent, consultant, recording artist, concert promoter, music teacher, and nonprofit administrator. As the music conservatory continued to grow, I found a replacement manager and focused on building Star Services Inc.

Relocating to Las Vegas in 1989 required selling my business and seeking new opportunities as a professional violinist and music therapy advocate. As my family life in St. George, UT, was fraught with my absence, I convinced my husband to find a new job, and we moved back to Las Vegas in 1996. Immediately facing false rumors that affected my Las Vegas show orchestra work, I pivoted to find my first music therapy job at Catholic Charities of Southern Nevada, which evolved into my required internship. When not being a certified music therapist blocked my nonprofit work, I quickly engaged in a long-distance certification (music therapy equivalency) program in 1999 and eventually resigned as Director of Youth and Family Ministry at my church.

In 2004, when my vocation as a professional violinist no longer satisfied me, I pivoted to grant writing to grow music therapy programs and revenue. Internal challenges at my nonprofit music therapy agency in 2010 led me to focus on building the Music4Life® brand. Recognizing a revenue shortfall in 2012, I continued my partnership with REMO, Inc., establishing the drum circle business. As I explored serving new populations, I learned best practices for treating Substance Use Disorders, evolving the Music Medicine Protocol.

In 2019, when American Addiction Centers shut down Solutions Recovery, I quickly pivoted, suspending services at Desert Hope Treatment Center due to past-due invoices and finding new offices to support staff and build new contracts outside of addiction. Realizing Music 4 Life Inc. was not set up for mass consumption, I started Music 4 Life Technology Inc. in 2016 to exclusively distribute Music4Life's products and programs, which required conversions into digital and virtual formats. I also found a co-author and submitted a patent to scale the business through a music app.

When my daughter gave birth in 2019, my husband and I pivoted to accept custody and later adopted our (grand)daughter. The COVID pandemic in 2020 required another pivot to support my aging parents in another state, leading to co-locating between Southern Nevada and Northern Idaho, with Music4Life® becoming mostly virtual and digitized (storing significant drum inventory).

Innovation and thinking outside the box have been crucial throughout my entrepreneurial journey. Vision aligned with mission constantly drives me, pushing me to figure out who, what, where, when, and how while seeking mentors and colleagues for support. Friend and music therapist Jodi Winnwalker captures this sometimes lonely, image-conscious journey perfectly: "Judith is a sparkling jewel in a flowing gown. Scythe in hand, she forges forward blazing trails for our community. As a dynamic, respectful, and compassionate leader, Judith invites others to walk beside her encouraging creative thinking and collaboration."

Working alongside Alyssa Janney, as HealthRhythms Manager at Remo, Inc., was a pleasure. She innovated the Aroma Drum Stress Management System, incorporating the Music4Life Stress Brake CD I envisioned after working with military members in 2007-2008 (Pinkerton, 2010). From 2019-2023, we collaborated on Music4Life product development, creating new products and converting existing ones into virtual and digitized formats.

Alyssa's perspective on networking in entrepreneurship resonates deeply within ESTEAMHealth.com: "Networking in entrepreneurship is like filling an artist's palette, where each connection adds a unique color, blending resources and ideas into a masterpiece of collective success. The most astonishing realization about my networking success is that it began years ago, sparked by my admiration and appreciation for the work of experts who would later become my collaborators. Networking success is built on relationships."

These experiences taught me that embracing change and adapting fearlessly is crucial for long-term success and avoiding obsolescence. Innovating and pivoting are not just strategies but necessities for thriving in the ever-evolving entrepreneurship landscape.

Expanding the Reach of Music Therapy

In response to the evolving needs of the healthcare sector, I substantially broadened the scope of music therapy by developing the Music Medicine Protocol. This initiative began with training nurses and soon expanded to encompass a diverse array of non-music therapists. Gaining accreditation as a continuing education provider through the Nevada State Board for Nursing in 1990 was a strategic move that enhanced my credibility as a therapeutic musician. This accreditation allowed me to offer workshops to various professionals, including physicians, social workers, marriage and family therapists, and alcohol and drug counselors. This focus emphasized group continuing education workshops, which became particularly notable at Valley Health System with Music4Life's first Nurse Educator, Michele Nichols, RN, Chief Nursing Officer at Valley Hospital Medical Center Las Vegas.

As the Music Medicine Protocol evolved, I aimed to educate music therapists. However, with the shortage of music therapists predicted, it soon became apparent that the training could significantly benefit non-music therapists, such as psychologists, therapists, counselors, social workers, nurses, doctors, educators, coaches, caregivers, executives, musicians, parents, medical professionals, athletic trainers, nursing assistants, peer support specialists, and human resource professionals. The goal then expanded to differentiate the differences between music therapy and the Music Medicine Protocol. It became increasingly important to establish who the healing agent is.

As referenced in Chapter 1, a certified Music Therapist is the healing agent who utilizes music-based interventions within an established therapeutic relationship with the client to address agreed upon goals. In the Music Medicine Protocol, the music is the healing agent utilized by trained individuals for self-care, in their practice or supporting different environments.

The Music Medicine Protocol provides music therapy-informed strategies based on my work as a music therapist, which involves assessing, adapting, and innovating therapeutic applications across various populations, from birth to death, with methods refined through ongoing research and advanced training. This comprehensive approach has made the protocol invaluable for those who frequently use music in their work but may not fully understand how to optimize its therapeutic potential.

This path also highlights a common issue in the field—beginning practice before formal certification. I worked as a therapeutic musician for fifteen years prior to obtaining official certification in 2002, initially finding program certification support under the American Association for Music Therapy (AAMT), which later merged with the National Association for Music Therapy (NAMT) in 1998 to form the American Music Therapy Association (AMTA). This experience has instilled in me a deep understanding and patience for non-music therapists who incorporate music into their therapeutic practices.

The impact of these training initiatives has been profound, directly addressing the critical shortage of music therapists in the United States. While misleading online sources may claim there are 19,200 music therapists ("History of Music Therapy," n.d.), actual figures confirm there are only 10,368 (B. Dalsimer, Certification Board for Music Therapists, personal communication, June 12, 2024). The field is experiencing a significant deficit, with hundreds of jobs remaining unfilled annually, and the government now offering six-figure salaries to attract top talent. Additionally, music therapists are increasingly assuming supervisory roles, further signifying the growth and importance of this profession.

Music4Life is committed to authenticating the practice of music therapy and differentiating the work of certified music therapists from that of other health professionals who utilize music. Our certification training supports a broad spectrum of licensed clinicians and other health professionals, while our self-care and educational programs assist caregivers, executives, educators, students, parents, and musicians. These initiatives are designed to teach the application of music as a therapeutic tool grounded in the principles of neuroscience, psychology, and music therapy.

As we train both music therapists and those from other professional backgrounds to use the Music Medicine Protocol, we emphasize that music therapists do not own music; rather, it is a universal therapeutic medium. In today's turbulent times, both nationally and globally, understanding the impact of music listening habits on well-being is more crucial than ever. Music4Life's Protocol strives to equip music therapists with advanced training and to support other health professionals with appropriate skills to harness music's therapeutic power effectively, utilizing the Key2MEE Music App to address the urgent needs of diverse patient populations and, at the same time, advancing the field of music therapy.

The Future of Music Therapy

As we reflect on the evolving landscape of music therapy, the future holds exciting developments that promise to enhance its impact and reach. Innovative programming has emerged by mobilizing the expertise of music therapists and health professionals, inspired by personal experiences with Alzheimer's and dementia care. Research is increasingly focused on integrating music therapy into comprehensive healthcare solutions, specifically targeting these conditions.

A unique approach to networking in entrepreneurship has also played a crucial role, likened to filling an artist's palette with each connection and adding a distinctive color. This blend of resources and ideas creates a masterpiece of collective success, built fundamentally on strong relationships cultivated over time. This perspective underscores the importance of meaningful connections and collaborative efforts in advancing the field.

Moreover, the effectiveness of music therapy is being validated through new research, particularly in military and neuroscience contexts. Initiatives like Creative Forces, NeuroArts Blueprint, and Sound Health Network, championed by Renee Fleming and in collaboration with major organizations such as the American Music Therapy Association and Johns Hopkins University, are paving the way for significant advancements (Sima, 2021; "Sound Health Initiative," 2022; Fleming, 2024).

Encouraging an entrepreneurial spirit and innovative approaches in therapeutic practices is essential. Feedback from audiences and session participants serves as a portal to new information, allowing for continuous improvement and adaptation. Each interaction is an opportunity to learn and enhance future endeavors, ensuring the field remains vibrant and responsive to changing needs.

The music therapy industry has grown remarkably. It is now valued at $2.62 billion in the USA and is projected to reach $5.73 billion by 2031 ("Music Therapy Market Insights," 2024). This growth reflects the increasing recognition and demand for music therapy's therapeutic benefits.

Collaborative visions have driven much of this progress. For instance, the International Foundation for the Healing Arts, co-founded with two dear friends, exemplifies the entrepreneurial spirit that propels the industry forward. Though the foundation only survived up to ten years, it supported the groundwork for many private practices.

Notable figures like Barbara Reuer, PhD, MT-BC, CEO and Founder of MusicWorxInc.com, and Helen Dolas, Founder/CEO of AbleArtsWor k.org, have made significant contributions to the field of music therapy. Barbara's collaborations, such as our mutual inclusion in training manuals and the review of a colleague's book "Music of Hate, Music of Healing" (Pinkerton et al., 2007; Reuer, n.d.; Reuer et al., 2022), and graduating more than 170 music therapy interns, highlight her entrepreneurial passion and innovative insights, as she emphasizes the importance of risk-taking and robust processes. Helen's vision of inclusive, diverse communities has turned her creative arts therapy agency into a thriving enterprise, emphasizing strategic community-building and substantial team investments.

The Music4Life® system, known as the Music Medicine Protocol, trains teams of clinicians and connects them through the Key2MEE® Music App to users who request support managing moods with prescriptive playlists to reclaim joy, peace, and purpose in life. Promoting music's universal nature across genres, generations, and cultures, this holistic approach will support music therapy's continual evolvement by advancing contributions to the growing demand for published research.

The field of music therapy stands on the cusp of transformative growth, driven by innovative programming, comprehensive research, and a collaborative entrepreneurial spirit. By integrating music therapy into healthcare solutions, including Alzheimer's and dementia care, and validating its effectiveness through rigorous research, the scope and impact of this therapeutic modality are set to expand significantly. Networking and strong relationships play a vital role in this evolution, as illustrated by the collaborative success described by experts in the field.

The industry's impressive growth trajectory, backed by significant market value and projections, underscores the increasing recognition of music therapy's benefits. Contributions from pioneering figures and organizations have laid a solid foundation for future advancements, ensuring that music therapy remains a dynamic and essential component of holistic healthcare.

As music therapy evolves, it continues to address the increasing health and wellness needs of diverse populations across various cultures and generations. However, with only 10,368 qualified music therapists in the United States, there is a clear need to expand their capacity to support the estimated 58 million people experiencing mental health conditions (Pramanik, 2023). The holistic approach of the Music4Life® Music Medicine Protocol, facilitated by the Key2MEE® Music App, demonstrates the potential to scale music therapy-informed strategies effectively. This approach will manage moods, promote wellness, and enrich lives, ensuring a vibrant and impactful future for mental health care.

CONCLUSION

As you conclude "Thriving Through Adversity," it's time to reflect on the core themes that have shaped your journey. Start by becoming more aware of your music listening habits and be open to exploring new ones to avoid falling into Chronic Comfort Zones™. Your habitual listening patterns can either support or hinder your emotional well-being. By practicing prescriptive listening techniques regularly, you can actively build emotional fluidity, resilience, and intelligence. Repetitive use of these skills reinforces confidence, assertiveness, and creative problem-solving abilities, essential tools for navigating life's challenges.

The Key2MEE® Music App is an excellent resource to help you on this journey. The App increases awareness of Emotional Profiles and connects you to programs that strengthen critical thinking about music listening habits, prescriptive playlists, Chronic Comfort Zones and their impact on your emotional and mental health. While the Key2MEE Music App will eventually allow you to create prescriptive playlists to monitor your progress, minimize unsettledness, improve relaxation, and ignite joy as you follow your purpose in life, this feature is part of Phase 2, which is expected to launch by December 2024, pending funding. For real-time updates and progress, please refer to Key2MEE.com.

Integrating prescriptive music playlists into your healing journey can lead to lasting transformation. By using music intentionally, you can enrich your life, helping you thrive through adversity and reclaim joy, peace, and purpose. Sharing strategic uses of prescriptive music can support cathartic emotional processing, fostering a more harmonious world. Discover your passion and purpose using the SMILE process to nurture your entrepreneurial spirit. Turn lemons into lemonade by finding strength in transforming obstacles into growth opportunities. Incorporate core values in both your business and family life to align with daily challenges and balance life more effectively. Bounce back from rejection quickly, pivoting with remarkable agility and a resilient, innovative mindset.

In my work with major artists challenged by addiction, I have seen the insidious path they often tread. They create music from trauma and then endure relentless tours to cover production costs, reliving their trauma with each performance. This cycle often leads to substance use and, tragically, suicide. The music industry thrives on this model, creating complex confusion among fans and artists alike. The unsettled emotions of today are far more intense than those of three decades ago, requiring more intense musical matches. We must change the culture of music creation and consumption by following evidence-based music therapy-informed methods in the Music Medicine Protocol. This approach can help you thrive through adversity.

I encourage you to take specific actions after finishing this book: download the Key2MEE® Music App, share this book with others, and start a social circle where you can share music interests, listen actively, build empathy, and potentially save lives. To speak the Music4Life® language and communicate effectively with others about music, consider completing a Music4Life training. This will prepare you to discuss music from an educated perspective and deepen your connections with family, friends, colleagues, and strangers.

Recently, I connected with a young man who was delivering me home from the dealership's service department while awaiting the repair of my car. I immediately asked about the music he loved, which he shared. I played it on my phone, loved it, and surprised him with my candor and inquisitiveness. He shared more deeply about a book he was writing. It was a precious 15 minutes I will not forget. When I saw him at the dealership again, I was instantly recognized, with a smile and a twinkle in his eye. Building harmonious communities, one person at a time. One Lyft driver saved a young man from death by suicide, sharing meaningful conversation and music. Do your part.

If you're tired of feeling trapped, take some time to reflect on the book's content. Ask others about their favorite music, why they like it, when and where they play it, and how it makes them feel. As you build your prescriptive playlists, seek recommendations from others to fill in gaps, creating new friendships and dismantling barriers through shared music interests.

I am deeply grateful for more than eleven thousand clients, transported from all over our country, and dozens of therapists whom I had the privilege of working with in Las Vegas, Nevada, primarily at Desert Hope - American Addiction Centers and Solutions Recovery, among others.

Thank you for joining me on this journey where all things sound and music fall under our framework, bringing a comprehensive approach to your healing journey. May the power of Music4Life's Music Medicine Protocol and the Key2MEE® Music App guide you to emotional balance, resilience, and a thriving life that ignites a new world brightly.

APPENDICES

APPENDIX A: PERSONALIZED SURGERY AND RECOVERY PLAYLISTS

This preferred music playlist was compiled from participants in a cancer retreat I facilitated. I quickly assigned the songs to the U.S.E. mood categories and categorized them accordingly. This is not the sequence I recommend they be played as a prescriptive playlist. It is offered as a resource to consider as you populate music into specialized U.S.E. mood music playlists. Remember that a designation of UE may not recommend it for a Music Medicine playlist. U/E references the music vs the lyric. Whereas UE references a mix of music energy. There is a general mood music analysis to follow, and circumstances and memories can make a song the best choice. For instance, "Another One Bites the Dust" by Queen would not typically go into a U or E playlist, but in this cancer patient's experience, it is a perfect fit for her to feel like she's conquering cancer during chemo, and would recommend it for her "Theme Song" playlist. The prescriptive playlist, aka Music Medicine Pill®, would be different, first identifying the Mood Sequence Formula™ when populating specific U.S.E. music related to specific emotions in the best sequence.

Preferred Music	Music Title	Composer/Artist	Notes about cancer patient's use
U	Better Than a Hallelujah	Amy Grant	During a friends chemo
U	Nobody Knows the Trouble I've Seen	traditional	Klutz happens
U	Rite of Spring	Angels & Airwaves	During hard times
U	That Wasn't Me	Brandi Carlile	Transbronchial lung biospy
U/E	A Little Bit Stronger	Sara Evans	During divorce
U/E	Another One Bites the Dust	Queen	During chemo imagining each cell getting killed
U/E	I Hope You Dance	LeeAnn Wolmack	Transition of her daughter
UE	This Girl Is On Fire	Alicia Keys	All the time & during recovery
US	All of That Love From Here	Wynona Judd	During chemo
US	When You Walk Through the Storm "You'll Never Walk Alone"	Carousel	Sad times passing
S	Here I Am	Tom Booth	
S	Pachebel Cannon in D	Orchestral	During surgery & recovery
SE	Somewhere Over the Rainbow/What a Wonderful World	Israel Kamakawiwo'ole	During time of radiation
SE	The Circle of Life	Lion King Elton John	During chemo
SE	What a beautiful world "What a Wonderful World"	Louis Armstrong	Private moments distressing
E	Blue Danube	Johann Strauss	Stressed moments during chemo, after chemo
E	Fight Song	Rachel Platten	During chemo & recovery
E	Girls Just Want to Have Fun	Cindi Lauper	Recovering from chemo
E	Madre Tierra - Mother Earth	Chayanne	Mornings & during down spirited times
E	Marine Corps Hymn	cadence	
E	You Gotta Be	Desiree	All the time and through chemo
USE	Take Me Back Home Again	John Denver	Skiing

Surgery Playlist of 15 music selections = 1 hour 42 minutes

Advisement: This playlist (or something similar) is meant to have an absence of beat, be very soothing, and have no words. It is intended to act as an analgesic, which may reduce the amount of anesthesia needed during surgery. Request the pre-op nurse tape your earbuds to your ears so they don't accidentally fall out, and tape your audio device to your gown, in an area that does not interfere with the surgical area so that it does not fall to the ground when transported, moving from bed to operating table back to bed. Make sure you have enough music timed for the length of the anticipated operation. Or, put one song on repeat.

Summer Space (not available - find similar music that is nature-based, i.e., babbling brook, birds, gentle, long, layered flute sounds)

Sleep Soundly (Pt.2) by Steven Halpern

Cellular Awakening by Kelly Howell

Ortho-7 from "Egg of Time" by Dr. Jeffrey Thompson

Yiomz (9 Rings) from "Egg of Time" by Dr. Jeffrey Thompson

Yik from "Egg of Time" by Dr. Jeffrey Thompson

Egg of Time by Dr. Jeffrey Thompson

Namizy by Dr. Jeffrey Thompson

Yziman from "Egg of Time" by Dr. Jeffrey Thompson

Adagio for Strings, Op. 11 by Samuel Barber

Forever by Hilary Stagg

Surgery - Recovery Playlist of 14 music selections = 1 hour 21 minutes

Advisement: Request the pre-op nurse to inform the recovery nurse that you have a surgical recovery playlist you would like to listen to after you arrive in recovery. The music playing will help to awaken you. The music chosen needs to be gentle on your body, with tempos gradually quickening. The music will also block any negative conversations in the recovery room that you may subconsciously mistake as the medical team talking about your condition. You want to be positive and soothed, shifting gradually into mildly energizing. Make sure lyrics are ALL positive, and music supports your heartbeat, doesn't oppose it, i.e. no anapestic beat. This playlist is my preference, with my focus on loving the violin. Choose your favorite instrument and populate your playlist with it, following the instructions above.

Air on G by Johann Sebastian Bach

Violin Concerto in E: Adagio by Johann Sebastian Bach

The Four Seasons, Violin Concerto in F minor, Op. 8 No. 4 "Winter:" 2. Largo by Antonio Vivaldi

Guitar Concerto in D Major: Largo by Antonio Vivaldi

Introduction et Rondo Capriccioso for Violin and Orchestra, Op. 28 by Camille Saint-Saens

Violin Concerto in E minor, Op.64 by Felix Mendelssohn

Double Violin Concerto in D Major by Johann Sebastian Bach

Violin Concerto in E Allegro by Johann Sebastian Bach

Brandenburg Concerto No. 3 by Johann Sebastian Bach

Capriccio Espagnol, Op.34: I. Alborado by Nikolai Rimsky-Korsakov

Holberg Suite: Prelude by Edvard Grieg

Hungarian Rhapsody No. 2 by Franz Liszt

Double Violin Concerto in D Major by Johann Sebastian Bach Arr. by Time for Three

Sinfonia in D by Johann Sebastian Bach

APPENDIX B: EFFECTIVE MUSIC FOR WALKING, JOGGING, AND POSITIVE MINDSET

This appendix presents Music4Life® and my personal curated prescriptive and specialized playlists designed to support various activities and emotional states, including Nellis Air Force Base service members. The recommendations include a balanced selection of tracks from Colby Buzzell's "My War: Killing Time in Iraq" (2005) and additional music to enhance mood management, safety, and unit cohesion. The playlists cover different purposes, such as cardio exercise, surgery, and recovery, demonstrating the application of music for both physical and emotional well-being. Each playlist is tailored to meet specific needs, ensuring a balanced music diet to maintain alertness and emotional stability.

KEY2MEE

Music4Life Sample Recommendations for Air Base Defense
Nellis Air Force Base, 2007, Security Forces

"My War" by Colby Buzzell - music selections

U Music		Genre
Wagner	Ride of the Valkyries	classical
Metallica	Star Wars Imperial March	heavy metal/soundtrack
Rob Zombie	Let the Bodies Hit the Floor	alternative
Staind	Hidden Song - Excessive Baggage	alternative
Bagpipes	Amazing Grace	folk
U/S Transition Music		
David Arkenstone	Cello's Song	new age
S Music		
Native Spirit	Cloud of Tears	nature/native american
Mozart Effect	Double Piano Concerto in D Major, K448: Andante	classical
Louis Armstrong	What a Wonderful World	jazz
S/E Transition		
Chariots of Fire	Titles - Theme Song	soundtrack
E Music		
Lee Greenwood	God Bless America	pop
John Lennon	Give Peace a Chance	pop
Nomad	Nomad	world
Tchaikovsky	Piano Concerto No. 1 in Bb Major: 1. Allegro non troppo	classical
Ennio Morricone	The Good, The Bad, The Ugly	rock
John Phillip Sousa	Stars & Stripes	classical
other E possibilities		
The Surfaris	Wipe Out	oldies
Toby Keith	Courtesy of the Red, White & Blue	country
ZZ Top	Low Rider	rock
The Clark Sisters	Hallelujah	gospel
Proyecto Uno	Esta Pega'o	world/hispanic
Cirque du Soleil	Kunya Sobe	world/Las Vegas show
Rossini	William Tell Overture	classical
Nicholas Gunn	Ritual	new age
Steppenwolf	Born to be Wild	rock
Survivor	Eye of the Tiger	soundtrack/rock

Walking /Jogging Playlist of 33 music selections = 2 hours 21 minutes

I always start my cardio with the first three songs, and then I may manually shuffle music selections to match the mood, tempo, and rhythm desired for the length of exercise time. Allow this playlist to inspire your own personal music choices focused on mood enhancement, oxygenation, and motivation to stay engaged longer.

Promontory form "The Last of the Mohicans"by Trevor Jones, Joel Mc-Neely & Royal Scottish National Orchestra

Come Along by Vicci Martinez & Cee Lo Green

Roar by Katy Perry

Shining Star by Earth, Wind & Fire

Golden Rule by Soji

Footloose by Kenny Loggins

Smooth by Santana (featuring Rob Thomas)

Chasing Coyotes by Rick Dusek & Daniel Hamilton

Best Day of My Life by American Authors

Rather Be by Vitamin String Quartet

Sing a Song by Earth, Wind & Fire

Happy from "Despicable Me 2" by Pharrell Williams

Somewhere Over the Rainbow by Israel "IZ" Kamakawiwoʻole

Holberg Suite, Prelude by Grieg

Sinfonia in D by Edvard Grieg

Violin Concerto in D Major, Op. 77: Allegro giocoso, ma non troppo vivace by Johannes Brahms

Symphony No. 7 in A Major, Op. 92: II. Allegretto by Ludwig van Beethoven

Santorini by Yanni

Wake Me Up Before You Go-Go by Wham!

One Minute More by Capital Cities

Every Good Thing by The Afters

Around the World by Daft Punk

Thunder Feet by Rick Dusek & Daniel Hamilton

Porscha by Russ Freeman & The Rippingtons

(Your Love Keeps Lifting Me) Higher & Higher by Jackie Wilson

Unwritten by Natasha Bedingfield

Violin Concerto in A minor, Op. 77: Allegro assai by Johann Sebastian Bach

Fairytales by Alice Deejay

Reach by Gloria Estefan

Wrapped Up in You by Garth Brooks

Can't Help Falling in Love by The Piano Guys

Hard to Concentrate by Red Hot Chili Peppers

Millenium Dance by Mehdi

ADDITIONAL RESOURCES

Key2MEE® Music App

Key2MEE®

The patented Key2MEE.com Music App (1.0) is THE recommended resource for accessing the Music4Life® Music Medicine Protocol and mastering your mood (Pinkerton et al., 2023). After downloading it from Apple or Google Play, log in and complete your Emotional Profile Quiz. This quiz evaluates your reported experience of twelve different emotions and relatedness to life conditions. After taking a few minutes to complete the quiz, you will instantly receive a unique code and image related to the report about your probable music listening habits and the potential existence of a Chronic Comfort Zone™.

Even though this personal assessment has been available on the Music4Life website for two decades, the Key2MEE App offers significant advancements:

- Key2MEE generates an updated report based on your Quiz input, reflecting my clinical experience with over 11,000 clients in the past decade.

- Many of these clients have been trapped in Chronic Comfort Zones™.

- The Emotional Profile report provides recommendations based on your results.

- Gain access to prescriptive playlists, Chronic Comfort Zone tutorials, research, Music Medicine trainings, and tools designed for empowerment, caregivers, and clinicians.

Phase 2 of the patented Key2MEE.com Music App (2.0) is planned to connect users with prescriptive playlist options. Hundreds of recommended Music Medicine selections from many genres, respecting all generations, will be available with your ability to request a Music4Life® Specialist's feedback about your preferred music being recommended or not, based upon the mood music analysis. You will be able to test the music's strength for YOU (YES - very individualized) before determining if it would be assigned to your specialized playlist. Once all algorithms are met, chosen music is populated into your specialized playlists culled to generate the prescriptive playlist, aka Music Exercise Regimen or Music Medicine Pill®, depending on your goals. The process follows advisements with our Specialists, who will respond to your Key2MEE® Music App input with an optimal Mood Sequence Formula™.

YOU are Your BEST Resource

In addition to the resources provided in Key2MEE®, there are several more that readers should consider. First and foremost, YOU are your best resource. While experts like physicians, therapists, and business consultants offer valuable advice and support, your proactive engagement in self-care is essential.

I'll be transparent here: being very public image-conscious, a trait instilled in me from a young age to uphold my family's reputation for excellence, I've faced certain challenges. Through these experiences, I've discovered keys to greater understanding that you might also recognize in yourself or others.

The following sections explore various aspects of health and well-being, each essential for a comprehensive approach to self-care. These include diet, technology, contemplation, and business. By exploring these topics, you'll gain insights into how each area influences your well-being and how integrating them can lead to a more balanced, fulfilling life.

Health: Diet

Understanding the impact of dietary choices on overall health and being mindful of what we consume can be transformative. When I co-authored "Protect and Serve: A 7 Day Gut Stress Program" with my husband, showcasing his chef talents, I realized I needed to be truthful about my own habits. Despite his efforts to accommodate my dairy and gluten/wheat intolerances, I often consumed these items when alternatives were unavailable.

This disconnect became apparent when I experienced angioedema. My face became swollen just two days before a violin performance. Urgent care administered a steroid to reduce the swelling, and a nurse brought saltine crackers to prevent nausea. In a moment of clarity, I wondered if my recent gluten/wheat consumption had caused the swelling. After monitoring my reaction to the crackers, the swelling extended to the right side of my lips. This incident informed me about the cause and the importance of dietary mindfulness.

I emphasize self-awareness and consulting both Western and homeopathic physicians for comprehensive self-care. While waiting in the doctor's office, I confirmed online that swelling can indeed result from gluten/wheat intolerance.

By staying in tune with your body and noting how different foods affect you, you can make more informed dietary choices that support your well-being. Additionally, noticing how music impacts your physiology, behavior, emotions, and mindset can enhance your self-care journey. Combining dietary mindfulness with other practices can lead to a more balanced and fulfilling life.

Health: Technology

Another aspect of self-awareness involves recognizing how our habits and dependencies, such as technology addiction, affect our overall health and quality of life. One morning, as words flowed effortlessly into my mind for this book, I realized I needed to monitor my technology "affinity" (aka addiction?), which began ten years ago when my son-in-law informed me that my daughter was a drug dealer. I became very connected to my phone, wanting to support her in figuring out life positively.

During a camping trip without cell phones, I experienced anxiety in the middle of the night, revealing to me that my phone had become an ineffective anxiolytic. I recognized that I was using game-playing to contain anxiety and problem-solving, yet it also led to issues such as experiencing urges to use my phone and loved ones complaining about its use. Recognizing and addressing our technology habits can help us find a healthier balance and improve our overall quality of life (All, 2018).

Health: Contemplation

Recognizing and addressing dependencies underscores the value of regular mindfulness practices such as meditation, yoga, Tai Chi, prayer, breathing techniques, sound baths, and so much more. These practices create space for personal reflection and connection to a higher power, promoting inner peace and clarity. They help ground us, providing a steady foundation from which to approach our daily lives and long-term goals.

By integrating these forms of inner support into our routines, we can maintain a balanced perspective, ensuring that our actions and decisions align with our core values and beliefs. These mindfulness practices are essential for maintaining inner peace and clarity amidst the challenges of everyday life.

Health: Business

Utilizing innovative strategies, including music therapy-informed methods, can enhance emotional intelligence and optimize business decisions.

Consider moving beyond traditional ways of thinking about music. Introduce fresh perspectives for mood management and recommend bold, disruptive patterns of action that address mood problems to enhance business decisions. Taking an online quiz to measure Emotional Intelligence (EI) can be a starting point. From there, using the Music Medicine Protocol may strengthen EI, helping you achieve business goals, whether it's to get a job, keep a job, or secure a promotion.

Initiate employee or client wellness programs that embrace DIY (Do-It-Yourself) prescriptive playlist strategies (Pinkerton, n.d.):

- Personalization respects preferred genres.

- Education overrides instinctive music listening habits.

- Motivation increases with healthy music listening habits.

- Perspiration increases with prescriptive playlists used during physical workouts.

- Repetition of highly empowered music listening processes transforms lives.

- Collaboration expands effective Music Medicine libraries with specialized playlists.

- Inspiration is contagious, spreading positive attitudes, collaboration, productivity, happiness, peace of mind, self-awareness, and empathy.

If you want to start or grow a business, consider resources like NxLeve L.org for small business start-up information, which has been upgraded from the in-person course I took 19 years ago. I also highly recommend CEOSpaceInternational.com, the high-level business group I joined in 2010.

Additionally, Music4Life's Music Medicine Protocol offers a wealth of resources for integrating music into therapeutic practices. Courses such as "Making Music Medicine" on Udemy.com, the Music Medicine Boot Camp, Music Medicine Advisor, and certifications like the Music Medicine Specialist and Clinical Specialist training provide strategies for using music to enhance health with clients at MusicMedicineAcademy. com. Current best practices, research, and recommended music are regularly featured in livestream podcasts and blogs at MusicMedicineClub. com. Future plans with the IRB-Approved Hospital Music Study on the stress-anxiety-resilience of hospital workers will further report on the impactful role of music in supporting health and quality of life.

I love featuring music therapists' creativity with published music and recommended songwriting courses. For example, "Daughters of Harriet" on Spotify and iTunes features five friends who are music therapists living in five different states: Barbara Dunn, Maureen Hearns, Lisa Jackert, Jodi Winnwalker, and Robin Rio, who believe in the power of voice and community singing. Dr. Tracy Richardson is an award-winning singer-songwriter and Director of Music Therapy at St. Mary-of-the-Woods College in Indiana with her music at tracyrichardsonmusic.com and her songwriting course at musictherapyed.com. TheSpiegelAcademy.com also offers a songwriting course with strategies for therapeutic impact.

Recognizing the creativity and dedication of these professionals, I am inspired to emphasize the role each of you can play in promoting and utilizing Music Medicine.

Health: Tools at theMusic4Life.com

Power Up Your Life Collection includes nine DIY (Do-It-Yourself) programs, Music4Life® Tools, and Curriculum specially priced for listening, viewing, reading, and daily engagement.

Survival Packs (DIY) include an eBooklet with a recommended Spotify music playlist when life gets tough and you need to calm your nerves or manage anger, with a caregiver focus on dementia/Alzheimer's, infants, anxiety, and validating life experiences.

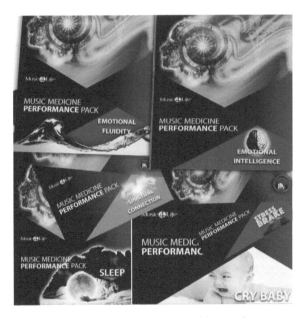

Performance Packs (DIY) include an eBooklet with a prescriptive music playlist to harness the Mood Sequence Formula™ within Music Medicine Pills® to mitigate problems with sleep, angst, anxiety, depression, crying babies, and connecting with higher power.

MAPP MEE™ Self-Assessment Kits (DIY) evaluate your emotional inventory and music responses to understand how music and emotions work together for a cathartic healing process supporting mental health. Complete the pre/post listening assessments, listen to the Music Medicine Pill®, then score and evaluate your responses to continue using Music4Life®. Each tool kit includes a Music Medicine Pill ("Stress Brake" or "MEE Concert") to address anger, anxiety, or depression. The workbook's special assessments, instructions, evaluations, recommendations, and diary support personal scoring, advisement, and next steps for treatment regimens utilizing Music Medicine Pills.

Music Medicine Pills® address anger, anxiety, and depression. They are called the MEE™ Concert, Stress Brake, and MEE in the Key of Peace. Featuring Mood Sequence Formulas™, each prescriptive playlist has been specially formulated to support a healing process and includes Judith Pinkerton's violin performance, either as a soloist or featured with her SoundSynergy ensemble.

Health: Curriculum at theMusic4Life.com

"Thriving Through Adversity: Prescriptive Playlists to Reclaim Joy, Peace and Purpose in Life" (2024) details the evidence-based practice of the Music4Life Music Medicine Protocol through dozens of case stories. Decades of entrepreneurial adventures chronicle narrations of Judith Pinkerton's life experiences.

"6 Habits of Music Medicine for Highly Empowered People" (2022) is summarized in Chapter 3 with six music listening habits taught eight different ways (i.e. listening, assessing, mindfulness, playlists, outreach, etc.). Separate boxed card sets and facilitator/participant manuals guide implementation of thirty therapeutic goals and activities.

"Power Up 365" (2022) daily texts engage empowering lessons over 365 days, with matching quotes, images, and Music Medicine selections from diverse genres to strengthen living each day.

"Music's Power to Heal: Your Emotional Mind" (2021) is the first in a series of books that updates research and music for each chapter within "The Sound of Healing" (1996).

"Brace for Impact: A Case for Emotional Fluidity" (2019) reports the efficacy of an IRB-approved research study conducted at the University of Nevada Las Vegas Student Health Center (2001).

"The Sound of Healing" (1996, 2003) unites medical science with music therapy to transform your music library into powerful music listening experiences for health and happiness. Read interviews of leading personalities in the music and health fields, hundreds of recommended music from sixteen genres, and dozens of healing stories.

"Protect and Serve: 7-day Gut Stress Program" (2021) is a short-term goal-setting, health improvement program utilizing 21 gluten and dairy-free recipes, meditative quotes, and music-listening recommendations for stress-free dining. Optimize gut health with enhanced relaxation and positive mindset written by husband and chef Dennis D. Burkhardt, D.C., and Judith Pinkerton.

Health: Advanced Training

Go to MusicMedicineAcademy.com to access training discounts through the Key2MEE® music app.

Practitioner Specialist - The "MMPS" credential requires 97 hours (includes pre-requisite MMCS training) plus continuing education to renew certification at MusicMedicineClub.com for certified music therapists.

Music Medicine Clinical Specialist - The "MMCS" credential requires 30 hours (includes pre-requisite MMS training) plus continuing education to renew certification at MusicMedicineClub.com for licensed health and therapy professionals.

Music Medicine Specialist - The "MMS" credential requires 18 hours (includes pre-requisite MMA training) plus continuing education to renew certification at MusicMedicineClub.com for certified education, sports, corporate and health professionals.

Music Medicine Advisor - 6 hours, "MMA" certificate only for students, musicians, caregivers, parents, and executives.

Musicmedicineclub.com

A monthly subscription for current research, strategies, and news with live stream events, podcasts, and blogs, also supporting Music4Life® continuing education requirements for MMPS, MMCS, and MMS certifications.

YOU are MY Best Resource

I'm counting on you to make a difference, whether it's daily, weekly, or monthly ("Herding experiment: Hundredth monkey phenomenon," 2021). Here's a WIN-WIN scenario that other mental health providers have requested: Earn passive income by promoting the Music Medicine training to your clientele. Our podcasts feature thematic discussions, including my BIG vision of Music4Life® changing the culture of music creation and consumption. Check out hundreds of our blogs and podcasts at MusicMedicineclub.com and subscribe for the cost of a cup of coffee. During live streams, interact with us!

Get your copy of "6 Habits of Music Medicine for Highly Empowered People" at theMusic4Life.com/shop. This boxed card set will remind you daily, weekly, and monthly of the 30 highly empowered processes you want to instill in yourself and others, transforming instinctive music listening practices that perpetuate Chronic Unsettled Comfort Zones.

Let's disrupt patterns of music listening habits trapped in Chronic Comfort Zones™ and grow channels that harness the power of music to generate empathy, cooperation, and compassion that nourish mental health. Allow me to support you as we build a strong network of powerful voices to "boil the ocean" - meaning an enormous effort - changing the culture of music creation and consumption by activating the "hundredth monkey phenomenon" for a New World.

REFERENCES

Chapter 1

Altshuler, I. M. (1948). The past, present, and future of musical therapy. In E. Podolsky (Ed.), *Music Therapy* (pp. 24-35). Philosophical Library.

Bowling, D.L. (2023). Biological principles for music and mental health. *Translational Psychiatry 13*, 374. https://doi.org/10.1038/s41398-023-0 2671-4

Cabrero, F.R., & De Jesus, O. (Updated 2022, September 30). Dysgraphia. StatPearls Publishing. Retrieved from https://www.ncbi.nlm.nih.gov/b ooks/NBK559301/

Chanda, M. L., & Levitin, D. J. (2013). The neurochemistry of music. *Trends in Cognitive Sciences, 17(4)*, 179-193. https://doi.org/10.1016/j. tics.2013.02.007

Chen, W.G., Iversen, J.R., Kao, M.H., Loui, P., Patel, A.D., Zatorre, R.J., & Edwards, E. (2022). Music and brain circuitry: Strategies for strengthening evidence-based research for music-based interventions. *Journal of Neuroscience 42(45)*, 8498-8507. https://doi.org/10.1523/JNEUROSC I.1135-22.2022

Cleveland Clinic (Updated 2022, June 2). *Neurodivergent.* Cleveland Clinic. https://my.clevelandclinic.org/health/symptoms/23154-neurodi vergent

Cook, T., Roy, A. R. K., & Welker, K. M. (2017). Music as an emotion regulation strategy: An examination of genres of music and their roles in emotion regulation. *Psychology of Music, 47(1)*. https://doi.org/10.1177 /0305735617734627

Hanser, S. (2021, January 12). *Music brings an antidote to toxicity.* Suzanne Hanser. https://www.suzannehanser.com/music-strategies-for-wellbein g/2021/1/12/music-brings-an-antidote-to-toxicity-1

Heiderscheit, A. & Madson, A. (2015). Use of the iso principle as a central method in mood management: A music psychotherapy clinical case study. *Music Therapy Perspectives, 33(1)*, 45-52. https://doi.org/10.1093/mtp/ miu042

Hennessy, S., Sachs, M., Kaplan, J., & Habibi, A. (2021). Music and mood regulation during the early stages of the COVID-19 pandemic. *PLOS ONE 16(10)*. https://doi.org/10.1371/journal.pone.0258027

Hodges, D. (2020). *Music in the human experience: An introduction to music psychology* (2nd ed., p. 261). Routledge.

Kim, S., Gabel, C., Aguilar-Raab, C., Hillecke, T.K., & Warth, M. (2018). Affective and autonomic response to dynamic rhythmic entrainment:

Mechanisms of a specific music therapy factor. *The Arts in Psychotherapy 60*, 48-54. https://doi.org/10.1016/j.aip.2018.06.002

Koivula, T. (2024, January 30). *Music's universal impact on body and emotion.* Neuroscience News. Retrieved from https://neurosciencenew s.com/music-emotion-body-25543/

Madsen, C.K., Cotter, V. & Madsen, C.H. (1968). A behavioral approach to music therapy. *Journal of Music Therapy, 5(3)*, 69–71. https://doi.org /10.1093/jmt/5.3.69

McFerran, K. & Grocke, D. (2022). *Receptive music therapy: Techniques, clinical applications and new perspectives* (2nd ed.). Jessica Kingsley.

Meymandi, A. (2009). Music, medicine, healing, and the genome project. *Psychiatry 6(9)*, 43–45. https://www.ncbi.nlm.nih.gov/pmc/article s/PMC2766288/

Moore, K. S. (2013). A systematic review on the neural effects of music on emotion regulation: Implications for music therapy practice. *Journal of Music Therapy, 50(3)*, 198-242. https://doi.org/10.1093/jmt/50.3.198

Pinkerton, J. (1996). *The sound of healing: Create your own music program for better health* (1st ed.). Alliance Publishing.

Pinkerton, J. (2003). *The sound of healing: Customize your music for enhanced well-being* (2nd ed.). Music 4 Life, Inc.

Pinkerton, J. (2019). *Brace for impact: A case for emotional fluidity.* Music 4 Life, Inc.

Putkinen, V., Zhou, X., Gan, X., Yang, L., Becker, B., Sams, M., & Num-menmaa, L. (2024). Bodily maps of musical sensations across cultures. *Psychological and Cognitive Sciences, 121(5).* https://doi.org/10.1073/pn as.2308859121

Reuell, P. (2018, January 26). Songs in the key of humanity. *The Harvard Gazette.* https://news.harvard.edu/gazette/story/2018/01/music-may-tr anscend-cultural-boundaries-to-become-universally-human/

Rider, M. (1985). Entrainment mechanisms are involved in pain reduc-tion, muscle relaxation, and music-mediated imagery. *Journal of Music Therapy, 22(4),* 183-192. https://doi.org/10.1093/jmt/22.4.183

Shatin, L. (1970). Alteration of mood via music: A study of the vectoring effect. *The Journal of Psychology, 75(1),* 81-86. https://doi.org/10.1080/0 0223980.1970.9916808

Stewart, J., Garrido, S., Hense, C., & McFerran, K. (2019). Music use for mood regulation: Self-awareness and conscious listening choices in young people with tendencies to depression. *Frontiers in Psychology 10.* https://doi.org/10.3389/fpsyg.2019.01199

Thaut, M. H., & Hodges, D.A. (Eds). (2018). *The Oxford handbook of music and the brain.* Oxford University Press. https://doi.org/10.1093/ oxfordhb/9780198804123.001.0001

Thaut, M. H., & Hoemberg, V. (Eds.). (2014). *Handbook of neurologic music therapy.* Oxford University Press.

Tomaka, J. (2024, June 29). *Brain health - adaptive or maladaptive*. Music4Life. Retrieved June 30, 2024, from https://themusic4life.com/brain-plasticity-adaptive-maladaptive/

Wellman, R., & Pinkerton, J. (2015). The development of a music therapy protocol: A Music 4 Life® case report of a veteran with PTSD. *Music and Medicine, 7(3)*, 24-39. https://doi.org/10.47513/mmd.v7i3.408

What is AMTA. (n.d.). American Music Therapy Association. Retrieved June 30, 2024, from https://www.musictherapy.org/about/whatis

Chapter 2

Borling, J. (2017). Stage two recovery for substance use disorders. *Music and Medicine, 9(1)*, 59-63. https://doi.org/10.47513/mmd.v9i1.525

Jackson, N. A. (2015). Music therapy and chronic mental illness: Overcoming the silent symptoms. *Music Therapy Perspectives, 33(2)*, 90-96.

Murphy, K. M. (2013). Adults with substance use disorders. In L. Eyre (Ed.), *Guidelines for music therapy practice in mental health* (pp. 449-501). Barcelona Publishers.

Music therapy and addiction treatment. (2021). American Music Therapy Association. Retrieved June 30, 2024, from https://www.musictherapy.org/assets/1/7/FactSheet_Music_Therapy_and_Addiction_Treatment_2021.pdf.

The Music4Life® USA. (2021, November 27). *Conquer Demons with Music Medicine* [Video]. Youtube. https://www.youtube.com/watch?v =X2qbPaSuBlA

Chapter 3

Altshuler, I. M. (1948). The past, present, and future of musical therapy. In E. Podolsky (Ed.), *Music Therapy* (pp. 24-35). Philosophical Library.

Bronson, H., Vaudreuil, R., & Bradt, J. (2018). Music therapy treatment of active duty military: An overview of intensive outpatient and longitu-dinal care programs. *Music Therapy Perspectives, 36(2)*, 195–206.

Clynes, M., & Panskepp, J. (Eds.). (1988). Generalized emotion - how it may be produced, and sentic cycle therapy, In *Emotions and psychopathol-ogy* (pp. 107-162). Plenum Press.

Conan, N. (Host). (2009, September 10). The impact of war: Army to train soldiers in emotional resiliency [Audio podcast episode]. In *Talk of the Nation*. NPR-National Public Radio. Retrieved from: https://www.npr.org/2009/09/10/112717611/army-to-train-sol diers-in-emotional-resiliency

Heiderscheit, A. & Madson, A. (2015). Use of the iso principle as a central method in mood management: A music psychotherapy clinical case study. *Music Therapy Perspectives, 33(1)*, 45-52. https://doi.org/10.1093/mtp/ miu042

Hodges, D. A. (2020). *Music in the human experience: An introduction to music psychology* (2nd ed., pp. 183-186). Routledge.

Holistic health and fitness, FM 7-22 (2020, October). Headquarters, Department of the Army. Retrieved from: https://media.defense.gov/2023 /Jul/27/2003268908/-1/-1/1/H2F-FM-7-22-2020.PDF

McFerran, K. & Grocke, D. (2022). *Receptive music therapy: Techniques, clinical applications and new perspectives* (2nd ed.). Jessica Kingsley.

Moore, K. S. (2013). A systematic review on the neural effects of music on emotion regulation: Implications for music therapy practice. *Journal of Music Therapy, 50(3)*, 198-242. https://doi.org/10.1093/jmt/50.3.198

Pinkerton, J. (n.d.). *Music wellness programs: Merging self-responsible strategies.* Corporate Wellness Magazine. Retrieved from: https://www.c orporatewellnessmagazine.com/article/music-wellness-programs-merging

Pinkerton, J. (1993). *Music as medicine: Rx (prescriptions) that heal.* SeminarConcerts International Inc.

Pinkerton, J. (1993). *Music: the stress-release system in three steps.* Seminar-Concerts International, Inc.

Pinkerton, J. (1996). *The sound of healing: Create your own music program for better health* (1st ed.). Alliance Publishing.

Pinkerton, J. (2003). *The sound of healing: Customize your music for enhanced well-being* (2nd ed.). Music 4 Life, Inc.

Pinkerton, J. (2010). *Stress brake: Music exercising emotions program booklet.* Remo Inc.

Pinkerton, J. (2014). *Music medicine boot camp.* Music 4 Life Inc.

Pinkerton, J. (2019). *Brace for impact: A case for emotional fluidity*. Music 4 Life, Inc.

Pinkerton, J. (2020, January 13). *Music 4 Life® pilot project*. Music4Life®. Retrieved June 30, 2024, from: https://themusic4life.com/wp-content/uploads/2021/09/SAFB-Music4Life-Report-AFWERX.pdf

Pinkerton, J. (2021). *Music's power to heal your emotional mind*. Music 4 Life, Inc.

Pinkerton, J. (Updated 2023, June 6). *Music powers potential: Good, bad and ugly*. Music4Life. https://themusic4life.com/music-powers-potential-good-bad-and-ugly/

Pinkerton, J. & Kelly, L. (1990). *Music: Can it stop pain*. Seminar Concerts International.

Shatin, L. (1970). Alteration of mood via music: A study of the vectoring effect. *The Journal of Psychology, 75(1)*, 81-86. https://doi.org/10.1080/00223980.1970.9916808

Team Tony (n.d.). *How do I change my state of mind*. Tony Robbins. Retrieved June 30, 2024, from https://www.tonyrobbins.com/mind-meaning/how-to-reset-your-mind-and-mood/

Team Tony (n.d.). *The 6 steps to master your emotions and live fully*. Tony Robbins. Retreived June 30, 2024, from https://www.tonyrobbins.com/mind-meaning/be-the-master-of-your-emotions

The power of pattern disruption as a vehicle for change. (2024). Gotham-Culture. Retrieved June 30, 2024, from https://gothamculture.com/20 16/04/07/the-power-of-pattern-disruption-as-a-vehicle-for-change/

The use of music for resilience-building (2021, August 20). IAMM - The International Association of Music and Medicine. Retrieved June 30, 2024, from: https://iammonline.com/2021/08/20/the-use-of-music-fo r-resilience-building-and-healing-trauma/

Wellman, R., & Pinkerton, J. (2015). The development of a music therapy protocol: A Music 4 Life® case report of a veteran with PTSD. *Music and Medicine, 7(3),* 24-39. https://doi.org/10.47513/mmd.v7i3.408

Chapter 4

Ackermann, K. (2024, January 3). *Warning signs of relapse: Depression, stress, and other triggers.* American Addiction Centers. Retrieved June 30, 2024, from https://americanaddictioncenters.org/adult-addiction-tr eatment-programs/signs-of-relapse

Cabotaje, A. (2020, February 24). *What do your food cravings reveal about your health?* Right as Rain by U.W. Medicine. Retrieved June 30, 2024, from https://bit.ly/foodcravingmeaning

Diamond, J. (1979). *Behavioral kinesiology.* Harper & Row.

Diamond, J. (1979). *Your body doesn't lie.* Warner Books.

Hawkins, D. (1995). *Power vs. force.* Veritas Publishing.

Hyde, K. L., Lerch, J., Norton, A., Forgeard, M., Winner, E., Evans, A. C., & Schlaug, G. (2009). Musical training shapes structural brain development. *Journal of Neuroscience, 29(10)*, 3019-3025. https://doi.org/10.15 23/JNEUROSCI.5118-08.2009

Miller, S. (2008). The peculiar life of sundays. *Harvard University Press.* Retrieved from https://www.jstor.org/stable/j.ctv1kwxdz5

Music medicine with military. (2019, December). Music4Life®. Retrieved June 30, 2024, from https://themusic4life.com/music-medicine-with-m ilitary/

National Center for Complementary and Integrative Health. (Updated 2022, September). *Music and health: What you need to know.* U.S. Department of Health & Human Services. https://www.nccih.nih.gov/hea lth/music-and-health-what-you-need-to-know

Pinkerton, J. (2020). *Music 4 Life® pilot project.* Music4Life®. Retrieved June 30, 2024, from https://themusic4life.com/wp-content/uploads/20 21/09/SAFB-Music4Life-Report-AFWERX.pdf

Pinkerton, J. (2022). The art of overcoming PTSD: Building resilience via music therapy. *Mental Health Spectrum, 2(2)*, 11-12. Retrieved from https://bit.ly/mentalhealthspectrumpinkertonPTSDarticle

Schlaug, G., Jancke, L., Huang, Y., Staiger, J. F., & Steinmetz, H. (1995). Increased corpus callosum size in musicians. *Neuropsychologia, 33(8)*, 1047-1055. https://doi.org/10.1016/0028-3932(95)00045-5

The Music4Life® USA. (2024, March 1). *One gangster's recovery* [Video]. YouTube. https://youtu.be/hhDAwjSkwFU

Wellman, R., & Pinkerton, J. (2015). The development of a music therapy protocol: A Music 4 Life® case report of a veteran with PTSD. *Music and Medicine, 7(3)*, 24-39. https://doi.org/10.47513/mmd.v7i3.408

Zhao, T. C., & Kuhl, P. K. (2020). Neural and physiological relations observed in musical beat and meter processing. *Brain and Behavior, 10(11)*. https://doi.org/10.1002/brb3.1836

Chapter 5

Belcher, C. (2013, October 6). Music 4 Life center plans didjeridu classes. *Las Vegas Review-Journal*. https://www.reviewjournal.com/uncategoriz ed/music-4-life-center-plans-didjeridu-classes/

Chen, L. (2023). Influence of music on the hearing and mental health of adolescents and countermeasures. *Frontiers in Neuroscience, 17*. https:// doi.org/10.3389/fnins.2023.1236638

Gonzalez, E. & Pinkerton, J. (2022, April 15). *Mood control in a changing world*. Music4Life®. Retrieved June 30, 2024, from https://themusic4li fe.com/mood-control-in-a-changing-world/

Herrity, J. (2023, October 31). *8 types of music to increase work productivity*. Indeed Career Development. https://www.indeed.com/career-advice/car eer-development/best-music-to-work-to

Hooks, E. (2022, January 14). *Music for big emotions: Emotion playlists*. The Sonatina Center. https://www.thesonatinacenter.com/blog-posts/2022/1/12/therap eutic-music-for-your-daily-life-mood-regulation-playlists

Mali, S. (2023, August 25). *The real meaning behind Taylor Swift's "Out Of The Woods."* Static Media. https://www.thelist.com/1374819/real-meaning-taylor-swift-out-of-the-woods/

Prior, H. M. (2022). How can music help us to address the climate crisis. *Music & Science, 5.* https://doi.org/10.1177/20592043221075725

Saavedra, E, & Alexander, H. (Updated 2022, February). *How can integrating music into your classroom benefit student learning and development.* National Center on Safe Supportive Learning Environments. Retrieved June 30, 2024, from https://safesupportivelearning.ed.gov/voices-field/how-does-music-benefit-your-classroom-or-school-community-most

Shultz, A. (2023, June 6). San Francisco Safeway blasted classical music 24/7 to 'deter loitering'. *SFGATE.* https://www.sfgate.com/local/article/san-francisco-safeway-blasts-music-in-parking-lot-18136448.php?IPID=SFGate-HP-Editors-Picks

Taylor, T. (2024, March 5). The psychology behind the earworm: An investigation into the world of 'default songs.' *Far Out Magazine.* https://bit.ly/defaultearworms

The Music4Life® USA. (2013, December 3). *Karen's journey* [Video]. YouTube. https://www.youtube.com/watch?v=ufmewrHMIyg

Chapter 6

American Psychological Association. (n.d.). Resilience. In *APA Dictionary of Psychology.* https://www.apa.org/topics/resilience

Our history. (n.d.). Anchorage Youth Symphony. Retrieved June 30, 2024, from https://www.alaskayouthorchestras.org/alumni/history/

Peterson, K. (2000, August 12). Woman promotes a healthy dose of music. *Las Vegas Sun*.

The Music4Life® USA. (2011, July 29). *Executive Reduces Pain* [Video]. YouTube.https://youtu.be/ZfVfeVmZ7no

Chapter 7

Dornan, G. (2007, February 22). Advocates drum up support for music therapy program. *Nevada Appeal*. https://www.nevadaappeal.com/new s/2007/feb/22/advocates-drum-up-support-for-music-therapy-progra/

McPherson, T.M. (1988, December 22). Focus interview: Sound therapy, sound body. *The Anchorage Times*.

Piper, S. (1982, August 26). Summer plaza series comes to end with chamber trio performance. *The Anchorage Times*.

Chapter 8

Cameron, J. (1992). *The artist's way: A spiritual path to higher creativity*. Penguin Random House.

Hall, G.C.N. (2017, February 7). The platinum rule. *Psychology Today*. Retrieved from https://www.psychologytoday.com/us/blog/life-in-the-i ntersection/201702/the-platinum-rule

Kleeschulte, C. (1984, February 27). Enterprising trio can set your business to music. *Anchorage Daily News*.

Piper, S. (1982, August 26). Summer plaza series comes to an end with chamber trio' performance. *The Anchorage Times*.

Vegas star opens civic center (1982, July 7). *Valdez Vanguard*.

Chapter 9

11 types of workplace harassment and how to stop them. (n.d.). Case IQ. Retrieved June 30, 2024, from https://www.caseiq.com/resources/11-ty pes-of-workplace-harassment-and-how-to-stop-them/

A history of sexual harassment laws in the United States. (Updated 2023, June). Wenzel Fenton Cabassa, P.A. Retrieved June 30, 2024, from https://www.wenzelfenton.com/blog/2018/01/01/history-sexual -harassment-laws-united-states/

Blakemore, E. (2023, June 2). Until 1975, sexual harassment was the menace with no name. *History*. Retrieved June 30, 2024, from https://www.history.com/news/until-1975-sexual-harassment-was -the-menace-with-no-name

Fisic, J. (2023, February 13). Self-advocacy at work: 7 tips to help you become a better self-advocate. *Pumble*. Retrieved June 30, 2024, from https://pumble.com/blog/self-advocacy/

Janove, J. (2018, August 28). Thwarting sexual harassment: 5 success stories. *Society for Human Resource Management*. Retrieved June 30,

2024, from https://www.shrm.org/topics-tools/news/hr-magazine/thw arting-sexual-harassment-5-success-stories

National Academies of Sciences, Engineering, and Medicine; Policy and Global Affairs; Committee on Women in Science, Engineering, and Medicine; Committee on the Impacts of Sexual Harassment in Academia; Benya, F. F., Widnall, S. E., & Johnson, P. A. (Eds.). (2018, June 12). *Sexual harassment of women: Climate, culture, and consequences in academic sciences, engineering, and medicine.* National Academies Press. Retrieved June 30, 2024, from https://www.ncbi.nlm.nih.gov/books/NBK50720 6/

Toomey, S. (1988, July 17). Alaska ear. *Anchorage Daily News.*

Workplace bullying statistics research & facts. (Updated 2024, January 7). MyDisabilityJobs. Retrieved from https://mydisabilityjobs.com/statistic s/workplace-bullying/

Chapter 10

McPherson, T.M. (1988, December 22). Sound therapy, sound body. *The Anchorage Times.*

Pinkerton, J. (1990, January). *Live musicians return.* New Dimensions of Las Vegas. Note: publication date verified by New Dimensions of Las Vegas owner/publisher/editor Darlene Mea, personal communication, July 3, 2024.

Pinkerton, J. (2020, January 13). *Music 4 Life® pilot project*. Music4Life®. Retrieved June 30, 2024, from https://themusic4life.com/wp-content/uploads/2021/09/SAFB-Music4Life-Report-AFWERX.pdf

Chapter 11

Kim, J. (2019, July 22). The psychology of the moon: With the lunar landing anniversary, what has the moon meant to humankind. *Psychology Today*. Retrieved June 30, 2024, from https://www.psychologytoday.com/intl/blog/culture-shrink/201907/the-psychology-the-moon

Pinkerton, J. (1993). *Music: the stress-release system in three steps*. Seminar-Concerts International, Inc.

Pinkerton, J. (1996). *The sound of healing: Create your own music program for better health* (1st ed.). Alliance Publishing.

Rosenblum, T.M. (1996, Jun 22). *In print*. Billboard Newspaper.

Chapter 12

Fleming, R. (2024). *Music and mind: Harnessing the arts for health and wellness*. Penguin Random House.

History of music therapy. (n.d.). American Music Therapy Association. Retrieved June 30, 2024, from https://www.musictherapy.org/about/history/

Kirtley J., & O'Mahony, S. (2020). What is a pivot: Explaining when and how entrepreneurial firms decide to make strategic change and pivot. *Strategic Management Journal 44*. https://doi.org/10.1002/smj.3131

Music therapy market insights. (2024). Skyquest. Retrieved from https://www.skyquestt.com/report/music-therapy-market

Pinkerton, J. & Reuer, B. (2007). *Project uplift*. Center for Creative Therapeutic Arts.

Pinkerton, J. (2010). *Stress brake: Music exercising emotions program booklet*. Remo Inc.

Pramanik, P. (2023). Music could hold the key to developing effective mental health interventions. *News Medical Life Sciences*. Retrieved June 30, 2024, from https://www.news-medical.net/news/20231206/Music-could-hold-the-key-to-developing-effective-mental-health-interventions.aspx

Reuer, B. (n.d.). Music-centered wellness in integrative medicine settings. MusicWorxInc. https://musicworxinc.com/product/integrative-medicine-settings-music-centered-wellness/

Reuer, B. & Pinkerton, J. (2022). Music of hate, music for healing. [Review of the book *Music of hate, music for healing: Paired stories from the hate music industry and the profession of music therapy*, by T. Ficken]. *Music and Medicine, 14(2)*, 133-135. https://doi.org/10.47513/mmd.v14i2.868

Sima, R. (2021, November 10). Veterans use creative forces to heal invisible wounds of war: How music and art therapies can help military service members. *Psychology Today*. Retrieved June 30, 2024, from https://www.psychologytoday.com/us/blog/the-art-effect/202111 /veterans-use-creative-forces-heal-invisible-wounds-war

Sound health initiative. (2022, May 10). American Music Therapy Association. Retrieved June 30, 2024, from https://www.musictherapy.org/r esearch/sound_health_initiative/

The job market for music therapists in the United States. (n.d.) CareerExplorer. Retrieved June 30, 2024, from https://www.careerexplorer.com/ careers/music-therapist/job-market

Additional Resources

All, S. (2018, February 12). Could you be addicted to technology? *Psychology Today*. Retrieved from https://www.psychologytoday.com/us/blog/ modern-mentality/201802/could-you-be-addicted-technology

Herding experiment: Hundredth monkey phenomenon. (2021, October 29). Cornell University. Retrieved June 30, 2024, from https://blogs.cornell.edu/info2040/2021/10/29/Herding-experim ent-hundredth-monkey-phenomenon/

Pinkerton, J. (n.d.). *Music wellness programs: Merging self-responsible strategies*. Corporate Wellness Magazine. Retrieved from: https://www.c orporatewellnessmagazine.com/article/music-wellness-programs-merging

Pinkerton, J. & Duggan, R. (2023). *Method and system for influencing emotional regulation through assessment, education, and music playlist applications* (U.S. Patent No. 11,806,479). U.S. Patent and Trademark Office. https://ppubs.uspto.gov/dirsearch-public/print/download-Pdf/11806479

ABOUT THE AUTHOR

Judith Ann Pinkerton is the visionary Founder and CEO of Music4Life®, a licensed, certified music therapist, online educator, and leader dedicated to harnessing the transformative power of music. Her journey began with the violin and classical music, eventually expanding to embrace all genres. Fueled by an adventurous and creative spirit within a supportive environment, Judith continually pioneers new ways to support others through music.

Throughout her career, Judith has received numerous accolades. She was honored as the first recipient of the Aflac & Academy of Country Music "Lifting Lives Honor" (2018) and the "Changemaker Award" for Music Therapy Advocacy from the American Music Therapy Association (2012). Her legislative advocacy led to securing significant funding (SB-579, Section 30, 2007) and licensure for music therapy in Nevada

(SB-190, 2011), including a $305,798 grant from the Fund for a Healthy Nevada (2008). In 2001, she received the Las Vegas Chamber of Commerce "Community Achievement Award in Arts & Entertainment."

As a TEDxUNLV speaker, "Music Powers Potential: Building Mental Fitness" (2014), Judith's discography reflects her deep commitment to music therapy, featuring titles like "Stress Brake" (2010), "MEE™ Concert" (1991), and "MEE™ in the Key of Peace" (1989). She has authored numerous publications and accredited curricula, including "6 Habits of Music Medicine for Highly Empowered People" (2023) and "The Sound of Healing" (1996, 2003). Her articles have appeared in Corporate Wellness Magazine, Music as Medicine, Mental Health Spectrum, and other reputable journals, with her podcasts on iTunes (Music 4 Life Podcasts).

She holds a B.A. in Music from Thomas Edison State University and the Music Therapy Equivalency from Arizona State University. Judith is a Nevada Licensed Professional Music Therapist (LPMT) and a Board Certified Music Therapist (MT-BC), having earned the first music therapy license issued in the USA on November 1, 2011.

Judith's passion for music therapy ignited in 1986 when her solo violin music replaced medication post-surgery for her husband. This passion was reignited in 2023 when music therapy played a crucial role in her father's remarkable recovery in the ICU, with his physician declaring it "scientifically unexplainable." With over twenty years of experience, Judith has treated a variety of client populations from womb to tomb, with more than 11,000 clients residing within addiction treatment centers.

Currently, Judith is immersed in several groundbreaking projects. She is working on an IRB-approved hospital study, long-term case studies, programs connecting mental health organizations with symphonies, and training mental health providers to support users through her patented music app Key2MEE®. Additionally, she spearheads the next phase of Key2MEE and will complete a book series with futuristic focus.

Judith's approach to life, seeking to serve, is encapsulated in her favorite phrase: "Challenged every day to enjoy life as a journey into more." This philosophy shines through in her hobbies, which include periodic family-driven hiking on scenic trails, camping under the stars, skiing down snowy slopes, exploring new destinations, volunteering in her community, and playing beautiful music in symphony and small chamber groups.

For inquiries or engagements, Judith can be contacted at info@themusic 4life.com.

More information about her work can be found on PsychologyToday, JudithPinkerton.com, theMusic4Life.com, and MusicMedicineAcademy.com

Follow her on:

patreon.com/musicmedicineclub

youtube.com/c/theMusic4Life

@yourmusicsage

linkedin.com/in/judithpinkerton/

 @JudithPinkerton

facebook.com/JudithPinkertonMTBC/

Made in United States
Troutdale, OR
05/27/2025

31706372R00196